Social Welfare in East Asia and the Pacific

Social Welfare in East Asia and the Pacific

EDITED BY

SHARLENE B. C. L. FURUTO

Columbia University Press   *New York*

Columbia University Press
Publishers Since 1893
New York   Chichester, West Sussex
cup.columbia.edu

Library of Congress Cataloging-in-Publication Data
Social welfare in East Asia and the Pacific / edited by Sharlene B. C. L. Furuto.
    p.   cm.
    Includes bibliographical references and index.
ISBN 978-0-231-15714-8 (cloth: alk. paper)—ISBN 978-0-231-15715-5 (pbk.: alk. paper)—
ISBN 978-0-231-53098-9 (e-book)
    1. Human services—Asia.   2. Human services—Pacific Area.   3. Social service—
Asia.   4. Social service—Pacific Area.   I. Furuto, Sharlene Maeda.
HV376.S634   2013
361.95—dc23

                                                                      2012028190

                                    ∞
Columbia University Press books are printed on permanent and durable acid-free paper.
This book is printed on paper with recycled content.
Printed in the United States of America

c 10 9 8 7 6 5 4 3 2 1
p 10 9 8 7 6 5 4 3 2 1

COVER IMAGES: © Shutterstock

References to Internet Web sites (URLs) were accurate at the time of writing. Neither the author nor Columbia University Press is responsible for URLs that may have expired or changed since the manuscript was prepared.

Contents

Contents

Foreword

It is a great privilege and honor to write a foreword to *Social Welfare in East Asia and the Pacific*. This book is important in many respects and a welcome addition to the existing literature on social welfare. It greatly appeals to me because its conceptualization and development were based on the need for it, identified during Sharlene Furuto's time spent teaching social work/welfare/development students. As development occurs across the Asia Pacific region in a highly varied manner in every sense, the need for welfare provisions and programs is growing. In response, programs in social work, social welfare, and international social development are expanding rapidly in much of the region, along with student numbers. For both reasons, this book is timely. Although welfare services, provisions, and practices in different forms, both formal and informal, exist in almost all Asia Pacific countries, very little has been written on them. Thus knowledge about welfare and its operation, strengths and weaknesses, adequacies and inadequacies, and unique features has remained undeveloped. This book breaks that barrier and opens up the welfare practices of many countries for readers to learn about.

The sample of countries selected for this volume is both insightful and interesting. It reflects a great variation in the trajectory of development, poverty levels, political systems, struggles, level of freedom experienced by people, and social and cultural practices in Southeast Asia, East Asia, and the Pacific—from the emerging world power of China to small islands in Micronesia. The book discusses the formal and informal social welfare systems in these countries and how the systems are evolving. In the contemporary divided, unequal, and diverse world, people's welfare and adequate mechanisms to ensure it are vital. The unfortunate reality is that welfare is closely linked to and often dependent on national and international politics, economic development, war, and defense, disregarding the needs of local people.

To understand the welfare conditions of the countries selected for this volume, it is necessary to understand their past. Therefore, historical contexts, different forms of colonization, sociocultural values and social problems rooted in socioeconomic and political structures, and the way states and civil society respond to the needs and problems of people do significantly matter. Without gaining that understanding, it is difficult for the social work profession, social workers, and welfare officials to effectively intervene and work with people in their respective contexts. The authors have firsthand experience in their respective countries and have authoritatively unearthed historical and current conditions and future challenges for social welfare. Their analysis and discussion of the issues engaged me and helped me to be better informed about social welfare in Cambodia, China, Hong Kong SAR, Indonesia, Malaysia, Micronesia, the Samoan Islands, South Korea, Taiwan, and Thailand. Shrinking or stagnating welfare systems in some developed countries in the Americas and Europe and emerging social welfare in Asia and the Pacific provide an interesting contrast for international scholars and social workers.

The book is a gateway for exploring and understanding social welfare in Southeast and East Asia and the Pacific, and I highly recommend it to educators, students, and practitioners in the field of social work, social welfare, social and community development, and human services, and for that matter, to anyone interested in the issue of welfare of people.

Manohar Pawar
Professor of Social Work, Charles Sturt University, Australia
President, International Consortium for Social Development Asia-Pacific

Preface

The undergraduate Social Work Department at Brigham Young University–Hawaii is unique for its high concentration of international students from Asia and the Pacific, a characteristic that is reflected in the overall university population. In 2011, of the total population of university students, 60 percent were from the United States; 23 percent were from Asia (predominantly South Korea, Japan, Hong Kong Special Administrative Region [SAR], the Philippines, Taiwan, and China but also Mongolia, Malaysia, Cambodia, Indonesia, Thailand, India, Singapore, Vietnam, Macao SAR, Myanmar, Laos, Sri Lanka, Nepal, and Pakistan); 12 percent were from the Pacific (predominantly Tonga, Fiji, Samoa, New Zealand, and Australia but also American Samoa, Marshall Islands, Kiribati, Papua New Guinea, French Polynesia, Federated States of Micronesia, Cook Islands, New Caledonia, Northern Mariana Islands, Tuvalu, Niue, Palau, and Vanuatu); and 5 percent were from other nations.

It is not surprising, then, that social work majors are required to pass courses in International Social Welfare in Asia and the Pacific and Social Work Practice with Asians and Pacific Islanders. Perhaps the most difficult aspect of teaching these courses is locating a textbook that provides the needed content. For a while, we used international textbooks that focused on Europe from a U.S. perspective along with journal articles specific to Asian and Pacific Island nations. About two years ago I finally decided to do what was right: to edit a book about social welfare in Asian and Pacific Island states. Everyone I talked with—academicians, publishers, students, practitioners—strongly encouraged me to fill this void in the social work literature.

As I began to conceptualize the book, I knew I wanted to make it somewhat broad so that it could be used not only in social policy, social work practice, and diversity courses on the baccalaureate and master's levels but also for practitioners living in Asia and the Pacific or living anywhere and practicing with Asians and Pacific Islanders. It seemed logical to start each chapter with the history of social welfare, values and culture, current social issues, government and not-for-profit social welfare programs, the social work profession, and education, and to end with a look at future challenges.

In contemplating contributors for this book, several thoughts were at the forefront: my gratitude to Kenji Murase for helping me, as a junior faculty member, edit my first book and my desire to help others publish also; a preference for contributors from Asia and the Pacific who understand not only the profession but also the people and programs; and my intention to tap the knowledge and expertise of my own BSW Asian and Pacific Island graduates, many of whom have become academicians or practitioners themselves.

The result is this book, *Social Welfare in East Asia and the Pacific*—ten chapters that focus on political entities that are not usually visible in the social work professional literature—Cambodia, China, Hong Kong SAR, Indonesia, Malaysia, the Micronesian region, Samoa and American Samoa, South Korea, Taiwan, and Thailand—preceded by an introduction and ending with a chapter that contrasts social welfare in that part of the world.

The contributors are all from the countries they write about or have lived and practiced or interned there. Some contributors are well-published academicians while others are practitioners publishing for the first time. Five have attended or graduated from BYU Hawaii. All contributors are highly regarded by their peers and are very familiar with social welfare in their respective political entities.

My support system over the past two years has been my husband, David, and our children, Linda, Matthew (and his wife Leah), Michael (and his wife Solaen), and Daniel; John Reeves, my social work colleague who has been a knowledgeable Pacific Islander consultant; and John Bailey, the College of Human Development dean, who has been instrumental in fiscal support. My *mahalo* (thank you) and *aloha* to all.

Social Welfare in East Asia and the Pacific

Overview of Social Welfare in East Asia and the Pacific

SHARLENE B. C. L. FURUTO

The part of the world known generally as Asia and the Pacific contains rich and geographically beautiful lands, but it can also be desolate and have few or untapped natural resources. Together, Asia and the Pacific (including Australia) comprise about half of the world's landmass and 60 percent of the world's population. Australia and New Zealand, two more developed countries in the Pacific, are notably different from other Pacific political entities in terms of population, landmass, and social welfare services and so are not examined in this book. Without them, the Pacific nations have a population of about 9.5 million and a landmass about the size of France in a water mass that encompasses 46 percent of Earth's oceans.

This chapter gives an overview of eleven East Asian and Pacific states. (Throughout this and the final chapter, the words *state* and *nation* are used interchangeably and refer to various types of political entities.) The Pacific nations consist of Samoa and American Samoa and islands in the Micronesian region, including Guam, the Federated States of Micronesia (namely, the four states of Yap, Chuuk, Pohnpei, and Kosrae), the Republic of the Marshall Islands, the Republic of Palau, and the Commonwealth of the Northern Mariana Islands. These island nations have diverse forms of government, resulting in a noticeable difference in availability of social services. American Samoa and Guam are unincorporated territories of the United States and benefit from most of the U.S. federal social welfare programs. The Federated States of Micronesia, the Republic of the Marshall Islands, and the Republic of Palau have constitutional governments in free association with the United States and are eligible for some federal social welfare programs. In this book, the social welfare system in the sovereign

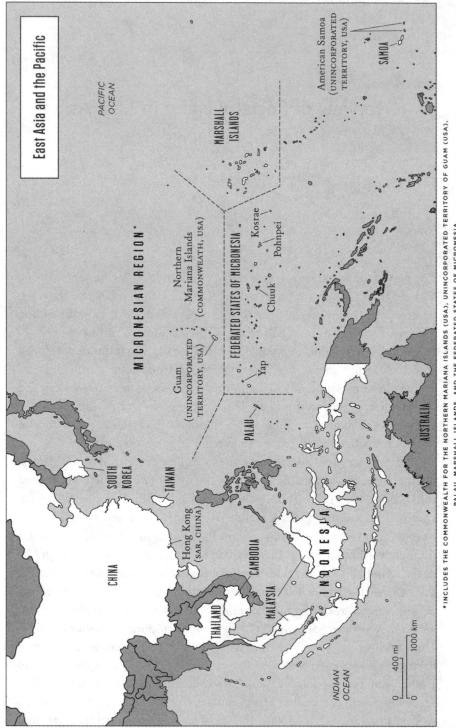

East Asia and the Pacific

PACIFIC
OCEAN

MICRONESIAN REGION*

Northern
Mariana Islands
(COMMONWEATH, USA)

MARSHALL
ISLANDS

Guam
(UNINCORPORATED
TERRITORY, USA)

FEDERATED STATES OF MICRONESIA

Kosrae

Pohnpei

Chuuk

Yap

PALAU

American Samoa
(UNINCORPORATED
TERRITORY, USA)

SAMOA

SOUTH
KOREA

TAIWAN

Hong Kong
(SAR, CHINA)

CHINA

THAILAND

CAMBODIA

MALAYSIA

I N D O N E S I A

AUSTRALIA

INDIAN
OCEAN

0   400 mi
0   1000 km

*INCLUDES THE COMMONWEALTH FOR THE NORTHERN MARIANA ISLANDS (USA), UNINCORPORATED TERRITORY OF GUAM (USA),
PALAU, MARSHALL ISLANDS, AND THE FEDERATED STATES OF MICRONESIA

nation of Samoa, a parliamentary democracy, is contrasted with that of American Samoa.

Asia, meanwhile, is the world's largest and most populous continent, located primarily in the Eastern and Northern Hemispheres. Asia covers 30 percent of Earth's total land area, and its population, now at four billion, nearly quadrupled in the twentieth century. Asia comprises fifty-three states in four areas: North, South Central, West and Middle East, and Southeast and East, or simply East. The Asian countries discussed in this book include, in Southeast Asia, the Kingdom of Cambodia, the Republic of Indonesia, Malaysia, and the Kingdom of Thailand, and, in East Asia, the Hong Kong SAR, which is a territory of China, the People's Republic of China, Taiwan (or the Republic of China), and South Korea (or the Republic of Korea). The states in the Southeast and East are part of the greater East region and are referred to as such in this book.

There is wide diversity in the forms of governments of these lands in East Asia as well: Taiwan has a multiparty democracy, Cambodia has a multiparty democracy under a constitutional monarchy, and Hong Kong SAR has a limited democracy. Malaysia and Thailand have constitutional monarchies, Indonesia and South Korea are republics, and China is a communist state. Recently China has had a stable government, while Thailand has been in the midst of a political conflict that has already cost a number of lives. Transparency International (2010) claims that "corruption remains an obstacle to achieving much needed progress," as is evidenced in Cambodia, Indonesia, China, and Thailand. The form of government, its leaders, and the level of corruption in government all affect the growth or stagnation of political and social development in each of these nations (Seyf 2001).

Social welfare is an integral aspect of the well-being of a population, and the development of social welfare is based on multiple factors, including geography and physical features of a country, government and political leadership, the economy, and culture and traditions. Each state has unique and yet universal social issues.

Social Challenges in East Asia and the Pacific

In general, while most East Asian and Pacific political entities discussed in this volume have made developmental progress in the recent past, some continue to battle a number of challenges in government leadership, economic stagnation, environmental fragility, unmet basic human needs, and social depression. There is a wide discrepancy in the average income of people in East Asian and Pacific nations. Many families in the tiger lands of Hong Kong SAR, Singapore, South Korea, and Taiwan live comfortably, while their counterparts in rural Cambodia and farming communities in China are steeped in poverty. Many Pacific Islanders rely on remittances for daily livelihood from family members working abroad. Global climate changes and major earthquakes are also taxing the well-being of nations and are suspected reasons for sinking atolls such as Caberet Island, Tuvalu, Kiribati (Alley 1998), the two Samoas, Micronesia, and the Marshall Islands as the sea level rises. Since much of the land in the Pacific is inherited rather than purchased, farmers who leave their ancestral lands for another island are homeless and unable to farm and support themselves on arrival.

Universal human rights as declared by the United Nations are not preserved when child sex-trafficking flourishes, a growing elderly population lives in squalor, and free speech, employment, primary education, and fundamental health care are lacking. From human-rights violations in China and accusations of misuse of power by the Cambodian, Indonesian, and Thai governments to the democracy in Guam and the economic boom in South Korea, Hong Kong SAR, and Taiwan, there is indeed much diversity in how East Asian and Pacific nations are governed and how social welfare has developed.

Global Impact of Social Welfare in East Asia and the Pacific

For many readers, East Asian and Pacific nations are on the other side of the world. So why do we need to know about the social welfare conditions of these global neighbors? Mapp (2008:v) cautions us, "While it is easier to prioritize the needs of those who are close to us over those who are further away, this approach will hurt us all in the long run." Indeed, with the globalization of our world, the social, economic, and political forces in one region do affect other parts of the world, and injustices experienced in local communities can be caused or affected by forces beyond national borders (Diaz, Mama, & Lopez 2006).

In addition, East Asia and the Pacific Islands encompass ancient civilizations that have been historically at both the peak and the abyss of worldly achievements. They have gained wisdom throughout the centuries that we can profit from today. China, Hong Kong SAR, and Taiwan, for example, are ancient enough to actually be celebrating their lunar year 4711 in 2013! These nations, at the vanguard of social issues, could also be the leaders of social solutions as they share their social welfare knowledge and models beyond Asia.

Residents of many East Asian and Pacific states depend on family, clan members, and fellow villagers for help using traditional and indigenous methods, in large part because government services are unavailable. An impressive number of Pacific families have members who have migrated to New Zealand, Australia, Hawaii, or the continental United States for employment and who regularly and frequently send remittances home to help support their families (Ware 2005). Perhaps the rest of the world and particularly those in the field of social work could consider revisiting the power of the family, clan, and village as initial resources to cope with social problems on the micro level. All local social problems can end up having a global impact: problems in villages affect a country, a country influences the status of a region, and eventually the well-being of the world is affected. Global social issues can best be addressed through international social welfare collaboration—learning about and learning from the social welfare problems and solutions of other countries.

International Social Development Theories

The terms *underdevelopment* and *development* were initially used in the 1950s and 1960s to reflect the emergence of newly independent countries in Africa, the Caribbean, Asia, and South America. Several social development theories came to light at that time.

In the more recent past, several authors have described social work theories. Payne (1997) promulgated three categories of social work theories and models: reflexive-therapeutic, socialist-collectivist, and individual-reformist. These three categories are helpful in organizing social work theories and approaches. Mapp (2008) and Healy (2008) discuss two development theories: the neoclassical approach, or modernization theory, and the dependency theory. When introduced about fifty years ago, the modernization theory viewed development as an end result, and the dependency theory viewed development as a process of impoverishment, although both espoused that development is dependent on economic growth and development.

Modernization theorists believe that underdevelopment and poverty in a nation are due to internal causes, including the state's lack of democratic institutions, capital, technology, and citizen initiatives. Furthermore, modernization theory supports the idea that an increased gross national product (GNP) will eventually trickle down and benefit the entire population, despite evidence that this has not been the result in Costa Rica and Brazil (Healy 2008). Mapp (2008) argues that capitalism and a freer market economy specific to a country's culture are basic to economic development. Wealthier nations can help less wealthy nations in various ways, such as limiting population growth, increasing food production, providing foreign aid, and increasing technology (Macionis 2006).

Dependency theory posits that development is a struggle between the have and have-not nations, where the wealthier nations, perhaps initially through colonization, have taken advantage of the less wealthy states (Healy 2008; Mapp 2008). Today financially poorer nations continue to be dependent on industrialized nations for markets, imports, technology, and information. These less powerful states often suffer from lack of infrastructure and lack of control over prices, trade conditions, and currency valuation. To change this unequal status, radical reforms are needed in the relationships between the have and have-not political entities. Wealthy nations, understandably, maintain this dependence imbalance to preserve their financial self-interests, and poor states have little recourse in opposition. Instead of internal conditions, dependency theory focuses on the external causes of underdevelopment, such as war, corruption, natural disasters, or noncoastal borders.

Meanwhile, Cox and Pawar (2006) discuss international social welfare using a comprehensive integrated-perspectives approach with global, human rights, ecological, and social development perspectives. The global perspective suggests the unity of one world, or the global village. The human-rights perspective consists of the values, ethics, and rights inherent to all human beings. The ecological perspective looks at the environment in terms of holism and unity in complex interconnecting relationships, diversity, equilibrium, and sustainability through astute management of natural resources. The social development perspective depends on intervention that is value based, proactive, multidimensional (not only by developing economic, social, political, cultural, legal, and ecological dimensions in an integrated and holistic sense but also by envisioning society in terms of social structures, social relations, social processes, and social values), and multilevel (for example, in terms of the local, regional, national, state, and global levels or the individual/family/community sector).

Finally, the global perspective is integral to social work as it broadens our perspective by including worldwide economic and political structures. Midgley (2008) describes four perspectives on globalization and culture that can make practice more effective in international settings: globalization as creating chaos and destroying local cultures; as fostering the emergence of a single, world culture based on Western values; as generating a powerful cultural backlash; and as promoting the development of new, hybrid cultural forms that incorporate both existing and new cultural patterns. Perhaps all four perspectives can be found in the states studied here at different times or locations.

Samoans living in the capital city Apia, for example, are more exposed to Westernization and seem to be losing some of their culture, while Samoans living in New Zealand, Australia, or the United States have taken on a regional culture based on Western values. Still other Samoans who left the islands twenty years ago are now sending their teenage sons back to Samoa to shape up, while other Samoans have been allowed to let their dual cultural experiences mix and develop into a flexibility that allows them to be more culturally Samoan with their elders, more Western with their peers, and to move in and out of their Samoan culture as needed with their parents and work colleagues. Social workers need to be aware of the dynamism of culture as a result of globalization.

Status of Social Welfare

The status of social welfare differs widely in East Asia and the Pacific, with variations not only in the nature and severity of social issues but also in the support available from the government, nongovernmental organizations (NGOs), and the international community. Other variables that affect the social well-being of a country are politics, the economy, and natural and human-caused disasters.

The human development index (HDI) (see appendix), which ranks a country by life expectancy, education, and income, can also be used to gauge the social well-being of a nation. Some of the nations discussed in this book are on the fringe of development according to the HDI. Others, like South Korea and Hong Kong SAR, are in the very high human development category. Malaysia is in the high category, and China, Thailand, Micronesia, Indonesia, and Cambodia are in the medium category. American Samoa, Samoa, and Taiwan are not ranked (UN Development Programme 2010).

Many peoples in the medium human development category, especially those in rural areas and on small islands and atolls, continue to struggle without potable water, a variety of nutritious food, and basic health care and education for reasons such as warfare, corrupt governments, limited government income, frequent natural disasters, poverty, and isolation. There is little in the social work literature that describes the plight of peoples with these social issues in much of Asia and most of the Pacific, thus minimizing attention to solutions for these problems.

Purpose and Scope of This Book

Some international social welfare books have been published recently that begin to address aspects of social welfare in limited parts of Asia and the Pacific. These books seem to focus on social work education or on major social issues (Noble 2009), including human trafficking, child soldiers, women's issues, and refugees (CQ Researcher 2010); forced labor, child welfare, war, and women's issues (Mapp 2008); indigenous social work (Gray, Coates, & Yellow Bird 2008); poverty, conflict, and migration (Cox & Pawar 2006); international social work values, practice, and policy (Healy 2008); and aging, child welfare, social security, poverty, and mental health (Hokenstad & Midgley 2004). Usually the social issues are presented in detail but with much less attention devoted to the broader context of the relevant countries. In addition, only a few East Asian and fewer still Pacific states surface in this literature.

To move toward worldwide collaborative solutions to social welfare problems, I believe we need to understand social welfare from a wider perspective and as experienced by broader global neighbors. This book offers a more expansive model for studying social welfare and the social development progress of political entities that are seldom seen in the literature.

The first purpose of this book is to broadly describe social welfare in selected East Asian and Pacific Island states by reviewing their social welfare histories, current social issues, and responses from the government and NGOs, highlighting unique, indigenous social solutions. Chapters also examine how the local culture affects attitudes and social programs, ending with a discussion of the status of the social work profession and social work education in the country, with a look toward the future. This is the only book available today that covers so many aspects of social welfare and social work for each of these nations.

The second purpose is to highlight some places in the world usually not found in the social work literature and to give the perspective of professional social workers who are from the area or who have lived and worked in that country.

The third purpose is to look beyond Europe and the United States to some distant lands for social work knowledge and solutions, encouraging social work educators and practitioners to be more inclusive in manifesting our mantra for equity and social justice. Every state has its strengths, and these social welfare successes should be shared with academicians and practitioners in other parts of the world.

The political entities studied, in the order that social work was introduced to their shores, are China, South Korea, Hong Kong SAR, Taiwan, Thailand, Indonesia, Malaysia, the Micronesian region, Samoa and American Samoa, and Cambodia. Most social issues in East Asia and the Pacific today are also those plaguing many countries in the Southern Hemisphere, termed the Global South: poverty, limited health and education facilities, lagging economies, child laborers, aging, drugs, an insufficient number of jobs, and migration and immigration. Similarities and dissimilarities between countries are discussed in the concluding chapter and in the Samoa and American Samoa chapter as well.

Brief Summary of the Chapters

China. China became a communist country in 1949 and managed to establish some forms of social security in the 1950s. The Cultural Revolution, from 1966 to 1976, set China back in a number of areas, including social welfare development. In 1978 Deng Xiaoping's policy of opening to the outside world led to a new age of economic reform and later to a socialist market economy. In 1978 the Chinese Communist Party approved the one-child policy, which requested that party and Communist Youth League members in urban areas aim for one child in their family; a generation later this now permanent policy successfully continues to curb population growth.

The social security program in China has undergone several major expansions and cuts. Chapter 2 is written by Minjie Zhang, a social work professor at Zhejiang Gongshang University in Hangzhou, Zhejiang Province, China. After addressing the social reforms of the past, Dr. Zhang gives an update on social welfare regarding aging, people with disabilities, children, and poverty, followed by a discussion of how the government is improving and expanding social programs in rural areas.

South Korea. Following the Korean War (1950–53), South Korea was under an authoritarian leadership, but in 1993, after years of military rule, it became a capitalist liberal democracy. Since the 1960s South Korea has transformed from an agricultural-based to an industrial-based economy and has made remarkable economic progress. But despite a robust economy, the poverty rate in South Korea has increased annually since 2000. Written by Jun Sung Hong of the University of Illinois at Urbana-Champaign, Young Sook Kim of the University of Tennessee at Knoxville, Na Youn Lee of the University of Michigan, and Ji Woong Ha of Dong Rae Middle School in Busan, South Korea, chapter 3 explains how youth crime and delinquency, poverty, and the aging population are problems challenging the South Korean social welfare system. A significant achievement for South Korea is that major conglomerates have partnered with the government to provide various social services on a large-scale basis.

Hong Kong SAR. Two major events occurred in July 1997 that have had far-reaching effects on the current status of social welfare in Hong Kong SAR. First, the Asian financial crisis occurred. While Thailand, Indonesia, and South Korea were especially affected, all Asia suffered, including Hong Kong SAR. The second major event was the transfer of Hong Kong sovereignty from the United Kingdom to the People's Republic of China. This return reunited Hong Kong with mainland China as a Special Administrative Region. How have the Asian financial crisis and the "one country two systems" governance changed social welfare policies since 1997? In chapter 4 authors Venus Tsui of Our Lady of the Lake University, Alvin Shiulain Lee of Boston University, and Ernest Chui Wing-tak of the University of Hong Kong indicate that the social welfare system remains the same, but there is a growing neoconservative orientation. The chapter also introduces the viewpoint that the government may be attempting to contain welfare expansion and take control of the nonprofit sector. The social welfare system in Hong Kong SAR remains budget driven and largely residual and conservative despite piecemeal welfare reforms in recent decades.

Taiwan. During the ancient and colonial periods, most of the social welfare services in Taiwan were performed by foreign missionaries, such as medical doctor James Laidlaw Maxwell and special education teacher William Campbell. Local wealthy scholars, such as members of the Fu Chang Society, also provided emergency relief. In more modern times, the Taiwan Bureau of Social Affairs was established when the Chinese Civil War ended in 1949. Since then, the government and NGOs have implemented an impressive array of social services. Li-ju Jang of National Pingtung University of Science and Technology and Pei-jen Tsai of National Chi Nan University describe in chapter 5 a number of innovative programs ranging from services provided by nannies to those provided by attorneys helping senior citizens.

Thailand. Chapter 6 spotlights Thailand and was authored by Jitti Mong-kolnchaiarunya of Thammasat University and Nuanyai Wattanakoon of Huachiew Chalermprakiat University in Bangkok even as the capital was immersed in semi–civil war. There are a number of reasons that the Thai people are dissatisfied with their government, including structural injustices in income and social inequality. Thailand, the only Southeast Asian nation that has never been colonized, may be at the cusp of major political changes that could affect its social welfare system and social development. The authors describe a number of possible social welfare schemes, including corporate social programs, private and community tax incentives, and government-matched funds for community-based welfare projects. Wats, or temples, are important traditional institutions that support social welfare by providing a number of services, including meals, education, drug treatment, and aid to final-stage HIV/AIDS patients.

Indonesia. While much of the world is aware of the earthquakes and resulting tsunamis that hit Indonesia in 2004 and 2005, killing about 131,000 individuals, few people are aware of social conditions there. Indonesia, a former Dutch colony, gained independence in 1945. The government began to pay special attention to social welfare programs in 1968. The programs faltered but were restored in 2001 under President Megawati Soekarnoputri. In chapter 7 Adi Fahrudin of Bandung College of Social

Welfare describes issues of poverty and malnutrition, unemployment, care for older people, street children, child workers, and sexually exploited children. He calls on the government, NGOs, indigenous practitioners, social work professionals, and social work educators to work collaboratively for solutions to these issues in the context of indigenous practices.

Malaysia. Malaysia, a former British colony, is another country less familiar to people in the United States and Europe. In chapter 8 Azlinda Azman of the Universiti Sains Malaysia and Sharima Ruwaida Abbas of the Universiti Utara Malaysia strongly emphasize the critical need to hire trained social work practitioners and to move toward social work education accreditation. They believe that sustainable development in the twenty-first century for Malaysia requires collaborative efforts of trained social workers and relevant social welfare stakeholders with appropriate social work policies and competency standards in place.

The Micronesian Region. Chapter 9 encompasses the Micronesian region, where a population of about 300,000 live on some 2,000 small islands with a total land area of about 1,615 square miles (2,600 square kilometers) in the western Pacific Ocean between Hawaii and the Philippine Islands. Vivian Dames, Joliene Hasugulayag, LisaLinda Natividad, and Gerhard Schwab, all of the University of Guam, describe diverse societies on islands and atolls well-known during World War II and now struggling with social problems rooted in their colonial histories and associated with the development of their young island nations. Problems facing the region include fragmentation and transformation of indigenous kinship and familial structures, public and environmental health problems, loss of land due to U.S. nuclear bomb detonations, unplanned and uncoordinated patterns of in- and out-migrations, and problems associated with the planned U.S. military buildup.

The authors contend that the region's social problems (as well as potential solutions) are largely driven by the unresolved, uncertain, and still-evolving political statuses and relations of these island societies. Solutions so far are primarily based on these islands associating themselves with the United States and benefiting from U.S. federal welfare programs. However, the question remains as to the problematic implications of Micronesian peoples becoming less self-reliant and more dependent on the United States. The people of the Micronesian region receive U.S. federal welfare benefits in exchange for allowing the U.S. military to use their islands for its global military missions. Hence the authors conclude that cultural and political efforts are constitutive of social work.

Samoa. In chapter 10 Kenneth Galeai of Brigham Young University–Hawaii contrasts the sovereign nation of Samoa with the U.S. territory of American Samoa, two political entities with the same culture and language but with marked differences in their method of government. In 1962 Western Samoa gained independence from New Zealand. Eight years later it became a member of the Commonwealth, and in 1997 Western Samoa formally adopted the name the Independent State of Samoa, or Samoa. The Samoan government head of state and the prime minister are selected by the forty-nine-member unicameral legislature, and all fifty-one government leaders are chiefs, or *matai.* The government addresses social issues predominantly through privatization, and NGOs are funded by internal and external sources. This model allows for government resources to be used in other areas by the community.

American Samoa. American Samoa, meanwhile, has been a U.S. territory since 1900 and was strategically important to the United States prior to and during World War II. Since then, American Samoa has developed a modern, self-governing political system with a unicameral legislature and chiefs holding all seats in the Senate. Today American Samoans benefit from social service programs available in the United States. Dr. Galeai introduces *fa'a Samoa,* or "the Samoan way," with intriguing examples of cultural manifestations and comparisons of social welfare in Samoa and American Samoa.

Cambodia. Pol Pot led the genocide from 1975 to 1979 that killed almost 25 percent of the Cambodian population. The civil war immediately followed, and this devastation finally ended in 1990. Free elections were held in 1993, and in 2010 the international tribunal found Duch (or Kaing Guek Eav), the director of Tuol Sleng prison, to be guilty of heinous death crimes against humanity, war crimes, torture, and premeditated murder. Chapter 11, written by Thy Naroeun of the Royal University of Phnom Penh, with Ammon Padeken of Kaaawa, Hawaii, and Sharlene Furuto of Brigham Young University–Hawaii, describes how, in the aftermath of genocide and warfare, the lesser role of government social services is overshadowed by human services provided by NGOs, wats or temples, village chiefs, and natural healers. The conclusion is that the encouraging, fairly recent progress made in economic and social work education is revitalizing the country. It seems that the resilient survivors of the Khmer Rouge are struggling to rebuild Cambodia despite corruption inside and outside the government.

The final chapter represents an analysis and comparison of social welfare in the states discussed in the preceding chapters. The many similarities and differences among the nations, beginning with their histories of social welfare, have resulted in a number of intriguing components in their social welfare systems today. The chapter also discusses some thriving indigenous social service models that the local populations have accepted and that could be considered for implementation in the United States and Europe. It ends with a discussion of future social welfare challenges

Learning from East Asia and the Pacific

In ancient times, each of these East Asian and Pacific political entities depended on a traditional welfare system that included indigenous cultural practices (Chi 2008) such as the wats. Later, Western colonial powers and missionaries arrived and, together with industrialization and urbanization, introduced the industrial charity model to Asia and the Pacific. Today some of the states are actively engaged in indigenizing the Western methods and models while others are anxious to begin. Students who study abroad using social work textbooks and literature published in Europe or the United States may return home and attempt to bridge their new knowledge with their traditional culture.

According to Chi (2008), some social workers who have studied abroad now have perspectives that conflict with those of colleagues who studied at home. While those who studied abroad are creating institutionalized responses to their local problems, the locally trained practitioners who react against the European and Western models are now generating authentic local models of social work education and practice that are based on principles of social development (Ferguson 2005).

I believe there is yet another course of action that is concomitantly ongoing in Asia and the Pacific. Some Asian and Pacific Island social work practitioners and academicians who have studied abroad are able to successfully transition from their European or U.S. perspectives to a dual worldview, consisting of both global and local perspectives. These professionals who have dual perspectives are able to work with their locally trained colleagues in developing indigenous paradigms. Thailand is already in the process of developing its own indigenous social work models and approaches. As part of that process, I have collaborated with local authors to write this book in which social work practitioners, academicians, and social welfare leaders who were trained abroad and locally share our knowledge with colleagues and students.

References

Alley, R. M. (1998). *The United Nations in Southeast Asia and the South Pacific*. New York: St. Martin's Press.

Central Intelligence Agency (2011). "Government Type." In *The World Factbook*. Retrieved March 24, 2011, from https://www.cia.gov/library/publications/the -world factbook/fields/2128.html.

Chi, I. (2008). "Social Work in China." *International Social Work* 48 (4): 371–79.

CQ Researcher (2010). *International Issues in Social Work and Social Welfare*. Los Angeles: Sage.

Cox, D., & M. Pawar (2006). *International Social Work: Issues, Strategies, and Programs*. London: Sage.

Diaz, L., R. Mama, & L. Lopez (2006). "Making the Social Work Profession an Essential Partner in International Development." Paper presented at the biennial conference of the International Federation of Social Workers, Munich, Germany, August.

Ferguson, K. (2005). "Beyond Indigenization and Reconceptualization: Towards a Global, Multidirectional Model of Technology Transfer." *International Social Work* 48 (5).

Gray, M., J. Coates, & M. Yellow Bird, eds. (2008). *Indigenous Social Work Around the World: Towards Culturally Relevant Education and Practice*. Surrey, UK: Ashgate.

Healy, L. (2008). *International Social Work: Professional Action in an Interdependent World*. 2nd ed. New York: Oxford University Press.

Hokenstad, M.C., & J. Midgley, eds. (2004). *Lessons from Abroad: Adapting International Social Welfare Innovations*. Washington, D.C.: NASW Press.

Macionis, J. J. (2006). *Society: The Basic*. 8th ed. Upper Saddle River, N.J.: Pearson/ Prentice Hall.

Mapp, S. (2008). *Human Rights and Social Justice in a Global Perspective: An Introduction to International Social Work*. Oxford: Oxford University Press.

Midgley, J. (2008). "Perspectives on Globalization and Culture: Implications for International Social Work Practice." *Journal of Global Social Work Practice* 1 (1) (November/December).

Noble, C., M. Henrickson, & I. Y. Han, eds. (2009). *Social Work Education: Voices from the Asia Pacific.* Victoria, Australia: Vulgar Press.

Payne, M. (1997). *Modern Social Work Theory.* London: Macmillan.

Seyf, A. (2001). "Corruption and Development: A Study of Conflict." *Development in Practice* 11 (5): 597–605.

Transparency International. (2010). "Corruption Perceptions Index 2010." In *Transparency International: The Global Coalition Against Corruption.* Retrieved March 20, 2011, from http://www.transparency.org/policy_research/surveys_indices/cpi/2010/results.

United Nations Development Programme. (2010). "Human Development Index (HDI)—2010 Rankings." In *Human Development Reports.* Retrieved March 21, 2011, from http://hdr.undp.org/en/statistics/.

Ware, H. (2005). "Demography, Migration and Conflict in the Pacific." *Journal of Peace Research* 42:435–54.

2

China's Changing Social Welfare

MINJIE ZHANG

Situated in eastern Asia and on the western shore of the Pacific Ocean, the People's Republic of China covers a land area of 9.6 million square kilometers (5.9 million square miles), or about the size of the United States. China's population was recorded at 1.3 billion in the 2000 census. China's economic progress in the past thirty years is unprecedented in world history. In just a few decades China has gone from one of the poorest countries in the world to a regional and global leader with a vibrant economy. Since 1980 China's average annual growth rate has been more than 10 percent, and China's economy is now the world's third largest.

According to the Constitution of the People's Republic of China, China is a socialist state based on the alliance of workers and peasants. Chinese citizens exercise the state's power through the National People's Congress and the local congresses at different levels. The State Council is the executive body of the highest organ of state administration. The rights of Chinese citizens, which are specified in the constitution, are well protected by the law and have a direct bearing on the citizens' vital interests. But as the largest and most populous developing country in the world and with a relatively low level of economic development, China is faced with the onerous task of meeting the needs of its people.

Culture and Social Support in Traditional Society

China has a written history of four thousand years, is one of the four oldest civilizations in the world, and has a central culture fundamental to the traditions of many East Asian countries. The Chinese culture has had an extensive impact upon social welfare issues and the provision of assistance.

Confucius has long been regarded as the representative and symbol of traditional Chinese culture. He was born in China in 551 B.C., a time of conflict, when there was dire need for social theory to reunite the nation and make it powerful. Many theories were proposed, but those of Confucius were the most successful. According to Confucius, society was in chaos because standards had deteriorated and people were not living up to their highest ideals. All would be improved if people would work more conscientiously to fulfill their roles in society. The ideal state of affairs that had once existed could be restored by using moral persuasion to put all on their best behavior. Confucius reasoned that if each individual were perfect in behavior, then society as a whole would likewise be perfect. Confucianism treats humans as social beings whose identities are determined by where they stand in relation to others in the web of social relations. The teachings of Confucius specialize not only in the orderly arrangement of society and relationships between people but also in self-perfection and self-development, humanism, and moral rectitude as the ultimate goals of every person. Confucian philosophy advocates that individuals put group needs above personal needs, placing a high value on family and family norms.

Confucianism teaches that the family is the cornerstone of society. The family in ancient China was the most fundamental social unit, for without good families, the nation could barely be ruled. Confucius also maintained that members of a family must keep harmonious relations with members of other families in the society. Being "friendly with your neighbors and having goodwill toward your acquaintances" continues to be a highly regarded value. Many families are still responsible for providing all types of security for family members, during births, illnesses, aging, accidents, disasters, and death. The mutual help and support among extended relatives is another factor that contributes to the strengthening of family security. The family prototype in traditional Chinese society was that of a stem family, consisting of the elder parents, their sons, daughters-in-law, and grandchildren. The older generation was responsible for fostering their children and sometimes even their grandchildren, who later could care for their elderly grandparents in a process called "counterfostering," considered a part of the natural order of things. The family was multifunctional and was involved in all aspects of family care—financial, emotional, medical, and so forth. Children were, and to a large extent remain, the main guarantee of social security for the Chinese people, especially for the farmers. The local government and patriarchal clans in some regions provided refuges for the aged, the sick, and the poor; free schools for poor children; free eating houses for weary laborers; associations for the distribution of secondhand clothing; and even societies that paid marriage and burial expenses for the poor and destitute (Farley, Smith, & Boyle 2006).

Today the state guarantees such security to those with no families to provide for them, and families and work units share long-term responsibility for the individual. The role of families has changed, but families remain important, especially in the countryside. Family members are bound, by law and custom, to support their members who are aged or disabled. The one-child policy, issued in 1980, promotes one-child families and forbids couples in urban areas from having more than one child. Families violating the policy are required to pay monetary penalties and might be denied bonuses at their workplace. However, in most rural areas, families are allowed to apply to have a second child if the first is a girl or has a physical disability, mental illness, or mental retardation. As the first generation of law-enforced only children come of age for parenthood, the one adult child is now responsible for supporting his or her two parents and four grandparents. This is called the "4-2-1 Problem." The 4-2-1 Problem, a severe financial strain on the one adult child/grandchild, makes retirement funds or charity the options for the six aging parents and grandparents.

The Chinese culture is essentially secular, but one of the main characteristics of Chinese religious beliefs is a practical approach to the role of religion in life. One of the features of Chinese folk religion is its promotion of collectivity and a sense of togetherness. Because people in an agricultural society are subject to many circumstances beyond their control, it is difficult to survive alone without some cooperation from others. Collectivity, not individualism, then becomes the common bond of social solidarity. In Chinese history, no philosopher or thinker of the classical period ever developed an ideal of individualism. Instead, in the family, all were taught to restrain themselves in order to avoid conflicts, and conflict had to be avoided because everyone had to live together. In the community, an elaborate system of ritual exchanges and obligations developed, under which even nonrelatives are tied to one another.

Buddhism also has played an enormous role in shaping the mindset of the Chinese people, affecting their politics, literature, philosophy, medicine, and social welfare. Buddhism was introduced to China in the first century A.D. and apparently was embraced by the rich before it was extended to the poor. Part of the success of Buddhism in China was that it taught its believers to be good people. Central to the Buddhist worldview is the concept of human suffering and ways to reduce and eliminate it. Buddhism teaches that with the right outlook and understanding, including living in the present moment, one can cultivate great peace and joy. Hence Buddhist organizations working with the sick and dying have been able to create an atmosphere congruent with clients' needs and expectations. Their commitment to the welfare of all sentient beings also involves them in activities on behalf of the welfare of animals and the physical environment. Buddhist welfare contributions in China are comprehensive and can be grouped into several categories, including palliative care, work with the sick and dying, revenue generation for poor and needy people, and the provision of food for refugees.

Development of Social Welfare in New China

After the establishment of the People's Republic of China in 1949, the new government focused more on social welfare. The new social welfare programs favored urban dwellers by giving them considerable welfare entitlements, whereas rural residents had to rely more on family care. Because this distribution system mainly covered part of the employees in state enterprises, Chinese scholars called it unity (*danwei*) welfare.

During the early 1950s China's social security system was established, and it provided benefits for retirement, industrial injury, birth, illness, and death. In 1951 the first legislative enactment of social security, the Labor Insurance Regulations of the People's Republic of China, came into effect, providing benefits for birth, disease, injury, medical care, unemployment, retirement, and death internment. This system was immediately put into practice in state, joint state-private, private, and cooperative enterprises or work organizations that employed more than one hundred workers. When an enterprise changed ownership, the security system went into effect in all state and joint state-private enterprises. Similar systems were also gradually established for collectively owned enterprises in urban districts. The social security system played an important role in rehabilitating and developing the national economy as well as guaranteeing the essential needs of the people.

However, this social security system was based on unit security (Zhang 2001). In China, the term *unit* originally referred to urban dwellers with employment in a work organization, such as an economic enterprise, professional institute, government bureau, school, or shop. These work units were not only specialized organizations for different divisions of labor but also providers of free, comprehensive, in-kind health, housing, and pension benefits designed to compensate for the low national standard wages. The state was responsible for arranging the employment of city and town dwellers. In principle, once an employee was hired, that person had a lifelong voucher for various welfare packages. Some large state-owned enterprises operated their own medical clinics, kindergartens, and schools. Employees could not resign to work in another work unit. The social security system for these work units is described as small and comprehensive or work unit managing society, in terms of the comprehensiveness of the benefits. Without the work unit, Chinese society would not function properly. The social security system provided coverage for those working in state agencies and institutions, state-owned enterprises, and some collective enterprises. Workers in other collective enterprises, the self-employed, and farmers, together comprising 70 percent of the population, had no social security coverage.

The work unit social security system was not administered in a unified way. All social security expenditures were funded by the state and state-owned enterprises. Chinese farmers and laborers outside this security system relied excessively on their children for security during accidents, calamities, and old age.

China's social welfare system included the following main characteristics:

- planned high employment rate
- planned low prices for grain, cooking oil, and fabric
- labor insurance (including pensions, free medical care, paid sick leave and maternity leave, occupational and nonoccupational injury benefits, disability benefits, and funeral expenses) for employees in state enterprises
- relief programs for the urban unemployed
- job security, free medical care, sick pay, and pensions available to urban employees in state enterprises

While the above provisions looked promising for urban dwellers, problems became increasingly apparent and severe as time went on. China's social welfare under the command economy had the following shortcomings:

- Coverage was limited and unfair; only 30 percent of the population was covered by social security.
- Though the social security system was first socialized in the 1950s, the degree of socialization was low.
- There was no jobless insurance or unemployment benefits.
- Laws and regulations were incomplete, and funding came only from the state, unit, or collective and not from employees.
- During the ten chaotic years of the Cultural Revolution, from 1966 to 1976, social-insurance work suffered serious setbacks as management agencies and trade unions were dissolved, social pooling from society for retirement expenses was canceled, and social insurance was turned into enterprise insurance.

Social Welfare Issues and Social Welfare Reform: 1984–2000

In 1978 China began a new age of reform when it opened its doors to the world. The Communist Party of China explicitly pointed out that the basic target of the reform was the establishment of a socialist market economic order. This breakthrough provided an important basis for establishing a new social welfare system that would be compatible with the development of the market economy and guarantee citizens their right to a livelihood. "The emerging social insurance program has the following advantages: it widens coverage, facilitates economic development, seeks a minimum entitlement, fosters social integration, and enhances individual participation and responsibility. The creation of an economically and socially viable social insurance program will support the economic development of the country in the twenty-first century" (Tang & Ngan 2001).

As China began its social security reform, some regions began exploring reforms of the old-age pension insurance system, including revenue generation for retirement pensions from state and collective-owned enterprises and an employee contribution system. Some regions even boldly explored ways to integrate social pooling with a personal account. Government institutions and some villages also conducted trial reforms in the pension system.

While the shortcomings of the social welfare system cited above could be traced back to the ineffective work unit security system, it was between 1984 and 1986 that this security system began to be regarded as an impediment to the market competitiveness of state-owned enterprises. The state-owned enterprises were regarded as having low economic productivity, and their employees were viewed as having low work incentives. These conditions resulted in a mounting burden on production costs. To address these problems, work unit security began to be dismantled in 1986 through a series of measures including the introduction of the contract worker system, bankruptcy law, open recruitment of labor, and the allowance of employee dismissal. Thereafter enterprises laid off their surplus and inefficient workers, and the enterprises themselves were liable for bankruptcy. During this process, some cities and counties practiced an old-age pension system in state-owned enterprises on a trial basis while others set up a retirement fund for contract workers with individuals contributing to the fund. Meanwhile, "waiting for a job" insurance, a form of unemployment insurance, was established for workers who had been laid off but were still officially listed as part of their state-owned enterprise's workforce.

From 1987 to 1990 a somewhat expanded social security program went into effect across the country on the county, city, and provincial levels to cover industrial accidents and medical care. This program blazed the way for the expansion of the old-age security system and strengthened the ability of social security in general to take risks.

Government support for social welfare was demonstrated in the work report to the First Session of the Seventh National People's Congress in 1988, when Premier Li Peng emphasized the need to accelerate reform of the social security system, establish and perfect various social insurance systems, and gradually form a social security system unique to China.

In 1990 Premier Zhu Rongji noted that reforms of the housing system, insurance system, and medical system should be priorities for the next ten years because they directly affected the well-being of the people. For the next two years, from 1991 to 1993, an overall social insurance reform focused on expanding the public provision program. The reform also promoted regulations managing all social welfare funds, new social security legislation, and contributions by individual workers to their own pensions.

The aim of social security reform was that the state financial department, institutions or companies, and employees would all collaboratively fund the program.

After 1994, as China's market-oriented economic reforms deepened, the urgent task to develop, standardize, and improve the social security system became most important, but it was difficult to visualize and implement a unified, standardized, social security system. During this stage China focused on providing security to enterprises by emphasizing the importance of such social insurance programs as old-age insurance, unemployment insurance, and medical insurance. Determining the kind of social security system for the countryside was another important theme at this time. The Policy Research Unit at the Ministry of Civil Affairs clarified that the rural security system to be developed should consist mainly of social relief, old-age insurance, social welfare, care to servicemen with disabilities, care to family members of revolutionary martyrs and servicemen, social mutual aid cooperative medical services, and a service network (Den & Liu 2007).

Reform of the social security system, which started in 1984, continues to move forward with the following aims:

- To gradually expand social security coverage. There is already a basic, unified insurance system for old age, unemployment, industrial injury, health care, and birth and maternity care in various types of enterprises. The environment now is favorable for changing the operational mechanism of the enterprises, readjusting the industrial structure, and being open to the world.
- To guarantee daily-life needs and promote production. The social security system must be both just and efficient while promoting enthusiasm, efficiency, and production.
- To establish a revenue-generation system with contributions from the state, enterprises, and individuals.
- To establish a social security management system whereby the state enacts unified legislation, government departments exercise unified leadership, social security agencies run the program, and financial and auditing agencies, as well as trade union and enterprise representatives, provide supervision. Commodity producers need to be free from the burden of completing specific social security operations (Zhang 2006b).

- To establish the social security system in rural areas while developing the rural economy. Meeting this goal will ensure stability and the implementation of the family-planning policy in the countryside. Use of social relief funds for helping the poor should be combined with developing production as much as possible.

Social security reform has achieved tremendous success since it was started in the mid-1980s (Wang 2004). The following changes have been implemented since 1984:

- An increased retirement pension fund for everyone
- Experiments with the old-age insurance system
- Insurance provided for the unemployed
- Experiments with health care plan reform
- A more equal, comprehensive, and economical industrial-injury insurance system

There are two current trends in the social security system. First, the government's control over the economy is relaxing, and urban residents are losing their price-subsidies benefits for food and housing. Second, state enterprises are being exposed to the market. Unemployment is becoming a serious issue; therefore, the most urgent task in urban areas now is to establish a new, rational, and effective social security system to address poverty.

During the Annual National Meeting on Financial Work on December 27, 2010, the Chinese finance minister disclosed that the 2011 central budget expenditure would reach nearly RMB 10 trillion, an increase of over RMB 1.3 trillion compared with 2010. The minister also announced that the financial inputs for social security and employment, education, social housing, and rural development would be further enhanced in 2011. A new item in the annual budget was extension of the coverage of the new rural pension insurance pilot program to 40 percent of the counties, a significant increase over the approximately 11 percent in 2009 and 23 percent in 2010. In line with a trend of approximately 10 percent annual increases since 2005, the average per capita monthly pension benefit nationwide for enterprise retirees was to be raised by RMB 140 in 2011 through budget support (Xie 2010).

Current Developments in Social Welfare

As social welfare systems disappeared or were reformed, the "iron rice bowl" approach to welfare changed. Article 14 of the constitution says that the state "builds and improves a welfare system that corresponds with the level of economic development." After years of exploration and practice, China has set up a social security system consisting of social insurance, social relief, social welfare, social mutual help, care for ex-servicemen with disabilities and family members of revolutionary martyrs, revenue generation through various channels, and the gradual socialization of management and services.

The social welfare system is one of the basic aspects of China's socialist market economic system. Under this system, elderly people are supported, patients with diseases are treated, workers suffering from industrial injuries are given insurance, disaster survivors are offered compensation, the unemployed are given relief, people with disabilities are properly placed, and poor people are provided with aid. Social welfare guarantees people essential life needs and ensures industrial and agricultural production, thereby guaranteeing social stability. Social welfare is a safety net that also helps compensate for the limitations of the market economy. Furthermore, the social welfare distribution system regulates the income distribution of different groups in society. Laws and regulations protect elderly people, children, and people with disabilities, and the state and society have adopted measures to improve their livelihood, health, and participation in social development. In recent years China's social welfare has focused on four populations: older people, people with disabilities, children, and those with low income.

Older People

A report presented by the China National Committee on Aging (2010) shows that at the end of 2009, the number elderly people in China reached 167 million, with 11 percent, or nearly 19 million, being 80 years old or above. Most of the 11 percent were wholly or partly unable to look after themselves. The number of wholly and partially disabled elderly people in China reached more than 10 million and 21.2 million, respectively, accounting for nearly 19 percent of the country's total aged population. Disabled elderly people need care services to different degrees. More than 50 percent of families in China are now empty-nest families (in which old people live without their children), and the figure exceeds 70 percent in certain large and medium-sized cities. There are about 40 million empty-nesters in the rural areas, accounting for 37 percent of China's rural aged population. There is clearly a lack of family and social support for old people in both urban and rural areas. In light of these problems, the Chinese government has decided to make more efforts to improve the governmental elder-care system.

In 2001 the state introduced the Starlight Plan, a program of community welfare service for elderly people. By June 2004 a total of 32,000 Starlight Homes for Elderly People had been built or rebuilt in urban and rural areas throughout China, for a total investment of RMB 13.5 billion (U.S.$2 billion). At the same time, the government has expanded the basic old-age pension system in urban areas, improved the pension system in rural areas, and attempted to include in these systems basic health care insurance and minimum living allowances (National Committee on Aging 2010).

China is establishing a subsidy system for elder-care services. Eligible elderly people will receive considerable government subsidies so they can be well cared for in rest homes or their own homes, and their living standards will not be lower than the average levels of local residents. In addition, residents over 80 years old will be entitled to a unified monthly old-age allowance across China. A community basic care program is also being established in all cities and towns so that low-income senior citizens who are physically challenged or live alone can move to rest homes or enjoy home-care services on government subsidies. At present there are 38,060 rest homes of various types in China, with nearly 2.7 million beds accommodating 2.1 million elderly people, but the total amount remains inadequate. The number of beds in China's rest homes represents just 2 percent of the total aged population, lower than the 5–7 percent in developed countries and even the 2–3 percent in some developing countries.

All levels of government include services for elderly people in their social-economic development plans; they gradually increase investments in services for elderly people and encourage investments from all sectors of society. Enterprises, private entrepreneurs, and others have also invested in and built welfare institutes. Recently a social service system for elderly people was established as the result of a campaign describing their needs. More elderly people now live at home because state and collective social welfare organizations are providing basic support.

People with Disabilities

The aim of social welfare for people with disabilities is to help them gain access to basic public services and eventually employment, income, medical care, pensions, and housing. The Law on the Protection of Disabled Persons, adopted in 1990 and enacted in 1991, is of significant importance to protect the rights of people with disabilities. This law consists of fifty-four articles and nine chapters that address rehabilitation, education, employment, cultural life, welfare, access, legal liability, and so on.

In 2004 the government announced that its Tomorrow Plan—Operations and Rehabilitation for Disabled Orphans—would provide ten thousand orphans with disabilities the necessary surgical operations and rehabilitation services; this goal was met two years later.

The successful 2008 Beijing Paralympics promoted the work of organizations serving people with disabilities and demonstrated the Chinese people's unprecedented enthusiasm to help people with disabilities.

Data regarding people with disabilities at the end of 2010 were reported by the China Disabled Person's Federation (2011) as follows:

- More than 4.412 million people with disabilities were employed in urban areas, and 13.473 million people were engaged in productive labor in rural areas.
- Some 9.271 million low-income people in urban and rural areas were enjoying income guarantees for life.
- A total of 605,000 rural people in residential facilities for seniors with disabilities were receiving concentrated support and the "five guarantees" (food, clothing, medical care, housing, and burial expenses).
- Some 2.92 million people were receiving temporary aid, regular allowances, and special allowances.

Despite significant progress, many challenges and difficulties remain. Owing to lack of awareness and resources, accessibility is uneven across different regions. Availability and accessibility of benefits for people with disabilities have progressed rapidly in big cities, but both need further promotion in the countryside and in small towns.

Children

China's children comprise one-fifth of the children in the world and 24 percent of the population of China. Children are the future of the world, and their well-being is an important part of the human life cycle.

According to a report by the National Working Committee on Children and Women under the State Council (2005), China has 192 special welfare institutions for children and 600 comprehensive welfare institutions with a children's department, accommodating a total of 54,000 orphans and children with disabilities. There are nearly ten thousand community services throughout China, for example, rehabilitation centers and training classes for orphans and children with disabilities such as mental retardation.

The State Council of the People's Republic of China (SCPRC) formally issued the Outline of the Program for Chinese Children's Development between 2011and 2020 in August 2011. This outline fully demonstrates the Chinese government's earnest and responsible attitude toward and concern for programs and services that benefit children. Likewise, all thirty provinces, autonomous regions, and municipalities directly under the central government have development programs for children based on the outline and respective local conditions. The measures and implementation have been executed effectively throughout the country. Under the outline, the mortality rate of infants and children under 5 years old is to be reduced to ten per thousand, and within nine years the educational program will cover 95 percent of all urban and rural children (SCPRC 2011).

Welfare homes play a special role in China's efforts to care for children. Welfare homes and some social welfare institutions care for orphans who have lost their parents because of natural disasters or accidents or who have been abandoned by their parents owing to serious illness or severe mental or physical disabilities.

Vigorous promotion of the programs by the government has helped such children enjoy the fundamental right to an education. The state also provides comprehensive welfare for children, including education and planned immunizations. Project Hope, the flagship program of China

Youth Development Foundation (CYDF), was founded in 1989. The main goal of the project is to ensure that children in rural communities today and in the future have the opportunity to matriculate in school. By the end of 2009 Project Hope had raised over RMB 5.7 billion in donations, helped 3.46 million children from poverty-stricken rural families continue their schooling, and built 15,900 Hope primary schools in poor, remote regions. (Wang 2009) In addition, the foundation has set up a Stars of Hope Award Fund to support top-ranked Project Hope students further their education, and a Hope Primary School Teacher-Training Fund allows teachers the opportunity to sharpen their skills.

In addition, the state takes special care to ensure the livelihood, recovery, and education of children with difficulties. Children with disabilities, orphans, and abandoned babies live in residential facilities and receive services.

Low-Income Groups

The poverty level was RMB 785 (U.S.$114.60) per person per year in 2008. According to the Ministry of Finance, the central government spent RMB 276.16 billion (U.S.$40.31 billion) on social welfare and employment programs in 2008, a 19.9 percent increase over 2007. In 2009 the monthly subsidy to low-income households was increased by RMB 15 (U.S.$2.19) for each urban citizen and RMB 10 (U.S.$1.46) for each rural citizen. The government hopes to strengthen social welfare and health care by providing higher subsidies for low-income people and a 10 percent increase in the basic retirement pension for enterprise retirees. In early 2011 Deputy Minister of Agriculture Fang Xiaojian said that China would raise the poverty line to RMB 1,196 (U.S.$184) and the monthly subsidy to low-income people to RMB 1404 (U.S.$216 (Fang 2011).

Currently most people with low incomes are workers laid off from state-owned enterprises, migrant workers living in cities, or farmers who lost their land because of industrialization or urbanization. Many employees were dismissed when their enterprises were restructured, and their income, usually quite low, was fixed at their dismissal. This income amount was unlikely to change even after their former employers saw huge increases in revenue. Migrant workers are often underpaid and usually are not covered by employee insurance and subsidies. Many farmers who lost their farmland to urbanization not only lost their source of stable income but also were not fairly compensated for their land. It is estimated that farmers usually received only 10 percent of all the revenues generated in land transference. If the government could grant higher compensation to farmers for lost land and as a general matter initiate policies to prevent these vulnerable groups from falling below the poverty line, the effect would be remarkable.

In November 2008 the Ministry of Housing and Urban-Rural Development issued a plan to make available more than two million low-rent houses and more than four million economical houses for low-income workers in three years. In addition, there would be more than 2.2 million houses in slum areas. In 2010 the government also raised the pension for enterprise retirees, improved treatment for those who receive special care as disabled former servicemen and family members of revolutionary martyrs, and offered more affordable housing to middle- and low-income families. This policy has increased the supply of affordable housing and promoted the rehabilitation of shantytowns and substandard buildings in urban areas.

Social Work Education

The history of social work education in China can be divided into four phases: adoption, suspension, reconstruction, and institutionalization.

Adoption

Social work entered China from the Western world. The earliest social work education was started in missionary schools in the early twentieth century. Hujiang University in Shanghai was the first university not only to perceive sociology as a systematic subject and profession but also to train social workers. This university, founded by the Christian Association of America, established a Department of Sociology with American short-term lecturers Daniel Kulp II, H. S. Bucklin, and J. Q. Dealey. Some of the courses included content in community work, child welfare, and social policy (Zheng & Li 2003). By 1949 more than ten universities in China had social work education programs. Most students who finished social work training were employed in welfare agencies and schools.

Suspension

Shortly after the Chinese Communist Party took power in 1949, the development of social work education was interrupted, and after 1952 social work courses were canceled altogether in universities and research institutes. There were likely several reasons for this: First, following the Soviet model of higher education meant halting sociology studies. Second, social historical materialism was perceived to be the true science of proletarians, and social work was labeled the "pseudoscience" of the bourgeoisie and thus had no place in socialist higher education. Finally, the new political leadership regarded the Chinese socialist society as a flawless white pearl, untouched by the problems social work was purported to address. From the early 1950s to the mid-1980s, social work education did not exist in universities in China.

Reconstruction

The reemergence of social work began in the mid-1980s. In 1984 a social work and management specialty program was established at Renmin University in Beijing, but no one enrolled. Three years later, Peking University initiated a social work education program in the Department of Sociology, and some students enrolled. Since the mid-1980s social work education has made great progress in China.

Since 2006 efforts have been made to develop social work education on the bachelor's, master's, and doctoral levels. The Ministry of Education is emphasizing the quality of social work education, including the practice element. The government has funded social work labs because of a lack of practice placements. Different colleges are concentrating on different specialist fields, such as social work with women, workers, and youth—made manifest by the names of the universities. The bachelor's program is general while specialization is taught at the master's level. According to statistics from the China Association for Social Work Education, in 2010 approximately 210 universities and colleges offered the bachelor's degree in social work, and several universities offered the master's degree in social work. Currently many colleges offer nondegree undergraduate training in social work as well.

The China Association of Social Work, CASW, was founded in 1988 and became a member of the International Federation of Social Work (IFSW) in July 1992. The CASW is the single authority with delegates from expert social groups and workers in China. It comprises sixteen professional committees, five special funds, eight functional departments, and three units directly under the guidance of the Ministry of Civil Affairs. The mission of CASW is as follows (China Association of Social Work 2011):

- To promote the construction process of specialization and vocationalization of social work under the guidance of the Chinese government
- To integrate various resources, develop the professional social service that mainly includes social welfare services and commonweal activity, and accelerate the socialization process of social work
- To strengthen theoretic study and practice innovation, develop social work education, and optimize the efficiency of social work
- To provide a sparkplug for the conception of social work, pursue social justice, and promote a harmonious and progressive society

This rapid development of social work evolved from increasing recognition of the use of social work knowledge to address social problems arising from the social and economic changes induced by China's open door policy. New initiatives were undertaken by government departments, academic institutions, and service providers to explore the possibility of reforming service delivery models for older people, children and youth, women, and other vulnerable groups. The development of social work has created demands for personnel with new skills and knowledge. It also led to the promulgation of government policies in 2006 to establish a strong workforce for the social work profession by setting up an accreditation system for social work as a vocation and making funds available for service development and the setting up of NGOs (Law & Gu 2008).

Institutionalization

While considerable progress has been made in social work education, there are some problems that require attention. There is a need to further reform and modernize the field. The principal issues in social work education in China are the following:

- Current social work faculty cannot satisfy the need for the development of social work education. Although many young faculty members have received systematic sociology education, they still must study social work to be better able to teach it.
- We need to develop social work theory and practice models that reflect the concepts, categories, and indexes of the reform and progress of Chinese society.
- Social work education methods need to better integrate knowledge with professional practice skills.
- Social work practitioners should be part of the policy-making process because they have close contact with people, understand their needs, and can reflect their reality to policy makers (Zhang 2001, 2004).

In addition, it may be appropriate to give systematic thought, reflection, and action to the following issues:

- Identifying more explicitly the domain of professional social work practice and education and linking this conceptualization to the development of a refined base of social work knowledge and skills for China
- Relating the characteristics of an increasingly diverse society to the development of curricular and practice models
- Reinforcing the relevance of social work research as a political instrument in the definition and solution of social problems
- Promoting social work knowledge and social work education programs and committing to involving the community in social change (Zhang 2001, 2004)

Early in the new century, the Ministry of Civil Affairs, the Chinese Association of Social Work Education, and numerous social work training institutions in China asked the Department of Applied Social Sciences at Hong Kong Polytechnic University to offer a master's-level training program for social work educators. In a collaborative effort, the Department of Applied

Social Sciences launched a master's of art social work program to create a critical mass of professionals able to assume leadership in the future development of social work education in China (Zhang 2004, 2005, 2006a).

China could learn also from the experiences of developed countries while simultaneously taking the initiative to develop social work education and a social work profession that is indigenous to China and other developing Asian countries. China does not have the burden of a historically established social work structure; therefore it can take any direction to develop its own national social work theories and practices to meet the specific needs of its unique society. This fact not only benefits China but also has the potential to contribute to the development of social work education globally.

The Social Work Profession

During the traditional planned economy period, China formed a social work model whereby all social services were controlled by the government. The transformation process was the result of serious challenges during the social transformation period. This transformation has made some advances owing to its adaptation to social change and service objectives. Social work is now accepted as a profession.

China lacks a sufficient number of social workers, and most social workers have not received professional training. Incomplete government statistics show that there are about 200,000 social workers in the Chinese mainland. Of these, though, only about a quarter have a professional background, and they must take further training to be licensed to do social work. Most social workers are concentrated in Beijing, Shanghai, and other big cities, while vast rural expanses, especially those in the country's center and west, are home to hardly anyone in that line of work (He 2011). Following the central government's enthusiastic promotion of building a strong team of social workers, social work as an occupational position has gradually been established in different government departments and communities. The number of social work positions has been increasing. In this time of rapid development, China's social work profession has broken through many fundamental barriers, such as insufficient teaching materials and unqualified teaching staff (Yin 2011).

In June 2008 the first qualification test for social workers was held. Of the more than 133,000 people who took the test, only about 20,000 were subsequently qualified as professional social workers to work in various fields of public service. The establishment of this test was an important step in the development of the social work profession and social work education. Social workers now have the beginning of credentials that attest to their readiness and competence as professional social workers. Continued professional development and lifelong learning are encouraged.

Existing in a developing country with its own historical, cultural, and political background, China's social work profession provides important values, attitudes, and services for the country's development. China is creating its own indigenous social work education and profession to help vulnerable populations and to promote respect for democracy, social justice, and human tolerance within the Chinese context.

After the Wenchuan earthquake in Sichuan province in 2009, services were oriented toward social work for development. The Community Livelihood Project was established at a local transitional housing area, and services focused on helping injured and disabled people through cultivation and development of mutual support groups for livelihood (Chen 2011). Today, with stronger government support and increasing participation of local and external NGOs, social workers are focusing on community network building. In addition, social workers are playing more important roles in natural disaster relief and crisis intervention work. There is great anticipation that indigenous practice and training approaches suitable for the social context of China will develop more quickly.

According to a circular released by eighteen central governmental departments in November 2011, the government has pledged to ensure that social workers will have more professional training and education opportunities. It intends to adopt payment guidelines and other policies to enable local government departments to purchase the services of charitable and nonprofit organizations, thus encouraging the employment of more social workers. It is planned that two million qualified social workers will be employed on the mainland by the end of 2015 (He 2011).

In summary, during the past one hundred years, China has undergone a number of changes, including going from a government that did not provide social services to a government that is concerned about the social welfare of its people, including vulnerable populations such as orphans and people with disabilities. The early social welfare unit security system, which exclusively favored only urban government employees, has changed markedly to a social security system today that not only is more equitable and comprehensive but also has a broader revenue source based in a market economy.

China faces the problem of an aging population. Family planning and a change in lifestyles have reduced the function of the family as an insurance factor. This fact requires improvement of the social security system and development of the insurance industry. It is imperative that China develop a social welfare system embodying the principles of universality, justice, and regard for individual worth and dignity.

Social welfare has progressed in China in a number of ways. Social security and services and benefits for older people, children, and people with disabilities are more readily available in urban areas; plus, there are currently some plans to expand these services and benefits to the vast rural regions. In addition, social work education, after a thirty-year absence, is now offered in more than two hundred institutions of higher education around the country, and the profession is moving in the direction of credentials with the establishment of the social work qualification test.

Although the outlook for social welfare appears much more promising now than ever before for client needs, social work education, and the social work profession, more attention needs to be focused on the aging population. Toward this end, social work practitioners and scholars may want to collaborate on the issue of aging through joint research projects, dual efforts in policy formation, and the sharing of practice wisdom.

As social work practitioners and academicians in China strive to achieve a stronger social welfare system, social work education, and social work professionalization, they should consider extending their boundaries to include various existing and newly emerging human service practitioners with similar values and social functions. A dialogue among these interested parties may offer a broader perspective for the further emergence and consolidation of the social work profession.

The only conclusion to be drawn at this point is that speedy changes are forthcoming, and the social welfare sector in China has to be more proactive with regard to the continuously changing social, economic, and political situation of China. The state is in a strategic position to continue expanding its social welfare. Collaborative work among the government, social work educators, and social work practitioners could well result in powerful strides being made in social welfare, not only in China but in Asia and the world beyond.

References

Chen, T., F. Chen, & X. Wang (2011). "The Practice of Livelihood Project in Post-earthquake Community and Exploration of Developmental Social Work: Experiences and Reflections of Qinghong Social Work Service Station in Mianzhu." *Social Work* 2:14–18.

China Association of Social Work (2011). "About China Association of Social Work (CASW)." Retrieved November 5, 2011, from http://www.cncasw.org/cncasw/gywm/xhgk/.

China Disabled Persons' Federation (2011). *2010 Statistical Bulletin of China Undertakings for Disabled People's Development*. Retrieved March 24, 2011, from http://www.cdpf.org.cn/sytj/content/2011–03/24/content_30316232.htm.

Den, D. S., & C. P. Liu (2007). *Study on Social Security System in New Rural Areas*. Beijing: People's Publishing House.

Fang, X. J. (2011). "China Will Raise Poverty Line." *Old Areas Construction* 6: 26–27.

Farley, W. O., L. L. Smith, & S. W. Royle (2006). *Introduction to Social Work*. Boston: Pearson Education.

Gao, L. Z., & X. C. Hu (2005). "Overview of and Reflections on Chinese Practice of Microcredit for Poverty Alleviation." *Social Development Issues* 3:35–48.

Gu, X. B., & H. Q. Yuanzeng, eds. (2004). *Research, Practice and Reflection of Social Work in Indigenous Chinese Context*. Beijing: Social Sciences and Documents Publishing House.

He, D. (2011). "1.8 Million Jobs Open for Social Workers." *China Daily*. November 9.

Information Office of the State Council of the People's Republic of China. (2002). "Labor and Social Security in China." *People's Daily*. April 30.

Law, A. K., & J. X. Gu (2008). "Social Work Education in Mainland China: Development and Issues." *Asian Social Work and Policy Review* 1:1–12.

Li, Y. S. (2005). "What Kind of Social Security for China? A Review of China's Social Security System." *Social Development Issues* 3:1–13.

National Committee on Aging (2010). "China to Establish Subsidy System for Elder Care Services." Retrieved November 17, 2010, from http://www.cncaprc.gov.cn/en/info/618.html.

National Working Committee on Children and Women under the State Council (2005). *National Report on Chinese Children's Development (2003–2004)*. Retrieved May 30, 2010, from http://www.china.com.cn/zhuanti2005/node_5875376.htm.

Qian, N. (2004). *Modern Social Welfare*. Beijing: Higher Education Press.

Shi, Z. X., ed. (2000). *Report on China's Social Welfare and Social Progress*. Beijing: Social Sciences and Documents Publishing House.

Si, B. N., ed. (2004). *Introduction to Social Security*. Beijing: Higher Education Press.

State Council of the People's Republic of China (2011). *The Outline of the Program for Chinese Children's Development (2011–2020)*. Retrieved August 8, 2011, from http://news.sina.com.cn/c/2011–08–08/175122955681.shtml

Tang, K. L., & R. Ngan (2001) "China: Developmentalism and Social Security." *International Journal of Social Welfare* 4:253–59.

Wang, D. J., ed. (2004). *The Reform and Development of the Social Security System in China*. Beijing: Law Press.

Wang, Q. (2009). "The Weight of Hope." *Business Watch Magazine* 5:31–39.

Wang, S. B., ed. (2004). *Introduction to Social Work*. Beijing: Higher Education Press.

———— (2006). "The Professionalization of Social Work in Transformation." *Journal of University of Science and Technology (social science edition)* 1:1–5.

Weiss, I. (2005). "Is There a Global Common Core to Social Work? A Cross-national Comparative Study of BSW Graduate Students." *Social Work* 2:101–10.

William, H. W., & C. F. Ronald (2003). *Social Welfare in Today's World*. Beijing: Law Press.

Xie X. R. (2010) "Report at the Annual National Meeting on Financial Work." Retrieved May 30, 2011, from http://www.gov.cn/gzdt/2010–12/28/content_1773935.htm.

Yang, T., & G. Yang (2005). "Chinese Policies on Social assistance in Rural Areas." *Social Development Issues* 3:24–34.

Yin, M. Z. (2011). "Profession, Scientific and Indigenization: Three Conundrums of Social Work in China in Last Ten Years." *Social Sciences* 1:63–71.

Yip, K. S. (2004). "A Chinese Cultural Critique of the Global Qualifying Standards for Social Work Education." *Social Work Education* 5:597–612.

Zhang, M. J. (2001). "The Development of Chinese Social Work in the 20th Century." *Journal of Zhejiang Social Academy* 2:62–66.

———— (2004). "Social Work Education in China: A Brief Review and Recent Developments." Paper presented at the International Conference of Social Welfare Issues and Social Worker's New Roles in the Era of Globalization, Kangnam University, South Korea, and University of South Carolina, Youngin, South Korea.

———— (2005). "Social Work and Social Work Education in a Global Age." *Journal of China Women College* 6:40–45.

——— (2006a). "Three Obstacles of Social Work Development in Contemporary China." *Journal of Zhejiang Gongshang University* 4:73–77.

——— (2006b). "Workfare Policy and Its Revelation to China." *Journal of Zhejiang Social Academy* 4:91–97.

Zheng, G. C. (2008). *The Strategy of Social Security System Reform in China: Principles, Goals and Action Plans.* Beijing: People's Publishing House.

Zheng, H. S., & Y. S. Li (2003). *A History of Chinese Sociology.* Beijing: China Renmin University Press.

3

Understanding Social Welfare in South Korea

JUN SUNG HONG, YOUNG SOOK KIM,
NA YOUN LEE, AND JI WOONG HA

Situated between the People's Republic of China and Japan, the Republic of Korea—commonly called South Korea—is a relatively small country of 98,480 square kilometers (61,193 square miles), only slightly larger than the U.S. state of Indiana. South Korea consists of a population of more than forty-eight million. More than ten million people reside in Seoul, the capital (U.S. Government Statistics 2009; Ministry of Foreign Affairs and Trade 2009). Despite its relatively small size, South Korea has the fourth largest economy in the Asia Pacific region and the fifteenth largest in the world, with a nominal GDP of U.S.$929,124 (1,040,191,457 KRW) (International Monetary Fund 2008). South Korea became a member of the Organization for Economic Cooperation and Development (OECD) in 1996 and is classified as a high-income economy by the World Bank and an advanced economy by both the International Monetary Fund and the Central Intelligence Agency (Central Intelligence Agency 2008). Although rapid population growth was a serious concern during the 1960s when industrialization took place, successful family-planning campaigns and policies, as well as changing lifestyles and attitudes, substantially reduced the fertility rate. Population growth is no longer a threat. For instance, the annual rate of population growth declined from 3 percent[during the 1960s to 0.31 percent in 2008. The declining fertility rate has generated public fear that the younger population is shrinking relative to the growing aging population.

After its independence from Japanese colonial rule was achieved in 1945, South Korea experienced many forms of government before it successfully developed into a stable democracy in the late twentieth century. Currently

South Korea is a republic with powers shared among the executive branch, led by the president; the unicameral legislative branch, called the National Assembly; and the judicial branch, with the Supreme Court and its appellate courts and the Constitutional Court. It is a unitary state with nine provinces and seven administratively separate cities, such as Seoul, Pusan, and Incheon. South Korea also has a multiparty political system, including the current ruling party, the Grand National Party (GNP), and the major opposition party, the Democratic Party (DP).

South Korea is among the world's most ethnically and linguistically homogeneous countries, with only a small Chinese population of about twenty thousand. However, the country has experienced large rates of immigration in recent years. Despite South Korea's homogeneity, it tolerates diversity in religion and consists of 49 percent Christians, 47 percent Buddhists, 3 percent Confucianists, and the remaining 1 percent others (U.S. Government Statistics 2009). In spite of the small percentage of Confucianists in South Korea, Confucianism remains an influence on South Korean values, norms, beliefs, and traditions. Thus it is more of a guiding philosophy than a religion to most South Koreans.

Despite marvelous achievements in becoming an economically strong country and joining the ranks of world powers, South Korea's rapid economic development during the past several decades and the ever-expanding role of globalization since the end of the cold war have cultivated a myriad of social problems, most of which are new to South Korean society. Decreasing fertility rates, an increase in population of older adults, growing income inequalities, rising rates of youth crime and delinquency, and discrimination against foreigners and immigrants are among the most pervasive problems in South Korea today. Because of these new challenges, the government has created social welfare policies and the infrastructure to carry out social programs and services. As a result, there has been rapid development in the social work profession, and various welfare policies have been devised and implemented. Nevertheless, the demands outpace the supply of social welfare.

The need for prevention, intervention, and policy efforts to ameliorate these problems necessitates a close look at the evolution and formation of a social welfare system in South Korea. In this chapter we first examine the historical developments in South Korean social welfare and then move on to explore the current problems the country has faced since the Asian economic crisis in the late 1990s. We summarize the rising influences of globalization, economic integration, and economic development on societal changes such as a rapidly aging population, growing income inequality, and an influx of foreign laborers. Third, we discuss the development of social work education and the social work profession because of rising demands for a systematic response to societal problems. Last, we identify some potential challenges for effective social work practice in South Korea.

History of Social Welfare in South Korea

South Koreans began adopting the term *social welfare* in 1948, when the South Korean government was first established. However, social welfare in South Korea can be traced back to ancient times. During the Three Kingdoms period (57 B.C. to A.D. 668), monarchs provided relief for the common people, who had experienced hardship due to natural disasters that continued during the Silla dynasty (668–918), when the Korean peninsula was unified. In the period of the Koryo dynasty (918–1392), a number of kings provided relief to the poor as well as medical services for commoners. For example, King Yejong (1105–22) established in 1109 Kujedo'gam, a welfare organization that provided free medical and funeral services for poor and suffering people, including those devastated by natural disasters. He later established Hyeminso, an organization that expanded free medical services for the common people as well as the poor and downtrodden (Goo 1970). During the Chosŏn dynasty (1392–1910), the majority of kings established welfare systems for impoverished, widowed, and orphaned people by expanding health care services.

During the Japanese colonial period (1910–45), when the Korean peninsula was colonized by the Japanese imperial army, Koreans had little or no access to social or medical services because of the Japanese seizure of the Korean government. In fact, less than 1 percent of Koreans received any form of social services (In 2000). After World War II, which officially ended Japanese imperialism in the Asia Pacific region, the Korean peninsula was under the control of the U.S. military government from 1945 to 1948. Although Koreans made great efforts to provide social services for those in need during the process of decolonization, lack of resources was a major barrier. Because of devastations caused by World War II, persisting socioeconomic problems and lack of resources made it difficult for the peninsula to provide social services, and so international NGOs such as the Red Cross were the driving force behind social welfare in Korea. These organizations arrived on the peninsula to provide relief assistance and medical treatment. Around this time the Korean peninsula was divided along the 38th parallel, and on June 25, 1950, the Korean War broke out; an armistice was signed three years later on July 27, 1953. The Korean War devastated both North and South Korea, and children in particular suffered tremendously during and after the war, as pillaging and ravaging swept the peninsula. The UN Korean Reconstruction Agency estimated there to be 100,000 orphans in 1951, and in 1953 there were 293,000 widows with 516,000 children; of these, 12,280 were offspring of American troops and South Korean women. International organizations from the United States came to South Korea and established orphanages (Hubinette 2005).

It was not until 1960 that the South Korean government and international organizations focused primarily on providing relief assistance for war sufferers. The welfare state also began to develop around this time. On May 16, 1961, General Park Chung Hee (1917–79) assumed the presidency. The government provided free meals to poor people, older people, and people with disabilities. At the same time, however, the government also focused on economic modernization and poverty eradication. Park argued that the most effective way to end poverty was not welfare spending but job creation, which would be possible only if the economy grew. True to his words, Park produced jobs, but he offered little social protection to the workforce (Kwon 2003). Until the 1970s welfare and social services in South Korea were virtually overlooked by the government.

In the 1970s, as South Korea made significant progress in economic development, Park began to focus on welfare-related policies. He implemented the Free and Subsidized Medical Aid Program in 1977 for citizens who fell below the poverty line and medical insurance policies for all employees and their dependents in large firms of five hundred or more people. Expenses were shared between the employer and the employee. The medical insurance policy was later extended to those working in a company with three hundred or more employees, as well as civil servants and private-school teachers. However, the president refused to ratify the newly legislated health insurance law, which delayed the implementation of universal health insurance (Aspalter 2005). The government nevertheless implemented the New Medical Protection Law in 1976, which is similar to Medicaid in the United States. This new social assistance law provided in-kind benefits to low-income earners and people below the poverty line. Park's government came to an end in 1979, shortly after he was assassinated.

Subsequent to Park's demise, Chun Doo Hwan (b. 1931), head of the Security Command, assumed leadership in South Korea in 1980. Chun restructured social welfare with the intent to strengthen families and achieve South Korean self-sufficiency. At the same time, the government felt obliged to extend the national health insurance plan to dependents of military personnel and pension recipients (Aspalter 2005). The Chun government created a social security system, implemented a minimum wage policy, and established public medical insurance to assist families to live independently. Major progress in social welfare was made in 1988 when South Korea implemented a universal health care system, or National Health Insurance (Lee 2003).

But it was not until 1993, when Kim Young Sam became the president of South Korea and established a civil government, that social welfare became a major part of the government's agenda. South Korea became a democratic nation, unlike the previous years of military dictatorship governance. This political change evoked people's desire for social reform and the development of a welfare system (Lee 2005), and demand for social workers increased significantly. In response, the government began to focus on providing social services for all citizens rather than just for marginalized groups such as orphaned children, poor families, or people with disabilities. The government presented "new Korea creation" as a political slogan, emphasizing the importance of welfare in order to achieve its welfare goals. However, a concrete welfare strategy was not considered until 1994 (Shin 2001).

In 1995 the Kim government announced that globalization was an effective strategy for achieving "new Korea creation" (Kim 2011); the government focused on economic growth and global competition, which once again took precedence over social welfare development (Lee 2005). The government plan for globalization was realized shortly after President Kim's participation in the Asia-Pacific Economic Cooperation (APEC) Summit in 1993 (Kim 2011) and the UN Social Development Summit in Copenhagen, Denmark, in 1995 (Lee 2005). The government ultimately announced that a productive welfare model, which balances welfare and economic development, would be adopted as a strategy for globalization (Sung 2001). Although the productive welfare model emphasized the importance of welfare, the focus was mostly on economic development, and welfare benefits were regarded as "unnecessary spending" (Kim 2011). As a result, the number of welfare beneficiaries decreased from 5.5 percent of the total population in 1992 to 3.3 percent in 2006 (Chung 2007).

In the beginning of Kim Dae Jung's presidency (1997–2002), countries in the Asia Pacific region—including South Korea—experienced a major financial crisis, which resulted in the devaluation of local currency and an increase in unemployment rates. These events widened the income gap between rich and poor. Demands for welfare reforms grew as the Korean Confederation of Trade Unions (KFTU) and the Federation of Korean Trade Unions (FKTU) coalesced and made demands for reforms in employment insurance, the social safety net for the unemployed and impoverished, the national pension, and the social security program. Recognizing these needs, the government substantially raised its welfare budget from U.S.$5.2 million (600 billion KRW) to U.S.$86.2 million (10 trillion KRW) (Lee, 2005). Further, the government launched public labor enterprises (i.e., employment in the public sector for the unemployed), job training, and a loan system for the unemployed. The Kim administration extended the pension system to self-employed people, and it was nationalized in 1999 (Lee 2005).

Roh Moo Hyun's administration (2003–08) was characterized as welfare-oriented, which reflected his attempt to develop a welfare state in South Korea. Key goals for Roh were to foster social integration and to ameliorate social displacement by facilitating distributive justice (Song 2003). Roh expanded the poverty policies of Kim Dae Jung via tax reform, which included increasing taxes for the rich and offering tax benefits to the working class. He also expanded social insurance to temporary workers (Song 2003). Despite the expansion of the social welfare system under this administration, the state did not play a major role in providing social services to citizens. Moreover, according to the OECD Social Expenditure Data 2003, South Korea's spending on health services and pensions was 6.9 percent of its GDP in 2005—the lowest among thirty OECD countries (Adema & Ladaique 2009).

Roh's presidency ended in 2008 when Lee Myung Bak, a former Hyundai executive and the mayor of Seoul, was elected as South Korea's next president. Lee's presidency, with its resurgence of conservatives, brought an end to a decade of progressive government. Lee's administrative government promised to reduce taxes and to bolster South Korea's global competitiveness by liberalization, deregulation, and free trade agreements. In his effort to pursue a growth-oriented welfare reform (under the slogan "growth first and distribution later"), he created a market-friendly welfare model, replacing Kim's and Roh's redistribution-based welfare model (Kim 2009). The financial crisis in the United States in 2008, however, forced Lee's government to reduce the target rate of economic growth from 7% to 2%, and to realize that pursuing welfare along with economic growth may be difficult (Kim, 2009). It remains to be seen to what extent social welfare in South Korea will be developed under Lee's government.

Social Problems and Social Welfare Today

Although South Korea has had a long history of social welfare, social welfare as a profession is relatively new (Hong & Han 2009). In recent years demands for social welfare professionals have grown in South Korea owing to a host of social problems, such as increasing rates of youth crime and delinquency, poverty, discrimination against foreigners, and an aging population in conjunction with significantly low birthrates.

Youth Crime and Delinquency

The number of youth-related crimes and delinquencies has risen in South Korea since rapid urbanization and the migration to metropolitan areas in the 1970s. Criminal activities in South Korea have become increasingly more violent (Korean Institute of Criminology 1994). Reducing criminal activities in the urban areas has required strong government intervention, enthusiasm for high educational attainment, and prohibition of firearms. In the 1990s social and environmental changes affected the character and attitudes of youths, which has resulted in family, school, and gang problems (Korean Institute of Criminology 1994). In the late 1990s, when South Korea experienced the Asian economic crisis, the devaluation of currency combined with massive company layoffs and the increasing gap between rich and poor broke the social fabric of society. Social problems, criminal activities (such as juvenile delinquency, violence, and property crimes), and suicide rates rose significantly as a result (Hong & Eamon 2009; Lee, Hong, & Espelage 2010).

Delinquent acts such as assault, peer victimization, fighting, and sexual violence in the schoolyards and neighborhoods have been increasingly reported by students, teachers, and parents. A number of recent studies (e.g., Hong & Eamon 2009; Kim, Koh, & Leventhal 2004) point out that peer victimization is highly prevalent in all educational levels of South Korean schools and has been frequently associated with behavioral, emotional, and social problems, as well as negative parent-child relationships and teacher-child conflicts (Hong & Eamon 2009; Shin & Kim 2008). Serious violent acts committed by young people, such as assault, gang involvement, homicide, and suicide, have also surged in South Korea. In 2006 there were 47,795 cases of juvenile delinquency, of which 39.3 percent involved youths between the ages of 14 and 15 (Mun et al. 2007). Suicide was also the second leading cause of death among young people in 2008 and is a major public health concern (Lee, Hong, & Espelage 2010). Because youth crime is a serious social concern, the government has established youth counseling centers nationwide in recent years. Several organizations, such as the YMCA and the Myongdong Info Zone of Youth (MIZY) Center, an organization that promotes cultural exchanges for young people, have also provided recreational opportunities. The government has offered a limited amount of funding to youth-based organizations and NGOs that establish youth centers (Lee 2003). Additionally, there are youth correctional centers in various municipalities, which are equipped with educational and recreational facilities and provide job training for incarcerated young people (Mun et al. 2007).

Several school-based intervention and prevention programs have been implemented in many school districts in response to the problem of school violence (Hong & Eamon 2009). Hwang and Kim's (2006) ten-session bullying prevention program for both victims and perpetrators of peer victimization is an excellent example of an intervention that enhances positive peer interactions. Unfortunately, many programs provide information only on school violence and how to cope with violence rather than on reforming the school environment (*Korea Herald* 2011). A number of suicide prevention and intervention strategies have also been implemented to assist young people in coping with academic stress (Lee, Hong, & Espelage 2010), to promote positive parent-child relationships (Doh et al. 2003), and to deal with peer victimization (Choi 2002). Because problems such as bullying and suicidal behavior are serious concerns, many school districts in

South Korea have also recently recognized the importance of school social workers. As a result, a limited number of school districts have social workers providing counseling services for students with emotional or behavioral problems, as well as for those with special needs (Mun et al. 2007).

Poverty

In 1959 more than 90 percent of the South Korean population lived below the poverty line owing to the Korean War. Despite South Korea's remarkable economic growth over the past several decades, the poverty rate has risen annually since 2000. This dramatic rise in poverty has been attributed to the Asian economic crisis, the economic recession in recent years, skyrocketing housing prices, and soaring unemployment rates. According to the Korea Development Institute (KDI), the national poverty rate in 2000 was 11.5 percent, which surged from 7.7 percent in 1999. In 2003 about 11 percent of the population (approximately 5.1 million people) were living below the poverty line. The number of social problems such as suicide, burglary, and theft has been increasing recently. For example, the number of reported cases of suicide because of poverty rose from 454 in 2000 to 600 in 2002 (Lee 2005).

The South Korean government has attempted to resolve the issue of poverty since the end of the Korean War. About 2.5 percent of the population receive free medical services. Of the population living in poverty, 5.7 percent receive welfare benefits or free medical services (Lee 2005). Additionally, social service programs for people with needs, such as women, people with disabilities, and children, have been at the forefront of the government agenda since the 1990s. The government has subsidized education, medical services, emergency funding, and public housing, in addition to providing financial assistance for people living below the poverty line (Korean Department of Health and Human Services 2008). The government also has joined forces with major conglomerates such as the Samsung Group to provide employment opportunities for people in poverty (Korean Department of Health and Human Services 2008) and to establish welfare programs. Moreover, the Samsung Group created the Samsung Foundation, which establishes and operates child-care centers and youth volunteer corps for orphaned teenagers with younger siblings, provides financial assistance for overseas training, and is actively involved in social welfare program development. In addition, NGOs and religious organizations such as Good Neighbors International, International Aid Korea, and Global Care provide free meals, temporary shelter, and medical supplies for poor and needy families in South Korea and abroad (Hong & Han 2009).

Discrimination Against Foreigners

In the late 1980s the labor shortage in the 3D (dirty, difficult, dangerous) job categories led to an influx of foreign laborers in South Korea (Lim 2002), many of whom migrated from countries such as China, Indonesia, Vietnam, the Philippines, Bangladesh, and Thailand. According to the Ministry of Justice, the number of migrant laborers (both skilled and unskilled) increased from 6,409 in 1987 to 243,363 in 2000 (Seol 2000). The Statistical Yearbook of Departures and Arrivals Control, 1991–2001, of the Ministry of Justice also recorded that the number of ethnic Korean laborers from China skyrocketed from 18,436 in 1991 to 93,736 in 2001 (Lim 2003). In response to the surging numbers of undocumented foreign laborers, the government coordinated an effort called the industrial trainees system to resolve the issue (Hong & Han 2009). This system was intended to train foreign workers employed in South Korean companies, which enabled employment of foreign unskilled workers in South Korea for the first time. As of 2006, foreign laborers numbered 360,000, or 1.5 percent of the South Korean workforce (Amnesty International 2008; as cited in Hong & Han 2009), of which 80 percent were undocumented laborers (Seol & Skrentny 2004).

Industrial trainees and undocumented workers frequently encounter human rights violations and exploitation in the workplace (Shin 2004). Foreign laborers also live below the poverty line. It is difficult for migrant workers to receive proper medical treatment when they have job-related injuries due to language and cultural barriers, as well as discrimination. Withheld wages, long working hours, dangerous working conditions, and prohibitions against organizing labor unions make it difficult for foreign laborers to live in South Korea. Additionally, female foreign laborers are vulnerable to sexual abuse by their employers (Hong & Han 2009).

To address the situation of foreign laborers in South Korea, sixty-three international NGOs and private-sector agencies, such as Bucheon Migrant

Workers, have provided counseling, medical services, and educational services for foreign laborers. To provide the needed financial support for immigrants and multicultural families in their adjustment to South Korean society, the government recently has provided financial incentives for programs that teach the Korean language to foreigners to assist them in overcoming language barriers. Some schools located in regions with a high number of ethnic minorities and multicultural families have offered afterschool Korean language classes to assist non-Korean children in their education. Major universities, such as Yonsei University and Ewha Womans University, have also provided merit-based scholarships for immigrants who demonstrate need and academic promise. To safeguard human rights of foreign laborers in South Korea, the Employment Permit for Migrant Workers was enacted in 2003, which permits foreigners to gain employment in South Korea (Hong & Han 2009).

Aging

A rise in the elderly population is currently one of the most pressing problems in South Korea. Until 1900 the population of people 65 years old and older was less than 1 percent of the population as a whole, increasing to 3 percent by 1950. The number of older adults in South Korea is estimated now at five million, which is about 12 percent of the total population. The elderly population is projected to increase to 14 percent by 2019 and more than 20 percent by 2026 (Kim 2004). The shift from an aging society to an aged society is happening faster in South Korea than in many other countries. For example, it took 115 years for France to make that shift and 85 years for Sweden to become an aged society. In contrast, South Korea, at the current rate of growth, will take only 19 years to move from an aging to an aged society. Unfortunately, South Korea is ill prepared for this eventuality (Howe, Jackson, & Nakashima 2007).

The care of older adults has gained attention from policy makers in South Korea in recent years owing to a major shift in social trends, including the increasing elderly population, geographic mobility of the young, growth of the female labor force, and a decrease in multigenerational households and a movement toward nuclear families. Family care for older people has declined significantly, while demands for costly public support for this group have increased, particularly in urban areas (Wong, Yoo, & Stewart 2007).

The South Korean government has recently begun to address the problem of aging and the decline in multigenerational households. In January 2008 the government provided approximately U.S.$84 (94,016 KRW) per month to citizens 70 years old and older and is planning to provide the same amount to those 65 years old and older (Korean Department of Health and Human Services 2008). The government also provides free medical services, public housing, and shelter for those living in poverty. A number of NGOs provide free meals and shelter for the elderly (Kim 2001). Additional social services for older people have been created in recent years, such as long-term care facilities and respite care providers, which have been keeping pace with the increasing number of older people (Choi, Choi, & Kim 2009). At the national level, several public campaigns, such as the Campaign for Respect for Elders, Respect for the Elderly Week, and Filial Piety Prize System, were established to preserve the traditional value of filial piety, which has been the keystone of social efforts in East Asian countries (Sung 1990).

Social problems such as youth crimes, poverty, discrimination, and lack of support for the older population necessitate effective prevention, intervention, and policy efforts. To address these problems, many nonprofit, private social service providers have been activated in South Korea. More than two thousand residential facilities provide services for vulnerable populations (Choi et al. 2009). At the community level, there are currently four hundred multipurpose, community-based, nonprofit social service centers operating, which are subsidized by the government and consist of ten to fifty full-time staff members. Because social workers play a critical role in addressing these issues and in providing needed social services, a close examination of the social work profession and education in South Korea is necessary.

Social Work Education

Demand for social welfare and social work education programs in South Korea has been greater than ever since the 1960s (Sung 1991). A social work education program in South Korea was first initiated in 1947 at Ewha Womans University, which offered classes in casework (Hong & Han 2009). This program was heavily influenced by social work education programs in the United States (Chon 2004). Seoul National University and Yonsei University subsequently established schools of social work in 1958 and 1980, respectively. Despite the establishment of social work programs in several universities since the late 1940s, social work was recognized as a legitimate profession in South Korea only in the 1980s, when increasing rates of income inequality and poverty due to rapid industrialization and urbanization became major concerns for many South Korean citizens, who demanded economic stability (Chi 1987). In response to the growing requests for social work professionals and researchers, the number of social work education programs in South Korea has rapidly increased. In 2001 there were 77 graduate and 101 undergraduate programs in social work and 64 vocational schools that offered a specialized social work program (Kwon 2004), and the number of social work programs increased substantially to more than 369 in 2009 (Korean Academy of Social Welfare 2007). These programs produced more than 15,000 graduates in 2004 and more than 45,000 licensed social workers in 2007 (Choi et al. 2009).

Social work education programs in South Korea—at both undergraduate and graduate levels—are structured similarly to programs in the United States, which primarily consist of social work classes and practicum. Core courses include the philosophy and values of social work, basic social welfare classes, human behavior in the social environment, methods of social welfare practice, social welfare law and policy, administration and program evaluation, survey methods and data analysis, and specialization (e.g., child welfare, youth welfare, aging, disability, women, and family). Social work students in South Korea are also required to fulfill 120 to 130 hours of practicum (Hong 2003). However, social work researchers in South Korea (e.g., Hong 2003) have pointed out the limitations in social work education. First, South Korean social work professors have yet to set standards for hands-on training, which is attributed to the fact that they typically supervise students in various specialties, from child welfare to aging. Additionally, as Yun (1997) noted, many social work professors in South Korea are research oriented, with little or no social work experience—particularly in the area of clinical social work. Sung (1991) also criticized the tendency to model American social work programs, given that American programs are practice oriented while South Korean programs are more theory based. Because many pioneering social workers and social work faculty members in South Korea were trained in the United States, the social work curricula have been strongly influenced by American social work educational programs (Choi et al. 2009). Another reason this can be problematic is that Western societies value individualism, which runs counter to the collectivist-oriented traditions of Asia.

Korean Academy of Social Welfare

The Korean Academy of Social Welfare (KASW) was founded in 1957 as the Korean Academy of Social Work and took its present name in 1985 (Korean Academy of Social Welfare, n.d.). Similar to the Council of Social Work Education in the United States, the goal of KASW has been to enhance understanding of social problems and to foster the development of social welfare in South Korea through dissemination of social welfare research. To achieve this goal, KASW has sponsored numerous conferences for researchers and practitioners, both domestically and internationally, published a quarterly journal on social problems and social welfare issues in South Korea, and supported major research projects about social welfare. For several decades KASW has made major contributions to the development of South Korean social work education and the social welfare system (Korean Academy of Social Welfare, n.d.).

The Social Work Profession

Articles 5 and 9 of the Social Welfare Law, first enacted in the 1970s, stipulate that social workers must have majored in an accredited social work program or be employed in a social service agency for at least five years (for high school graduates) to qualify for social work licensure (Kim et al. 2006). The social work licensure system in South Korea is divided into three levels: Level 1 certification is the highest level, in which applicants are required to pass an examination provided by the government in cooperation with the Korea Council of Social Work Education. Level 2 is the second highest, and level 3 certification is granted to applicants depending on their educational degree and number of years of social work experience (Yeom & Bae 2010). As of 2006 there were 157,228 licensed social workers in South Korea (Chung H.W. 2007).

Despite significant advances in the social work profession, social workers have not received the same degree of respect compared to other, more prestigious careers, such as medicine or law. According to H.W. Chung's 2007 study, social work was perceived by only 12.4 percent of the general population as a respectable profession, and 55.6 percent responded that social work is at the same level as teachers or nurses. The study also found that 18.9 percent recognized social work as a profession similar to nursery school teachers, and 13.1 percent felt that it is not a legitimate profession. H. W. Chung (2007) argued that social work has been identified as a volunteer activity rather than a profession. Moreover, Nho (2004) found that the average yearly salary for social workers in South Korea was approximately U.S.$1,600 (1,790,829 KRW), which is significantly lower than for other similar professions. A survey of 5,670 social workers also reported that 74 percent were dissatisfied with their salary, which remained low despite many years of work experience (Nho 2004).

Korea Association of Social Workers

The Korea Association of Social Workers (KASW) is a government-approved organization, which is equivalent to the National Association of Social Workers in the United States. Committed to 320,000 members, its mission is threefold: to improve the quality of the social work profession in South Korea, to provide opportunities for knowledge and skills development, and to influence laws that safeguard the employment rights of social workers and their clients. In accordance with the Social Welfare Law, which is under the direction of the Ministry of Health, Welfare, and Family Affairs, the activities of KASW include issuing licenses to social work professionals, administering level 1 of the social work licensing examination, providing continuing education, and cooperating with various organizations to develop training programs for social workers specializing in various fields (Korea Association of Social Workers n.d.).

Moreover, to enhance social workers' education and skills development, and to influence laws that safeguard their rights, KASW has been actively consulting with policy makers to improve social welfare; assisting social workers training in specialized fields; publishing a monthly magazine, *Social Worker*, with updated information on welfare issues; organizing communications among social workers; and circulating social work–related information on policy changes and new trends via weekly e-mail correspondence. KASW has also provided training abroad for social workers to increase networking opportunities with other countries and has cooperated with international institutions as a member of the International Federation of Social Workers by hosting conferences and international forums (Korea Association of Social Workers, n.d.).

Despite the advances in social work education and the social work profession in South Korea, there remain several cultural barriers to effective practice and service delivery, as we discuss in the following section.

Cultural Barriers to Effective Social Work Practice

Social work as a profession is relatively new in South Korea, so it is inevitable that long-standing and pervasive cultural factors such as social shame and patriarchy, as well as lack of a culturally competent social work practice, can pose a barrier to social work practice and social services.

Social Shame

In South Korea social shame (*changpi*) can be defined as a sudden feeling of embarrassment that brings a flush to one's cheek. The feeling of shame is linked with the dominant values of Korean culture, which were affected by the process of modernization (i.e., expansion of scientific knowledge, a democratic system, industrialization, and urbanization) during the late nineteenth century when Western cultural influences penetrated the Korean peninsula. Values considered important in modern South Korea include the insistence that individual efforts be made for liberty, egalitarianism, reason, and material wealth. Feelings of shame in contemporary South Korea are associated with the lack of these markers of success (Kim 2001).

People often try to avoid meeting or contacting the person who is aware of their shame. When people feel a sense of shame in public, they attempt to avoid the situation. Because South Korea is a collectivist society, individual shame is interpreted as an entire family's shame. For example, although the divorce rate has skyrocketed in South Korea, many South Koreans still perceive divorce as shameful and dishonoring to the entire family. A child's physical or mental disability is also perceived to be shameful for the entire family, and family members may not feel comfortable talking about the child in public (Kim 2001).

Given the effectiveness of family-oriented social work practice, there has been a major shift in the primary unit of attention in the United States, from the individual to the family (Early & GlenMaye 2000). In Asia, because one's identity is usually more linked to one's family, friends, and groups (Sue, 2006), traditional Western-based psychotherapeutic approaches that emphasize open verbal communication are not perceived as effective (see Chu & Sue, 2011). In addition, because of shame associated with help seeking outside the family in South Korea, many individuals and family members are hesitant to utilize mental health services or become involved in counseling sessions (Jang et al. 2007). Many are also reluctant to seek help because of the stigma attached to mental or emotional distress, and those who do seek help often utilize phone or Internet counseling, where they conceal their identity. Lauber and Rossler (2007) argued that compared to Western societies, in Asian countries there is a more widespread tendency to stigmatize and discriminate against people with mental or emotional disabilities, since they are perceived as dangerous.

Patriarchy and Women's Roles

The traditional Confucian value of patriarchy has dominated South Korean society for several hundred years, since the Chosŏn dynasty. According to this patriarchal system, the relationship between men and women is hierarchical, men and women having different social roles. Women occupy domestic roles (e.g., household tasks), while men dominate public roles. Women are also expected to be obedient to the three men in their lives—their father (prior to marriage), their husband (during marriage), and their son (after the death of their husband).Women's roles are expressed as "earth," and men's positions are frequently expressed as "heaven" (Sung 2003). According to the Confucian Rule of Three, men are endowed with superior authority compared to women. In traditional Korean culture, the ideal woman is characterized as a wise mother and good wife (Pak 2006). This is someone who devotes her life and maintains a subordinate relationship to her husband and children. In this traditional culture, women are also expected to conceal their true emotional expressions and their burdens (see, e.g., Kim 2001). Another salient feature of Confucian-based patriarchy is filial piety. A married woman is judged by how well she fulfills her role as a caregiver to her elderly parents-in-law (Sung 2003).

However, as South Korea has become more prosperous, and as increasing numbers of women have gained access to education and employment opportunities (Park 2001), these patriarchy-based relationships have changed dramatically (Sung 2003). For example, the number of female college graduates increased from 2.4 percent of college graduates in 1975 to 25.5 percent in 2005, and approximately half of the entire female adult population in South Korea is employed (Korean Women's Development Institute 2006). Despite these changes, the South Korean welfare policy still emphasizes the importance of women's household duties, and many South Korean working women experience the dual burdens of work and family as a result (Sung 2003).

For example, the government introduced the child-care leave system under the Equal Employment Opportunity Act in 1987, which allowed for two months of maternity leave. Employed women with a child 1 year old or younger became eligible for a one-year maternity leave without financial support. The act was revised and recognized in the equal opportunity registration in 1995, which changed the *maternity* leave to *parental* leave, to encourage fathers' involvement in child rearing. In reality, limited eligibility allows male workers to use the benefit only in the case of a spouse dying or becoming afflicted with a terminal illness. In 2001 employment insurance provided U.S.$200 (223,853 KRW) per month for parental leave for each working mother. The amount was subsequently increased to U.S.$300 (335,781 KRW) in 2003, U.S.$400 (447,757 KRW) in 2004, and U.S.$500 (559,689 KRW) in 2006. The goal of increasing the amount of parental leave benefits was to retain female employees in the workforce and resolve the problem of low birthrates. However, the amount has been insufficient for child-care needs (Presidential Committee on Aging and Future Society 2005; Sung 2003). Although the parental leave system is a step toward eliminating patriarchy and fostering gender equality, little has been changed to relieve women of the dual burden of work and family.

As of 2010 the child-care leave system has been extended to working women with children ages 6 years old or younger who do not attend elementary school. The government is also currently providing a monthly benefit of U.S.$500 (558,125 KRW) for employees with young children (Haengbokhan Il Gajeong ui Gyunhyeong n.d.). The number of employees who applied for the parental leave benefits was 68,526 in 2008, according to the Korean Women Workers Association (n.d.), an organization dedicated to ensuring human rights and gender equality for working women. However, the number of former employees seeking telephone counseling for job loss due to parental leave has also increased, from 34.8 percent in 2007 to 55.7 percent in 2008 (Korean Women Workers Association n.d.). Park (2002) noted that because of age and gender discrimination in South Korea, older women risk losing their jobs when they become pregnant because they are perceived as expendable.

Cultural Competency in Social Work

In response to the growing numbers of immigrants and international marriages in South Korea, a limited number of social work education programs have included international and multicultural curricula. Major universities in South Korea—for example, Ewha Womans University, Seoul National University, and Yonsei University—have recently included courses such as International Social Work and Cultural Diversity and Social Work Practice, to name just a couple. The South Korean government and many universities have also provided financial support to help immigrants and multicultural families adjust to South Korea. For example, Korean language programs for foreigners have been expanded with government subsidies and university scholarships (Hong & Han 2009).

Unfortunately, many migrants and foreign brides of South Korean men experience human rights violations such as spousal abuse and abuse in the workplace, which places them in a precarious situation with little or no recourse. Although international and multicultural classes have been incorporated in a limited number of social work education programs, these programs have not adequately prepared social work students to provide culturally relevant services for immigrants and ethnic minorities. Although a limited number of NGOs and other social service organizations such as Amnesty International have advocated on behalf of migrant workers' rights, service providers have been ill equipped to meet their needs owing to language and cultural barriers.

Recently demands for social work education and the social work profession have increased rapidly in South Korea. Despite the need for social work professionals, little has been known about the current state of social work education and practice. In this chapter we provided a historical overview of social work and social welfare in the South Korean society, which was followed by an assessment of such major issues as youth crime and delinquency, poverty, discrimination against foreigners, and aging. We then examined the current state of social work education and the social work profession as well as some barriers to implementing effective social work practice, including social shame, patriarchy, and the lack of culturally competent social work practice.

Developing the South Korean social work profession and education is crucial. To do so, social workers need to collaborate with grassroots and government organizations and be active agents in implementing social policies that promote the social and economic well-being of vulnerable and marginal groups. Researchers also need to conduct evidence-based research to enhance both social work practice and policy. In addition, researchers must collaborate with practitioners, NGOs, social service agencies, and the government.

Reflections and Directions

Social problems in South Korea require a close examination of the existing social work education and profession in South Korea, considering that social workers play a critical role in addressing these issues and in providing the needed social services. In recent years social workers and grassroots organizations in South Korea have made a major effort to advocate on behalf of vulnerable groups and to assist them in acquiring skills that enhance their ability to access social and economic resources and to integrate into mainstream society. Although South Korean social workers make a great effort to ameliorate social ills, social justice can be achieved only when policy and structural changes are realized. As Eamon (2008:327) argued, "Simply teaching relevant knowledge and skills to vulnerable groups . . . is insufficient to make many of the necessary policy and structural changes that are required to gain access to decision-making processes, social and economic resources, and equal opportunity." Advancing the South Korean social work profession and education is imperative; however, social workers must also effectively collaborate with grassroots and government organizations and be active agents in implementing policies that enhance the social and economic well-being of vulnerable groups. Only then will social justice be achieved.

South Korea is experiencing dynamic changes that present challenges as well as opportunities for future improvement and development. Social work researchers in South Korea are committed to developing and disseminating knowledge about effective intervention strategies and to bridging the gap between theory and practice through research, education, and consultation (Choi et al. 2009). It is crucial that scholars provide evidence-based findings to enhance social work practice and policy. Thus researchers must actively collaborate with practitioners, NGOs, social service agencies, and the government to ameliorate social problems and to promote social justice for all citizens. The first step is for social work faculty in the classroom to address the important social issues (such as discrimination, human rights violations, and exploitation) that affect the nation's vulnerable populations. It is our hope that this chapter provides directions for future research and knowledge development.

References

Adema, W., & M. Ladaique, M. (2009). "How Expensive Is the Welfare State? Gross and Net Indicators in the OECD Social Expenditure Database (SOCX)." *OECD Social, Employment and Migration Working Papers*, doi: 10.1787/220615515052.

Amnesty International (2008). "Republic of Korea: Migrant Workers Are Also Human Beings." *Amnesty International*. Retrieved June 13, 2008, from http://lib.ohchr.org/HRBodies/UPR/Documents/Session2?KR/AI_KOR_UPR_S22008 anx_Migrantworkersarealsohumanbeings.pdf.

Aspalter, C. (2005). "The East Asian Welfare Regime." In *The Challenge of Social Care in Asia*, ed. N. T. Tan. New York: Marshall Cavendish.

Central Intelligence Agency (2008). "Appendix B. International Organizations and Groups." In *CIA World Factbook*. Retrieved April 17, 2010, from https://www.cia.gov/library/publications/the-world-factbook/appendix/appendix-b.html.

Chi, Y. C. (1987). "Social Development and Capacity Building: A Case Example of a Social Welfare Center in Korea." *International Social Work* 30:139–49.

Choi, J. H. (2002). "Victimization by Peers in Early Adolescents: Relationships to Parent Attachment, Peer Rejection, and Friendships." *Korean Association of Child Studies* 21:307–22.

Choi, J. S., S. Choi, & Y. Kim (2009). "Improving Scientific Inquiry for Social Work in South Korea." *Research on Social Work Practice* 19:464–71.

Chon, S. Y. (2004). "A Study of the Relationship Among the Social Work Educations, Values and Advocacy," M.A. thesis, Seoul Women's University.

Chu, J. P., & S. Sue (2011). *Asian American Mental Health: What We Know and What We Don't Know*. Retrieved November 6, 2011, from http://scholarworks.gvsu .edu/orpc/vol3/iss1/4.

Chung, H. W. (2007). "Sahoe pokji illyŏk ŭi chŏnmunsŏng chegobang'an." *Wol'gan Pokji Tonghyang* 102:16–21.

Chung, M. K. (2007). "Globalization, Democratization, and the Restructuring of Production and Welfare Regimes in Korea." *Korean Social Policy* 14:6–79.

Doh, H. S., J. I. Kwon, B. K. Park, S. H. Hong, J. Y. Hong, & Y. E. Hwang (2003). "The Development of Intervention Programs Based on Characteristics of Children Victimized by Peers: Focus on Parent Education and Social Skills Training Program. *Korean Association of Child Studies* 24:103–21.

Eamon, M. K. (2008). *Empowering Vulnerable Populations*. Chicago: Lyceum Books.

Early, T. J., & L. F. GlenMaye (2000). Valuing Families: Social Work Practice with Families from a Strengths Perspective. *Social Work* 45:118–30.

Goo, J. H. (1970). *Social Welfare History in Korea*. Seoul: Institute of Korean Social Welfare.

Haengbokhan Il Kajŏng ŭi Kyunhyŏng (n.d.). *Chikjang poyuk sisŏl chiwon: Solchi piyongmusang chiwon*. Retrieved March 21, 2010, from http://www.happy balance.kr.

Heo, S. (1999). "Kukmin kichosaenghwal pojangbŏp'i chejŏngdoegikkaji." *Wol'gan Pokji Tonghyang* 15:6–9.

Hong, G. K., & M. Domokos-Cheng Ham (2001). *Psychotherapy and Counseling with Asian American Clients*. Thousand Oaks, Calif.: Sage.

Hong, S. M. (2003). "Sahoe pokji silchŏn kyoyuk esŏ ŭi chŏnmunsŏng." *Wol'gan Pokji Tonghyang* 54:12–14.

Hong, J., & I. Y. Han (2009). "Cultural Competency and Social Work Education in 'Multicultural' South Korea." In *Social Work Education: Voices from the Asia-Pacific*, ed. C. Noble, M. Henrickson, & I. Y. Han, 99–124. Victoria, Australia: Vulgar Press.

Hong, J. S., & M. K. Eamon (2009). "An Ecological Approach to Understanding Peer Victimization in South Korea." *Journal of Human Behavior in the Social Environment* 19:611–25.

Howe, N., R. Jackson, & K. Nakashima (2007). *The Aging of Korea: Demographics and Retirement Policy in the Land of the Morning Calm.* Retrieved April 18, 2012, from http://csis.org/files/media/csis/pubs/070321_gai_agingkorea_eng.pdf.

Hubinette, T. (2005). "Comforting an Orphaned Nation: Representations of International Adoption and Adopted Koreans in Korean Pop Culture." Ph.D. dissertation, Stockholm University.

Hwang, H. J., & J. U. Kim (2006). "A Study on the Development and Effectiveness of the Bullying Prevention Group Counseling Program." *Tong'a Non'jip* 42: 91–109.

In, K. S. (2000). *Ideals and Reality of Social Welfare in Korea.* Seoul: Nanam.

International Monetary Fund (2008). "IMF Advanced Economies List." *World Economic Outlook Database: WEO Groups and Aggregates Information.* Retrieved April 17, 2010, from http://www.imf.org/external/pubs/ft/weo/2009/02/weo data/groups.htm.

Jang, Y., G. Kim, L. Hansen, & D. A. Chiriboga. (2007). "Attitudes of Older Korean Americans Toward Mental Health Services." *Journal of the American Geriatrics Society* 55:616–20.

Kim, B. S., J. S. Hur, K. Y. Lee, & M. M. Choi (2006). "The Current Situations and Developmental Strategies of the National License of Social Workers." *Han'guk Sahoe Pokji Kyoyuk* 11:1–38.

Kim, M. (2001). "Exploring Sources of Life Meaning Among Koreans." M.A. thesis, Trinity Western University, British Columbia.

Kim, M. S. (2004). "Solution for the Aging Society." Paper presented to the Economic and Social Research Society Meeting, Seoul.

Kim, S. M. (2011). "The Impact of Neo-liberal Globalization on Preschool Day-Care Service in South Korea: Tensions and Dilemmas." *International Social Work* 54:7–20.

Kim, S. W. (2009). "Social Changes and Welfare Reform in South Korea: In the Context of the Late-coming Welfare State." *International Journal of Japanese Sociology* 18:16–32.

Kim, Y. S., Y. J. Koh, & B. L. Leventhal (2004). "Prevalence of School Bullying in Korean Middle School Students." *Archives of Pediatrics and Adolescent Medicine* 158:737–41.

Korea Association of Social Workers (n.d.). *Korea Association of Social Workers.* Retrieved July 5, 2010, from http://welfare.net/site/global/globalEng.jsp.

Korea Herald (2012). "Serious School Violence." January. Retrieved April 18, 2012, from http://www.koreatimes.co.kr/www/news/opinon/2012/01/202_102669.html.

Korean Academy of Social Welfare (n.d.). *About KASW.* Retrieved May 7, 2010, from http://www.kasw.org/Es_1.html.

——— (2007). *Fifty Years History of Korean Academy of Social Welfare.* Seoul: Kong Dong Che.

Korean Department of Health and Human Services (2008). *Basic Fund for Elderly People*. Retrieved March 1, 2010, from http://bop.mw.go.kr/bbs-front/?mode=view.

Korean Institute of Criminology (1994). *Crime and Criminal Justice in Korea: KIC Research Abstracts*. Vol. 1. Seoul: Korean Institute of Criminology.

Korean Women's Development Institute (2006). *2006 Annual Report*. Retrieved March 21, 2010, from http://www.riss.kr/link?id=A76465810.

Korean Women Workers Association (n.d.). *Korean Women Workers Association*. Retrieved March 21, 2010, from http://kwwnet.cafe24.com/index.php.

Kwon, H. K. (2003). "The Birth of a Welfare State in Korea: The Unfinished Symphony of Democratization and Globalization." *Journal of East Asian Studies* 3:405–32.

Kwon, Y. S. (2004). "Research on Establishing an Identity of Social Work Education in South Korea and Strengthening the Social Work Profession." *Sahoe Kwahak Nonchong* 21:155–66.

Lauber, C., & W. Rossler (2007). "Stigma Towards People with Mental Illness in Developing Countries in Asia." *International Review of Psychiatry* 19:157–78.

Lee, J. B. (2003). *Solution to Youth Problems*. Seoul: Nanam.

Lee, J. C. (2003). "Health Care Reform in South Korea: Success or Failure?" *American Journal of Public Health* 93:48–51.

Lee, S. Y. (2008). *A Study on the Parental Leave Effect on Women's Labor Force Participation in Korea: The Usage Pattern and the Effect of Employment Extension.* Retrieved March 21, 2010, from http://www.riss.kr/link?id=T113377933.

Lee, Y. H. (2005). *Han'guk sahoe wa pokji chŏngchaek: Yŏksa wa issue*. Seoul: Na'num ŭi chip.

Lee, S., J. S. Hong, & D. L. Espelage (2010). "An Ecological Understanding of Youth Suicide in South Korea." *School Psychology International* 31 (5): 531–46.

Lim, T. C. (2002). "The Changing Face of South Korea: The Emergence of Korea as a 'Land of Immigration.'" *Korea Society Quarterly*, Summer/Fall: 16–21.

——— (2003). "Racing from the Bottom in South Korea? The Nexus Between Civil Society and Transnational Migrants." *Asian Survey* 43:423–42.

Ministry of Foreign Affairs and Trade (2009). *Destination Korea*. Retrieved April 9, 2010, from http://www.mofat.go.kr/english/main/index.jsp?lang-eng.

Ministry of Labor (2000). "Employment and Control of Foreign Manpower." Ms.

Mun, S. H., C. S. Ku, M. C. Pak, & H. O. Kim (2007). *Han'guk sahoe wa adong chŏngsonyŏn pokji*. Paju: Yang Seo Won.

Nam, K. C. (2004). "The Education Process and Textbook in Social Work Practice." *Sanghwang Kwa Pokji* 17:47–88.

Nho, C. R. (2004). "The Issues and Tasks for Social Work Education." *Yonsei Sahoe Pokji Kyoyuk* 10:174–96.

Pak, J.H.C. (2006). *Korean–American Women: Stories of Acculturation and Changing Selves*. New York: Routledge.

Park, B. J. (2001). "Patriarchy in Korean Society: Substance and Appearance of Power." *Korea Journal* 41:48–75.

Park, S. (2002). "The Consequences of Life Events on Korean Women's First Entry into and Withdrawal from the Labor Market." *Korean Journal of Sociology* 36:145–74.

Presidential Committee on Aging and Future Society (2005). *Low Fertility: Gender Analysis and Policy Implications.* Retrieved March 21, 2010, from http://www.riss.kr/link?id=M11759548.

Seol, D. H. (2000). "Past and Present of Foreign Workers in Korea 1987–2000." *Asia Solidarity Quarterly* 2:6–31.

Seol, D. H., & J. Skrentny (2004). "South Korea: Importing Undocumented Workers." In *Controlling Immigration: A Global Perspective*, ed. W. A. Cornelius, T. Tsuda, P. L. Martin, & J. F. Hollifield, 481–513. Stanford: Stanford University Press.

Shin, D. M. (2001). "The Social Welfare Policy of the Kim Young Sam Government: Globalization and Social Welfare." *Yonsei Social Welfare Study* 6/7:1–24.

Shin, S. I. (2004). "Social Welfare Intervention for Low-Income Foreign Families." *Journal of Social Welfare* 27:113–39.

Shin, Y., & H. Y. Kim (2008). "Peer Victimization in Korean Preschool Children: The Effects of Child Characteristics, Parenting Behaviors and Teacher-Child Relationships." *School Psychology International* 29:590–605.

Song, H. K. (2003). "Politics, Generation, and the Making of New Leadership in South Korea." *Development and Society* 32:103–23.

Sue, D. W. (2006). *Multicultural Social Work Practice.* New York: Wiley.

Sue, D. W., & D. Sue (2003). *Counseling the Culturally Diverse: Theory and Practice.* 4th ed. New York: Wiley.

Sung, K. R. (2001). "Democratic Consolidation and Welfare State Development: A Comparison of the Kim Young Sam Government and the Kim Dae Jung Governments." *Korean Social Welfare* 46:145–77.

Sung, K. (1990). "A New Look at Filial Piety: Ideals and Practices of Family-Centered Parent Care in Korea." *Gerontologist* 30: 610–17.

Sung, M. S. (1991). "Social Work Field Education in Korea." *Research Journal* 1:259–79.

Sung, S. (2003). "Women Reconciling Paid and Unpaid Work in a Confucian Welfare System: The Case of South Korea." *Social Policy and Administration* 37: 342–60.

U.S. Government Statistics, Bureau of East Asian and Pacific Affairs (2009). *Background Note: South Korea.* Retrieved April 9, 2010, from http://www.state.gov/r/pa/ei/bgn/2800.htm.

Wong, S. T., G. J. Yoo, & A. L. Stewart (2007). "An Empirical Evaluation of Social Support and Psychological Well-being in Older Chinese and Korean Immigrants." *Ethnicity & Health* 12:43–67.

Yang, S., & P. C. Rosenblatt (2000). "Shame in Korean Families: An Ethnographic Approach." *Family and Culture* 11:151–67.

Yeom, H. S., & H. O. Bae (2010). "Potential Issues in Field Practicum Student-Exchange Between Korea and the U.S.A." *International Social Work* 53:311–26.

Yun, H. S. (1997). "Korean Social Welfare Education—Problems and Solutions: Towards a Development of Social Welfare Education." *Korean Journal of Social Welfare Studies* 9:37–73.

4

Social Welfare in Hong Kong

Colonial Legacy and Challenges for the HKSAR

VENUS TSUI, ALVIN SHIULAIN LEE, AND ERNEST CHUI WING-TAK

Social welfare, in its broad conceptualization, refers to people's well-being, including health, education, housing, employment, safety, and security. However, in its narrow sense, social welfare policy refers to the provision of governmental social safety nets that seek to alleviate poverty and distress (Dolgoff & Feldstein 2003:109) and provide benefits and services to people who require assistance in meeting their basic needs (Karger & Stoesz 2006:4). In the case of Hong Kong, social welfare is defined as a residual welfare state with its provision of a social safety net of minimum standards (Tang & Wong 2003). Social welfare development in Hong Kong, as in other welfare states, has been influenced by economic, political, and sociocultural changes that have occurred during the last 160 years, tracing back to 1842, when Hong Kong became a British colony. In this chapter we provide an account and analysis of the development of social welfare before and after Hong Kong's return to China in 1997.

A Brief Sketch of Hong Kong

Hong Kong is a metropolis well-known for its economic prowess within the greater China region and for its unique ability to integrate both Eastern and Western philosophies into its social and economic systems. Its prosperity is reflected in the following statistic: in 2009 the GDP stood at U.S.$215,355 million (HK$1,679,769 million), which was the thirty-eighth highest in the world (World Bank 2010). Hong Kong started off as a fishing village before it was ceded to Great Britain in 1842. In 1997 Hong Kong was reunited with mainland China to become a Special Administrative Region (HKSAR) of the People's Republic of China, which functions with a "one country two systems" approach. Although Hong Kong operates in a system that promotes a free-market economy that exercises human rights and individual liberties, China's government structure is based on socialist policies promoting an authoritarian government role. Despite its divergence in political and economic agendas, the central government of China has bestowed the HKSAR a high degree of autonomy to preserve the Hong Kong way of life.

Hong Kong, with its diverse terrain and complex geography, was home to approximately 6.89 million people in 2008 (HKSAR Government, Census and Statistics Department 2010b). The total area of Hong Kong encompasses 1,104 square kilometers (686 square miles). With a large population and limited space, the population density is 6,480 people per square kilometer (16,587 people per square mile). The population is 95 percent (6,522,148 people) of Chinese descent (HKSAR Government, Census and Statistics Department 2009) and 5 percent from various parts of the world. The early Chinese community in Hong Kong consisted of migrants from mainland China. This population had been transient, but the tumultuous times that arose in China, such as the Sino-Japanese War, World War II, the Chinese Civil War, and the Cultural Revolution, forced as many as two to three million people to migrate to Hong Kong and Taiwan (Skeldon 1996).

History of Social Welfare in Hong Kong

Evolution of the Welfare Regime

During the colonial era (1842–1997), local academics perceived the British colonial government's interest in social welfare as short-term, conservative, passive, and discouraging (Chow 2008:25). It was characterized by a non-interventionist approach and residual nature (Aspalter 2006; Chui 2007). The colonial government had no concern for long-term welfare developments and instead maintained a marginal role. But despite its distanced stance on social welfare, the Hong Kong government did provide financial subsidies to local agencies (Hong Kong Government 1948).

The first government white paper on social welfare revealed that the colonial government believed that too much social welfare would cause the family and its traditional functions to disintegrate (Hong Kong Government 1965). Further, the government feared the welfare state demand for a "free lunch" would breed dependence, jeopardize people's work incentive, resemble the neoconservative tenet of moral hazard, and destroy economic success (Barry 1999). Therefore, in maintaining low tax rates and laissez-faire policies for the sake of economic interests, the government justified its limited role in aiding poor and needy people. As such, social development in Hong Kong typically has been subordinate to economic development, which characterizes Hong Kong and other East Asian states, such as South Korea, Singapore, and Taiwan, as developmental states (Ramesh 2004; Tang 2000). The government has not viewed social welfare as a right for its citizens, and any services offered have been promoted as benevolent acts of the government for which people should be grateful (Lee 2009).

A key turning point came in the late 1960s and marked the beginning of progressive development for social welfare in Hong Kong. After major social riots in 1966 and 1967, the colonial regime launched a massive campaign to improve living conditions and social welfare that led to new programs for public housing, health care, free education, and social services. Hong Kong entered a golden era of welfare development in the 1970s, concomitant with the economic growth that brought more revenue to the government to improve living conditions. By the early 1980s the social welfare system had constructed a safety net to secure a basic standard of living for all Hong Kong people. Despite the lack of contributory social security schemes, the wide range of service provisions was comparable to those in other developed societies (Chow 2003).

Historically, welfare policy in Hong Kong was dominated by conservative elites and the authoritarian state, while the labor unions and social democratic parties were very limited, if not insignificant, in affecting social policy making (Goodman, White, & Kwon 1998). Hong Kong's belated and limited democratization (Chui 1997), which commenced in the 1980s, did not effectively empower the legislature to check on the executive arm of the administration, neither before nor after 1997. The political institution bestowed on the business sector a predominance that allowed it to effectively preserve a probusiness, and thus conservative, policy orientation.

Chinese Heritage Influence on Social Welfare

Cultural roots also engendered the configuration of social welfare in Hong Kong. An emphasis on the traditional virtues of self-help and family reliance, in both the ruling class and the general public, pervaded the society. Prior to the 1997 handover, there appeared to be congruence in welfare ideology between the state and the civil society, one that emphasized self-reliance and minimal state provision. Because of the influence of traditional Chinese culture, in particular familism, the family unit is regarded as the most important social and economic entity in society and plays a crucial role in care giving for its members. Chinese familism places family interests such as preserving and enhancing family honor and stability above individual interests. For example, filial respect is very important in Chinese families, where children, relatives, and even grandchildren have a reciprocal duty to care for elderly people. Traditionally Chinese are willing to sacrifice themselves for family members, and because of the value of self-sufficiency, the stigmatization of the concept of welfare (Mak & Cheung 2008), and the desire to avoid "loss of face," they tend to seek help from immediate and extended family members before turning to friends, community members, religious healers, or even professionals. While seeking this informal help is normal, asking for assistance from the government can be very shameful and intimidating. The evolution of social welfare in Hong Kong has been shaped not only by the cultural orientation but also by the complex socioeconomic and political changes of the unique context since colonial rule.

One of the most influential ideologies that has actively changed and shaped the Chinese culture in Hong Kong is Confucianism. Confucian principles have been ingrained into the fabric of China's culture, including in Hong Kong. The Chinese people condemn deviant behavior, emphasize individual responsibility to the family as well as to ancestors, and foster attachment to a community (Grange & Yung 2001). Confucian principles determine what responsibilities individuals have within the family sphere, and for many it involves the strict adherence to maintaining the family's welfare, such as looking after older people, other family members, friends, and even neighbors (Chau & Yu 2009). This emphasis on welfare provision at the family level, due to Confucian ethics that encourage familial support, may explain the underdevelopment of social welfare programs and is evident in the lack of transfer-payment programs to poor and elderly people (Grange & Yung 2001).

Welfare Delivery System

In the evolution of welfare provision, Hong Kong may be described as an NGO-based welfare system (Aspalter 2002). Historically voluntary agencies have been at the forefront in offering direct assistance to individuals, while the British colonial government generally remained uninvolved during the early days. The first welfare agencies were founded by religious groups that provided homes and training for abandoned children (Hong Kong Government 1954) and by traditional philanthropic organizations. For instance, the Tung Wah Group of Hospitals (established in 1870) has been prolific in providing medical, educational, and community services and has become the largest charitable organization in Hong Kong. Despite the absence of direct welfare services to the community, the Hong Kong government did provide financial subsidies to many of the agencies to assist them in their work. It was not until after the end of World War II in 1948 that the Social Welfare Office was set up to oversee welfare activities (Hong Kong Government 1948), followed in 1958 by the establishment of the Social Welfare Department (SWD) and its services to Chinese refugees in Hong Kong.

When the Chinese Communist Party assumed sovereignty on the mainland in 1949, a large number of church-based social service organizations moved their operations to Hong Kong. Together with the preexisting traditional charitable organizations, these service agencies participated in relief work and provided services to the Chinese refugees. Later a Committee on Voluntary Emergency Relief Council was established to coordinate voluntary welfare organizations and organize various welfare services (Hong Kong Council of Social Service 2009a). By 1947 the committee developed into the Hong Kong Council of Social Service (HKCSS), and it was incorporated in 1951.With the increasing number of welfare agencies in Hong Kong, the coordination efforts and role of the HKCSS have become more prominent. The HKCSS since has become an umbrella organization representing more than 370 member agencies that render more than 90 percent of the social welfare services and provide three thousand service units all over Hong Kong (HKCSS 2009a).

Existing Social Welfare Provisions

Currently welfare services in Hong Kong are delivered by the government's Social Welfare Department and a large number of NGOs. Below is a cursory review of the wide array of welfare services for individual and families.

Family and child welfare services. To preserve and strengthen the family, a new service delivery model was adopted in 2003 to provide a continuum of preventive, supportive, and remedial services for families in need. Currently there are sixty-one integrated family service centers and two integrated service centers in the territory. In response to the rising number of family and crisis cases in recent years, particularly domestic violence involving spouse and child abuse, services were revamped and reorganized. The government and NGOs now provide specialized services for individuals and families. For example, the Family and Child Protective Services Units, specialized units operated by the SWD, provide services for families dealing with child abuse, spouse battering, and child custody/guardianship disputes through outreach, investigation, early intervention, statutory protection, casework, and group work services. In addition, there are five refuge centers currently operated by NGOs, rendering temporary accommodation to women and their children in times of family crisis or domestic violence. The Family Crisis Support Center, established in 2002 by Caritas, an NGO founded by the Catholic Diocese of Hong Kong to offer relief and rehabilitation services during the Second World War, tackles family crises at an early stage by providing integrated and accessible services, such as twenty-four-hour hotline services, short-term emergency interventions with accommodations, referrals, and other support services.

Services for older adults. With the policy objective of promoting "care in the community" and "aging in place" for elderly people to help them live in the community as long as possible and to have a dignified and healthy life, the government over the years has subsidized NGOs to provide a wide range of community care and support and residential care services for older adults. For instance, Hong Kong Sheng Kung Hui Welfare Council operates the District Elderly Community Center, Neighborhood Elderly Center, a day care center for elderly people, residential services, home care, and home help services to provide diversified elder services in the community, including case management, community education, outreach and networking, a support team, and career services. Furthermore, to ascertain the needs of older adults and match them with appropriate services, a Standardized Care Needs Assessment Mechanism was introduced in 2003 to allocate subsidized long-term care services.

Services for young people. To respond to the multifarious needs of young people, a comprehensive and integrated model that incorporates both center-based and school-based approaches has been adopted under the management of integrated children and youth service centers. Other services such as Community Support Service Scheme and counseling centers for psychotropic substance abuse also help youths recovering from drug abuse and repeat offenses. The Hong Kong Federation of Youth Groups establishes youth networks and provides services and facilities for the social, educational, cultural, and physical development of young people, which include counseling, outreach, youth employment, parent-child mediation, leadership training, and volunteer services.

Rehabilitation services. There is a comprehensive array of rehabilitation services for those with physical and mental disabilities, including training and education, prevention and early identification and assessment, employment services and vocational training, social and medical rehabilitation services, as well as aftercare support services. For instance, New Life Psychiatric Rehabilitation Association advocates equal opportunities for people with mental illness by rendering a comprehensive range of community-based rehabilitation services via halfway houses, aftercare service, long-term care homes, sheltered workshops, supported employment service centers, and integrated community centers. Rehabilitation services are provided to assist individuals with disabilities in developing their physical, social, and mental capabilities to the fullest extent and by facilitating their integration into the community.

Community services. Services have been developed that focus on community problems, promote community cohesion and social harmony, and improve the quality of community life. Pioneered by NGOs, community development programs like Neighborhood Level Community Development Projects (NLCDPs) have been initiated in deprived and less privileged communities since the 1970s. Neighborhood Advice–Action Council, one of the active NGOs in the area, implements NLCDPs to provide services for residents living in the squatter and rural areas with a particular focus on community participation, community education, and utilization of community resources to solve community problems. To develop a support network and social capital for community residents, this organization initiated new community projects by providing services such as regular home visits, mutual support groups, referral services, job skills training, and outreach activities.

Transformation of Social Welfare

Welfare Changes During the Transition

The signing of the Joint Declaration regarding the future of Hong Kong in 1984 encouraged the colonial government to expand social services. This resulted in higher public expectations on the role of government in providing social welfare benefits. The following sections highlight the restructuring that took place during this time and a few social issues relevant to Hong Kong society.

Restructuring welfare services: Post–1997. In the attempt to preserve social stability during the critical period of political transition, the new HKSAR government maintained the preexisting welfare provisions in various aspects. As stated in the Basic Law, the development and improvement of the HKSAR social welfare system should be made only as a function of social and economic conditions. Thus no new social welfare system was expected with the establishment of the new government. In addition, having seen the ineffectiveness of Western welfare states, resulting in heavy fiscal crisis since the 1980s, Hong Kong has adopted stringent measures in its welfare provision. Before 1997 Hong Kong followed a Thatcherite neoconservative orientation with similar policies. At the time the government adopted tenets of managerialism and market-oriented principles, including such notions as the 3Es (economy, efficiency, effectiveness) and the 3Ms (market, management, measurement). The inauguration of the new HKSAR regime in 1997 coincided with the Asian financial crisis and led to massive unemployment that put a fiscal burden on the government. The Hong Kong government responded by deploying public resources to reprioritize its social commitments in addressing unexpected socioeconomic changes. The retrenchment of social programs and an emphasis on individual responsibility in welfare provision pervaded society at the time. To maintain its low tax policies and fiscal balance, the HKSAR government espoused the "small government and big market" approach by adopting stringent public-spending measures, limiting its commitments to social welfare provision (Chow 2004). Such initiatives can be traced back to the ascendancy of new public administration tenets that emphasized account-ability and control over public expenditures. These restrictive tenets were closely linked to neoconservative ideology.

Subordination of NGOs to stringent government control. Many NGOs in Hong Kong originated from overseas Christian missionaries stationed in mainland China and received funding from overseas religious organiza-tions. However, when Hong Kong developed its economy, these overseas funding sources gradually dwindled. Concomitantly the colonial govern-ment started to provide subsidies to the NGOs and sustained their op-erations. Since the 1970s NGOs and the Hong Kong government have worked collaboratively as partners while working for the community's wel-fare; however, in the 1990s nearly 90 percent of NGOs became financially dependent on government funding. With the spread of the neoconservative welfare ideology, financial support for individual NGOs was based strictly on their performance, using an output-monitoring approach. The govern-ment's 2001 introduction of the lump-sum grant (LSG) system signified this change. Under the LSG system, the service performance monitoring system assesses the performance of service units based on funding and service agreements and a set of service quality standards. The Social Wel-fare Department has taken a proactive and predominant role in funding and monitoring services while holding NGOs accountable for service qual-ity and delivery (HKCSS 2009d). In fact, the introduction of these mana-gerialist doctrines into the welfare sector could be framed as the govern-ment's attempt at containment of welfare expansion and control over the nonprofit sector (Lee & Haque 2006, 2008).

In addition to the LSG, the government also introduced competitive bidding for social service projects. Though competition among NGOs may foster the development of innovative projects and advance service provisions that are more sensitive and responsive to community needs, NGOs have had to cut expenses by reducing overhead, imposing more fee-for-service charges, and taking cost-minimization measures as allowed by the LSG.

Significant Contemporary Social Welfare Issues

Major social welfare issues in Hong Kong in recent years include economic restructuring leading to unemployment; poverty and disparities of wealth;

an aging population; discrimination against new immigrants; social exclusion of ethnic minorities; and a growing demand for social and political participation (HKCSS 2009c). Furthermore, with the increasing interface between Hong Kong and mainland China and a concomitant increase in Chinese migrants, Hong Kong social work professionals must also serve immigrants from mainland China who might not necessarily share the same socioeconomic and cultural features of the local Chinese community.

Economic restructuring leading to unemployment. Hong Kong experienced a structural economic change while preparing for the coming of a knowledge-based economy. Since the 1980s a tremendous number of factories have relocated to China, and this process of deindustrialization has led to a loss of low-skill jobs and resulted in high unemployment rates. In addition, because of a knowledge-based economy, the "digital divide" gap between those with access to information technology and those with very limited or no access continues to marginalize older people and less-skilled, less-educated, and disabled people. As a consequence of economic restructuring, less-skilled older laborers and new immigrants were the hardest hit, and many were forced to accept much lower pay, find other means of support, or become unemployed. To protect vulnerable groups from exploitation and sustain the living standards of low-paid workers, there have been extensive debates in the Legislative Council and among employers, employees, and trade unions, which finally led to the passing of the minimum wage bill in July 2010. The initial statutory hourly minimum wage rate of approximately U.S.$3.60 (HK$28) was passed in November 2010 and came into force on May 1, 2011. Some opposing voices claimed that the introduction of a minimum wage would further erode Hong Kong's free-market ways and cause a loss of an estimated 30,000 to 170,000 jobs, depending on the wage level (*Economist* 2010). Whether establishing a minimum wage will provide economic protection for vulnerable groups and low-paid workers or will increase demands for welfare subsidies is subject to further developments and the intervention strategies of the government. For now, the issue of a minimum wage has promoted social dialogue at various levels of society, which is crucial to long-term economic development and people's well-being.

Poverty and income disparity. Despite Hong Kong's economic success before 1997, income disparity has been spectacular in recent years. The Gini coefficient, which measures income distribution, rose from 0.451 in 1981 to 0.518 in 1996 and reached a new height of 0.533 in 2006, indicating the worsening of income disparity in Hong Kong. Contrary to the perception of widespread economic prosperity, economic benefits in Hong Kong affect only a small number of people (Tang & Wong 2003), as evidenced by the increased prevalence of low-income families and families living in poverty. There were 890,000 people living in low-income families in 1995 and 1.22 million in 2005, an increase of 50 percent (HKCSS 2009b). These disadvantaged groups include older adults, single parents, low-income and unemployed individuals, and people in poor health.

Aging population. Aging is a major social issue in many developed societies, and Hong Kong is no exception. As of mid-2009 approximately 13 percent of the population was age 65 or above, and it has been estimated that the figure will rise to 24 percent by 2030. This is to be expected since life expectancy is high: 79.8 years for males and 86.1 years for females (HKSAR Government, Census and Statistics Department 2010a). With advances in medical technology and increased awareness of the benefits of healthy lifestyles, it is inevitable that life expectancies will increase and therefore greater demands will be placed on health care services, including long-term care services.

Even with the increased demand for services, the government has yet to establish viable retirement protection plans for the present cohort of older people. Many of these, living in poverty and dependent on public welfare services without a retirement scheme, are further at risk for a lower quality of life. For instance, some 60 percent of the government's public assistance recipients are older people (HKSAR, Social Welfare Department 2010). As of 2008 more than half the inpatients of public hospitals under the auspices of the Hospital Authority were age 65 or older (Hospital Authority 2010). As a result of the changes in family structure and functions, the weakening of some traditional values, and diminishing filial piety (Chow 1999), Chinese families in Hong Kong may not be able to care for their elderly members. The paradox is that despite the promotion of care in the community, the government has failed to provide adequate support services for older people (Chow & Chi 2003).

Discrimination against new migrants. When the British and Chinese governments started discussing the transfer of sovereignty that would take place in 1997, the governments agreed to allow mainland migrants to enter Hong Kong and reunite with families. As a result, Hong Kong has been receiving 54,000 legal Chinese migrants annually since 1995. This increased population flow across the border is forging closer ties between

Hong Kong and the mainland, mostly in terms of cross-border marriages, schooling, employment, and investments, creating a large demand for social welfare services by Chinese migrants. However, the Hong Kong government's efforts to increase exclusivity in social welfare provision have resulted in institutional and social discrimination against the migrants.

Economic restructuring resulted in the reduction of less-skilled jobs in the labor market and exacerbated the existing competition between local citizens and migrants. The restructuring did little to provide support for those in need and failed to meet the requisite conditions for the successful integration of new immigrants into the Hong Kong community (Weiner 1996). Consequently, locals and immigrants entered into intense competition for jobs and welfare benefits, producing widespread sentiments of parochialism and rampant social dissent. Inevitably, discriminatory perceptions against new Chinese arrivals gradually permeated the society (Chui 2004). Studies show that new arrivals from China experience various forms of social and institutional discrimination and exclusion, such as failing to secure employment, earning lower wages, and more frequently encountering inferior service or treatment (SOCO, 2001, 2004, 2009). The seven-year residence requirement for migrants to qualify for welfare also created divisive social sentiments among local Chinese, who were against distributing scarce resources to the migrants. This aptly supports Walker's (2007:13) postulation that apparently there has been an "interface between neo-liberal globalization and Confucianism" in East Asian countries and regions, including Hong Kong, and that the emphasis on self-reliance has resulted in deep-rooted stigmatization of welfare dependency.

Social exclusion of ethnic minorities. Hong Kong can be described as an increasingly multicultural, cosmopolitan region with 5 percent of its population being non-Chinese, including other Asian and European ethnic groups. However, ethnic minorities suffer from high unemployment. Research has reported that more than 40 percent are jobless. The government has been blamed for not being able to create jobs for ethnic minorities or eliminate barriers they encounter in the labor market. Urged by NGOs and various ethnic groups, the government took steps to combat racial discrimination, and the Race Discrimination Ordinance (RDO) eventually came into operation in July 2009. The ordinance, enforced by the Equal Opportunity Commission, aims at eliminating racial discrimination in all forms within employment, education, and public services. Yet there is no explicit inclusion of new Chinese arrivals in the legislature because of policy failures in addressing discrimination against mainland Chinese migrants. What is problematic is the growing disparity within the local Chinese community. If the discriminatory situation is left unaddressed, the divisiveness may reinforce social exclusion, further segregate the groups, and eventually jeopardize social cohesion and harmony.

Growing demand for social and political participation. The prospect of transfer of sovereignty in 1997 provided an impetus for the outgoing colonial administration to buttress its dwindling legitimacy by increasing social policy provisions starting in the 1980s. These social policy provisions were met with rising expectations and called for accountability within public services. Since the 1970s these services also provided training opportunities for social workers to actively participate within the sociopolitical arena to help advocate for disadvantaged and less privileged groups. With the relaxing of the political system in later years, social workers were elected to the District Council and the Legislative Council, through which grassroots voices were channeled to address and improve the welfare of the people. There has been growing demand for the general public to participate in politics, and related literature has indicated a shift in people's attitude toward responsibility for welfare (Chow 2003). Despite an emphasis on family responsibility and self-reliance by both the previous colonial administration and the HKSAR government, contemporary society generally views welfare as a response to changing needs and as a shared responsibility between the government and family members.

The Social Work Profession

In Hong Kong social welfare and its services have been delivered mainly by a community of social work practitioners who were strongly influenced by Western missionaries from mainland China. This Western mode of operation was introduced to the welfare arena after 1949, and changes in the sociopolitical climate increased the need for social workers to transform from unskilled workers into professionals. This is signified by the Hong Kong government's stipulation in 1972 that only graduates with social work degrees could apply for social welfare officer positions (Chow 2008). According to Chow, this was generally regarded as one of the most important milestones in the professional development of social workers in Hong Kong.

Frontline practitioners beginning their careers are expected to be able to perform the full range of what constitutes social work practice: casework, group work, and community work, or intervention at the micro, mezzo, and macro levels. More recently, because of the government's promotion of integrated services in the youth, family, and elderly fields, there is an emerging trend that practitioners must adopt a holistic or eclectic approach in their interventions.

Currently Hong Kong has three professional social work bodies: the Hong Kong Council of Social Services (established in 1947, incorporated in 1951), which serves as a platform for coordinating the NGOs; the Hong Kong Social Workers Association (established in 1949, incorporated in 1975), which promotes professional development and is based on individual membership; and the Hong Kong Social Workers General Union (established in 1981), which works for practitioners' rights as employees of NGOs and the government. The Hong Kong Social Workers Registration Board, a statutory body set up in 1996, is vested with the authority to oversee the registration of social work practitioners. In 2010 an estimated fourteen thousand social workers were registered in Hong Kong.

Social Work Education

Social work education in Hong Kong began in 1950 at the University of Hong Kong. The colonial government at the time began to provide short-term inservice training programs for its staff in the Social Welfare Department. It set up the Social Work Training Advisory Committee in 1960, the Social Work Training Fund in 1961, and the Social Work Training Institute in 1973. Today six training institutes provide professional social work training ranging from the subdegree (i.e., associate degree and higher diploma) level to postgraduate-level degrees. Graduates of the training institutes can automatically register as social workers to begin work in the government or NGOs.

The various training programs' curricula have relied heavily on adaptation of their Western, particularly Anglo–American, counterparts. All undergraduate programs offered by local training institutes adopt a generalist orientation, which provides basic training to students and prepares them to serve a wide range of clientele. Nonetheless, after sixty years of evolution, the social work curricula in various training institutes in Hong Kong have gradually undergone indigenization to better meet the needs of the local Chinese community. There are also increasing exchanges and collaboration between Hong Kong and mainland universities, and Hong Kong training institutes now collaborate with their Chinese counterparts by offering social work programs in various cities in China. After 1997 the government pledged to promote higher education, resulting in the proliferation of self-funded community colleges and similar training institutes. A mushrooming of subdegree programs of social work training ensued (Mok & Tan 2004), resulting in the marketization, or "McDonaldization," of higher education (Mok 1999).

Social welfare in Hong Kong has always been influenced by its colonial history and, as in other welfare states, has been defined by social, political, and economic forces. As a residual welfare state (Tang & Wong 2003), Hong Kong maintained policies that aimed to reduce social and economic hardship but met only basic needs (Karger & Stoesz 2006). Prior to 1997 welfare policies were conservative since the colonial government at the time feared that too much welfare support would destroy family values and undermine economic stability (Hong Kong Government 1965; Barry 1999).

The early austere movements in welfare policies marked Hong Kong's beginnings; however, social unrest in the late 1960s, due to poor living conditions, gave rise to welfare reform and expanded welfare programs to include public housing, health care, free education, and social services. The programs rivaled those of other welfare states at the time (Chow 2003) and marked the golden age of welfare in Hong Kong. Despite the boom in welfare programs, Hong Kong society still held a probusiness stance that maintained conservatism in social policy—a result of limited democratization (Chui 1997), weak social democratic parties, and ineffective labor unions (Goodman, White, & Kwon 1998).

At the time the colonial government was not as involved in frontline work, whereas NGOs became the implementing arm of social welfare. In the beginning religious organizations were responsible for services; however, the creation of the Social Welfare Office provided additional support to NGOs in service implementation (Hong Kong Government 1948) and expanded oversight and capabilities of welfare provision. It was not until post-1997 that fears of restructuring welfare permeated society. To maintain social stability, the new HKSAR government chose to keep the old policies and structures, although with stricter fiscal controls (Chow 2004) to prevent the deficit spending that was so prevalent in Western countries. The 1997 handover saw a fluid transition; however, as financial markets become more interlinked and governments face greater financial scarcity, more austere measures can be expected in social welfare in Hong Kong—a place where residual welfare pervades society.

Recommendations and Conclusions

In the 1980s, when Hong Kong commenced its democratization, there was a simultaneous escalation of public demand and expectation for the government to provide more social welfare civil entitlements (Wong & Wong 2005). However, the people of Hong Kong apparently are not willing to pay a higher tax or take on more individual responsibility to support such welfare provision. For instance, recent attempts to set up contributory schemes for medical services have not generated enthusiasm. Despite the resistance, however, collaborative public-private welfare schemes that balance government and individual responsibility for welfare are needed.

Given the changing socioeconomic and political contexts in Hong Kong, as well as the new social problems arising from the transforming society, the social work profession is well positioned to enhance competence and devise more service strategies. Not only do social work education and training institutes have to provide students with quality practicum experiences and professional competence, they also need to instill in their graduates a higher level of commitment and passion to address the daunting challenges upon graduation. In addition, to strengthen the professionalism of social work in Hong Kong, social workers need to actively engage in fostering evidence-based practice and continuous research to affect practice and policy. It is imperative that social work professionals, including educators, practitioners, and researchers, broaden their knowledge and perspectives by incorporating evidence-based practice, remaining current in research, and adopting a more proactive role in developing innovative approaches to meet the diversified and ever-changing needs of the society.

Hong Kong underwent a generally smooth political, social, and economic transfer during and after the historic 1997 handover of sovereignty. Social welfare policies have largely been maintained, though increasingly tinted with more neoconservative orientations. As this chapter has stressed, the social welfare system in Hong Kong remains budget-driven and largely residual and conservative despite piecemeal welfare reforms in recent decades. The development of the social welfare system has been more a function of adaptive and incremental supports in response to political pressure and socioeconomic challenges (Lee 2006). The social provisions have been financed chiefly by taxation, and the level of service output is regulated by the revenue of the government (Lee 2005). Although there has been some broadening of social benefits to the entire population, before and after the HKSAR government was established in 1997, there is no indication that Hong Kong has abandoned its residual stance on social welfare. There are upcoming challenges that require responses from the government and the Hong Kong community at large to devise appropriate welfare policies and services. The social work professional community and institutes for education and training should also develop relevant services, models of intervention, and indigenous training programs that respond to such social needs.

References

Aspalter, C. (2002). "The Hong Kong Way of Social Welfare: An NGO-Based Welfare System." In *Discovering the Welfare State in East Asia*, ed. C. Aspalter, 115–37. Westport, CT: Praeger.

———— (2006). "The East Asian Welfare Model." *International Journal of Social Welfare* 15: 290–301.

Barry, N. (1999). "Neoclassicism, the New Right and British Social Welfare." In *British Social Welfare in the Twentieth Century*, ed. R. M. Page & R. L. Silburn, 55–79. New York: St. Martin's Press.

Chau, R.C.M., & S.W.K. Yu (2009). "Culturally Sensitive Approaches to Health and Social Care." *International Social Work* 52 (6): 773–84.

Chow, N. (1998). "The Making of Social Policy in Hong Kong: Social Welfare Development in the 1980s and 1990s." In *The East Asian Welfare Model: Welfare Orientalism and the State*, ed. R. Goodman, G. White, & H. Kwon, 159–74. New York: Routledge.

———— (2003). "New Economy and New Social Policy in East and Southeast Asian Compact, Mature Economies: The Case of Hong Kong." *Social Policy & Administration* 37 (4): 411–22.

———— (2004). "Social Welfare in Hong Kong—Post 1997: Opportunities in the Midst of Constraints.' *Journal of Societal & Social Policy* 3 (3): 63–76.

Chow, N. W. S. (1999). "Diminishing Filial Piety and the Changing Role and Status of the Elders in Hong Kong." *Hallym International Journal of Aging* 1 (1): 67–77.

———— (2008). "Social Work in Hong Kong—Western Practice in a Chinese Context." *China Journal of Social Work* 1 (1): 23–35.

Chow, N. W. S., & I. Chi (2003). "Catering for the Elderly." In *Fifty Years of Public Housing in Hong Kong: A Golden Jubilee Review and Appraisal*, ed. Y. M. Yeung & T. K. Y. Wong, 409–30. Hong Kong: Chinese University Press.

Chui, E. (1997). *Limited Democratization: Strategic Inclusion in Hong Kong*. Ph.D. dissertation, Chinese University of Hong Kong. Ann Arbor, MI: UMI Dissertation Services.

———— (2004). "Housing and Welfare Services for New Arrivals from China: Inclusion or Exclusion?" In *Immigration Law in Hong Kong*, ed. J. Chan & B. Rwezaura, 227–50. Hong Kong: Sweet and Maxwell Asia.

———— (2007). "The State of Welfare in Hong Kong." In *The State of Social Welfare in Asia*, ed. C. Aspalter, A. Aldosary, A. Dashkina, & S. Singh, 123–52. Taoyuan: Casa Verde.

Dolgoff, R., & D. Feldstein (2003). *Understanding Social Welfare*. 6th ed. Boston: Allyn & Bacon.

Economist (2010). "End of an Experiment: The Introduction of a Minimum Wage Marks the Further Erosion of Hong Kong's Free-market Ways." July 15. Retrieved July 25, 2010, from http://www.economist.com/node/16591088.

Goodman, R., G. White, & H. J. Kwon (1998). *The East Asian Welfare Model: Welfare Orientalism and the State*. London: Routledge.

Grange, A., & B. Yung (2001). "Aging in a Tiger Welfare Regime: The Single Elderly in Hong Kong." *Journal of Cross-Cultural Gerontology* 16 (3): 257–81.

Hong Kong Council of Social Service (HKCSS). (2009a). *Brief History of HKCSS*. Retrieved April 1, 2010, from http://www.hkcss.org.hk/abt_us/index_e.asp#.

———— (2009b). *Family and Community Service in Hong Kong*. Retrieved April 1, 2010, from http://www.hkcss.org.hk/download/folder/fc/fc_eng.htm.

———— (2009c). *Mission of Social Welfare in Hong Kong*. Retrieved April 1, 2010, from http://www.hkcss.org.hk/download/folder/socialwelfare/sw_eng.pdf.

———— (2009d). *Paper to the Lump Sum Grant Steering Committee: Issues of Concerns on the Implementation of Recommendations in the Review Report on the Lump Sum Grant Subvention System*. Retrieved April 1, 2010, from http://www.hkcss.org .hk/cm/lsgr/download/Paper_LSG_SteeringCommittee_20072009.pdf.

Hong Kong Government. (1948). *Hong Kong Annual Report*. Hong Kong: Government Printer.

———— (1954). *Hong Kong Annual Report*. Hong Kong: Government Printer.

———— (1965). *Aims and Policy of Social Welfare in Hong Kong*. Hong Kong: Government Printer.

Hong Kong Special Administrative Region (HKSAR) Government, Census and Statistics Department (2009). *Hong Kong 2006 Population By-Census: Summary Results.* Retrieved August 8, 2010, from http://www.censtatd.gov.hk/products _and_services/products/publications/statistical_report/population_and_vital _events/index_cd_B1120036_dt_detail.jsp.

———— (2010a). *Hong Kong Population Projections 2010–2039.* Retrieved August 8, 2010, from http://www.censtatd.gov.hk/products_and_services/products/pub-lications/statistical_report/population_and_vital_events/index_cd_B112001504 _dt_detail.jsp.

———— (2010b). *Key Economic and Social Indicators.* Retrieved April 13, 2010, from http://www.censtatd.gov.hk/hong_kong_statistics/key_economic_and_social _indicators/index.jsp.

Hong Kong Special Administrative Region (HKSAR) Social Welfare Department (2010). *Statistics and Figures on Social Security.* Retrieved March 15, 2010, from http://www.swd.gov.hk/en/index/site_pubsvc/page_socsecu/sub_statistics/.

Hospital Authority. (2010). *Hospital Authority Statistical Report 2007–2008.* Retrieved April 1, 2010, from http://www.ha.org.hk/upload/publication_15/106.pdf.

Karger, H. J., & D. Stoesz, D. (2006). *American Social Welfare Policy: A Pluralistic Approach.* Boston: Pearson/Allyn & Bacon.

Lee, E.W.Y. (2005). "The Renegotiation of the Social Pact in Hong Kong: Economic Globalization, Socioeconomic Change, and Local Politics." *Journal of Social Policy* 24 (2): 293–310.

———— (2006). "Welfare Restructuring in Asian Newly Industrialized Countries: A Comparison of Hong Kong and Singapore." *Policy & Politics* 34 (3): 453–71.

Lee, E.W.Y., & M. S. Haque (2006). "The New Public Management Reform and Governance in Asian NICs: A Comparison of Hong Kong and Singapore." *Governance* 19 (4): 605–26.

———— (2008). "Development of the Nonprofit Sector in Hong Kong and Singapore: A Comparison of Two Statist-Corporatist Regimes." *Journal of Civil Society* 4 (2): 97–112.

Lee, J. J. (2009). "The Colonial Government of Hong Kong's Development of SocialWelfare: From Economic and Social Service Perspectives." Hong Kong, China, Social Welfare Practice and Research Center, Department of Social Work, Chinese University of Hong Kong. Retrieved November 9, 2011, from http:// web.swk.cuhk.edu.hk/uploads/research/paper7.pdf.

Mak, W.W.S., & R.Y.M. Cheung (2008). "Affiliate Stigma Among Caregivers of People with Intellectual Disability or Mental Illness." *Journal of Applied Research in Intellectual Disabilities* 21:532–45.

McLaughlin, E. (1993). "Hong Kong: A Residual Welfare Regime." In *Comparing Welfare States*, ed. A. Cochrane & J. Clarke, 105–40. London: Sage.

Mok, K. H. (1999). "The Cost of Managerialism: The Implications for the 'Mc-Donaldization' of Higher Education in Hong Kong." *Journal of Higher Education Policy and Management* 21 (1): 117–27.

Mok, K. H., & J. Tan (2004). *Globalization and Marketization in Education*. Cheltenham: Edward Elgar.

Ramesh, M. (2004). *Social Policy in East and Southeast Asia: Education, Health, Housing and Income Maintenance*. London: Routledge-Curzon.

Skeldon, R. (1996). "Migration from China." (Contemporary China: The Consequence of Change.) *Journal of International Affairs* 49 (2): 434–55.

Society for Community Organization (SOCO) (2001). "Hong Kong Racial Discrimination Study Series 1: New Immigrants from Mainland China—Executive Summary." Retrieved September 2, 2010, from http://www.soco.org.hk/publication/publication_index.htm#3.

——— (2004). "Racial Discrimination in Hong Kong: A Focus on the Treatment of New Immigrants from Mainland China Under the Future Racial Discrimination Ordinance." Retrieved September 2, 2010, from http://www.soco.org.hk/publication/publication_index.htm#three.

Society for Community Organization and New Immigrants Mutual Aid Association (2009). "Discrimination Against New Arrivals in Hong Kong, Research Report." Press release of the conference on Hong Kong Government's disregard of human rights and grievances of new immigrants from mainland China. Retrieved September 2, 2010, from http://www.soco.org.hk/publication/publication_index.htm.

Tang, K. L. (2000). *Social Welfare Development in East Asia*. Basingstoke, UK: Palgrave.

Tang, K. L., & C. K. Wong (2003). *Poverty Monitoring and Alleviation in East Asia*. New York: Nova Science.

Walker, A. (2007). "Globalization and Welfare Reform East and West." *National Taiwan University Social Work Journal* 15:1–38.

Weiner, M. (1996). "Determinants of Immigrant Integration: An International Comparative Analysis." In *Immigration and Integration in Post-industrial Societies: Theoretical Analysis and Policy Implications*, ed. N. Carmon, 46–62. London: Macmillan.

Wong, C., & K. Wong (2005). "Expectations and Practice in Social Citizenship—Some Insights from an Attitude Survey in a Chinese Society." *Social Policy and Administration* 39 (1): 19–34.

World Bank (2010). *Hong Kong SAR, China*. Retrieved August 8, 2010, from http://data.worldbank.org/country/hong-kong-sar-china.

5

Social Welfare and Social Work Development in Taiwan

LI-JU JANG AND PEI-JEN TSAI

Taiwan, also known as Formosa, is located east of the Taiwan Strait, off the southeastern coast of mainland China. The mountainous island spans the Tropic of Cancer and is covered by tropical and subtropical vegetation. Japan had originally acquired Taiwan and the Penghu island group from the Qing Empire in 1895 through the Treaty of Shimonoseki. However, at the end of World War II in 1945, Japan renounced all claims over its former colonial possessions. Since then, the island group has been under the government of the Republic of China (ROC).

The economy, education, language, art, customs, and lifestyle of the people of Taiwan are influenced mainly by the Han Chinese culture, the indigenous cultures, and the Japanese culture. According to the Ministry of the Interior of the ROC (2010), at the end of June 2010, the population of Taiwan was estimated at 23,138,381, about 2.2 percent (508,380) being indigenous people. The government has recognized fourteen tribes. The other three major ethnic groups are the Minnan, Hakka, and mainlanders. Minnan (70 percent) and Hakka (15 percent) constitute 85 percent of the total population at this time. Mainlanders consist of Kuomintang (KMT) troops who were defeated by the Communist Party in the Chinese Civil War in 1949. They and their Taiwan-born descendants accounted for about 13 percent of the population in 2010.

The government of the ROC was founded on a constitution and the Three Principles of the People, which declares that the ROC "shall be a democratic republic of the people, to be governed by the people and for the people" (ROC Constitution, Article I, § 1). The government is divided into five administrative branches: the Control Yuan, Examination Yuan,

Executive Yuan, Judicial Yuan, and Legislative Yuan. The two major political parties are the KMT, the ruling party in 2012, and the Democratic
Progress Party.

Health care in the ROC is managed by the Bureau of National Health
Insurance (BNHI). National Health Insurance coverage requires copay-
ment at the time of most services unless it is a preventative health service;
a service for low-income families, veterans, or children under 3 years old;
or a service for catastrophic disease. Low-income households maintain
100 percent premium coverage by the BNHI, and copayments are reduced
for people with disabilities and some older people. The ten leading causes
of death in the ROC in 2009 were cancer, heart disease, cerebrovascular
disease, pneumonia, diabetes, accidents, chronic lower respiratory diseases, chronic liver disease and cirrhosis, suicide, and nephritis and renal
syndrome and nephrosis. The life expectancy for males was 75.9 years and
82.5 years for females, according to the Department of Health (2010).

Reports of the Directorate-General of Budget, Accounting and Statistics
(2010b) indicate that when comparing the second quarter of 2009 with the
second quarter of 2010, the total export value increased by U.S.$70.2 bil-
lion (NT$2,246.4 billion), or 46.4 percent, and the total import value in-
creased by U.S.$63 billion (NT$2,016 billion), or 54.1 percent. The trade
surplus during this period was U.S.$7.2 billion (NT$230.4 billion). The
Directorate-General of Budget, Accounting and Statistics (2010a) also
reports that in 2009 the value of machine tool output was U.S.$2.4 bil-
lion (NT$76.8 billion), putting Taiwan in sixth place in the world. The
export value of machine tools was U.S.$1.9 billion (NT$60.8 billion), a
decrease of 47.7 percent from the previous year. Regarding education, the
reports show that in Taiwan more than 13 million students were registered
in higher education, including 340,000 doctoral students and 183,000
other graduate students, in the 2009 academic year. By the end of 2009
only 23.3 percent of adults held junior high certificates, 34.5 percent were
high school graduates, and 42.2 percent held an undergraduate or higher
degree.

Since the early 1990s many foreign brides and laborers have moved to
China and such Southeast Asian countries as Vietnam, Indonesia, Thailand, and the Philippines. According to the Directorate-General of Budget, Accounting and Statistics (2008), of all couples that were married in
Taiwan in 2007, about 18 percent included a foreigner. In addition, for-

eign laborers have formed a strong labor force in Taiwan. According to the Council of Labor Affairs (2009), by the end of March 2009 there were 343,227 foreign laborers in Taiwan.

History of Social Welfare in Taiwan

Ancient Times to 1945

The earliest charitable organization in Taiwan might be considered the Fu Chang Society, which was established in Hinchu during the Qing dynasty (1644–1911). The society was a nongovernmental institution with six local scholars who served as directors. Most of its members were wealthy people who felt that it was their responsibility to take care of the poor and needy by providing them with financial aid.

In 1868 Dr. James Laidlaw Maxwell, a medical missionary from Scotland, established Jiu-lau (Old Building) Hospital in Tainan. The hospital provided free medical services for poor and needy families. In 1900 Dr. Maxwell and his son oversaw the construction of Sin-lau (New Building) Hospital, the first Western-style hospital in Taiwan. In 1891 the Scottish missionary William Campbell established Shin Gu Tang, a school for the blind. It was the first special education institute in Taiwan, and students with sight impairments were taught to utilize braille for reading, mathematics, and occupational training. Tuition and lodging were free for the poor, and the school depended heavily on donations from church members overseas.

Unfortunately, Shin Gu Tang was shut down in 1897 because of the war with Japan. However, Campbell negotiated with the Japanese government, hoping it would take over the school. In 1900 the Japanese government agreed to add a department of education for the blind to Tainan Cihhuei Sign Language School. In 1922 the Japanese government officially took over the school and changed its name to Tainan School for the Blind and the Mute, and it became the first public school for people with disabilities. The school was divided into two schools in 1968: the School for the Hearing Impaired and the School for the Blind. Students with hearing impairments stayed at the old campus in Tainan, while students with sight impairments were transferred to the new campus in Taichung.

In 1896 the Japanese government promulgated the Regulations for Social Services for the Sick and/or Deceased Travelers. The first social service for the homeless was established in Taiwan in 1895. In 1919 it was
divided into two divisions: the social department, which managed health
care, and the social enterprise, which took care of probation affairs. After 1918 neighborhood houses (multipurpose community centers) were
established to provide medical treatment, midwifery, public guidance, career consultations, life assistance, homelessness care, women protection,
and boarding. The district commissioner system was introduced to Taiwan in 1923. The Japanese government hired prestigious local people to
serve in the district commission. The duties of the commissioners were
to assess the needs of the residents and provide services such as health
treatment, child protection, mediation, residence records, and financial aid
(Lin 2006).

1946 to 1979

At the end of World War II, almost all the social enterprises established by
Japan that were taken over by the ROC government stopped functioning
until the Taiwan Provincial Social Affairs Department was established in
June 1947. The KMT chairman in Taiwan, Yi-chung Li, was appointed its
general-director, and he began plans to construct five new relief agencies
later located in the areas of Kaohsiung, Hualien, Hsinchu, Penghu, and
Pingtung. The ROC government subsequently adopted commonly used
Chinese social policy strategies and social welfare movements.

At the end of the Civil War in 1949, China was divided into two countries: the Republic of China (ROC), governed by the KMT, with territory
including the islands of Taiwan, Penghu, Kinmen, Matsu, and other minor
islands; and the People's Republic of China (PRC), governed by the Communist Party, with territory including mainland China, Hong Kong, and
Macau. Thus for years the mission of the Social Affairs Department was
to support the Three Principles of the People—democracy, human rights,
and livelihood—developed by Dr. Sun Yat-sen in 1905 as part of a philosophy to make China a free, prosperous, and powerful nation. Social work,
considered to be a part of politics during that time period, was meant to
fulfill the ROC government's political ambitions. Thus its emphasis was to

rebuild mainland China, construct Taiwan, and prepare the people to fight against mainland China.

To stabilize the emotions and ease the homesickness of the KMT troops who retreated to Taiwan in 1949, the ROC government made social policies regarding veterans' affairs a priority. The Homes for Veterans and the Veterans Health Administration were set up to serve the veterans shortly after they arrived in Taiwan. In the 1950s three major social insurance acts were enacted: the Military Insurance Act of 1953, the Labor Insurance Act of 1958, and the Government Employee Insurance Act of 1958.

During this time the government also initiated child, youth, and women's welfare services, as well as public assistance. Child welfare services included the establishment of orphanages and temporary day-care centers during harvest seasons. Youth welfare services consisted of halfway houses and group homes. For women's welfare services, the Protection of Adopted Daughter Act was enacted and a program of job counseling services for women in Taipei was established. Additionally, public assistance programs such as aid to families with emergency needs, disaster relief, and aid to low-income families became available to assist disadvantaged families.

In 1965 the Executive Yuan, which is responsible for enforcing the laws of the ROC, promulgated the Current Social Policy on Social Welfare for the People, which emphasizes the importance of social insurance and provided a new focus for promoting social welfare. In May 1968 the Executive Yuan started the Community Development Framework, which sets up community service centers, organizes committees with enthusiastic people, and hires professional social workers. The framework clearly defines professional social workers as those who receive degrees in social work or related fields. For current social workers, on-the-job training is available to improve their professional knowledge and skills. Besides the government's efforts, religious groups and nongovernmental organizations have provided financial assistance, family services, and youth services to high-risk families.

1980 to Present

The 1980s were an important period for the development of the social welfare system in Taiwan. The government passed a variety of social welfare policies, such as the Senior Citizens Welfare Act of 1980, People with Disabilities Rights Protection Act of 1980, Public Assistance Act of 1980, Vocational Training Act of 1983, Labor Standards Act of 1984, and Youth Welfare Act of 1989. In addition, the Department of Health started planning for national health insurance in 1988, and it was established in 1995 to serve the entire population.

The 1990s were called the ten golden years of social welfare development in Taiwan by the Control Branch (Lin & Shen 2008) because many important social welfare policies were passed, such as the Child and Youth Sexual Transaction Prevention Act of 1995, Sexual Assault Crime Prevention of 1997, Social Work Act of 1997, Regulations on Living Allowance for Medium- or Low-Income Senior Citizens of 1998, Education Act for Indigenous Peoples of 1998, and Domestic Violence Prevention Act of 1998.

Owing to societal changes such as the increase of female-headed households and the older population, as well as the promotion of gender equality and human rights, more social welfare policies were enacted in the next decade, including Aid to Women-Headed Single-Parent Families of 2000, Protection for Workers Incurring Occupational Accidents Act of 2001, Indigenous Peoples Employment Rights Protection Act of 2001, Gender Equality in Employment Act of 2002, Employment Insurance Act of 2002, Life Allowance for Senior Citizens of 2002, Children and Youth Welfare Act of 2003, Protective Act for Mass Redundancy of Employees of 2003, Sexual Harassment Prevention Act of 2005, Charity Donations Destined for Social Welfare Funds Implementation Regulations of 2006, People with Disabilities Rights Protection Act of 2007, National Pension Act of 2007, and Regulations on Special Care Allowance for Medium- or Low-Income Senior Citizens of 2007.

Taiwanese Culture and Social Welfare

Traditionally people in Taiwan believe that they should get help from immediate family, clan members, and neighborhoods first, and then local charitable and governmental entities. The following Taiwanese maxims for managing the home clearly depict the social values, beliefs, roles, and relationships of family members:

- Valuing wealth more than parents is unbefitting a son.
- Respecting and learning from older and more experienced people will serve in times of trouble.
- Even the deceased ancestors should not be worshipped insincerely.

The Twenty-Four Filial Exemplars has been published as a children's book and short stories to teach about filial piety. Taking care of parents in their old age is an essential traditional value to the Taiwanese people. Some policy makers were reluctant to pass the Senior Citizens Welfare Act of 1980 because they feared the demise of filial piety. Unfortunately the rising generation has less desire to preserve such a tradition.

Two maxims, "Even descendants are simple-minded; they must be educated" and "To take secret revenge when one has a grudge will bring disaster upon younger generations," remind parents to value children's education and examine their own conduct often. Childbirth and raising and protecting children are considered the main responsibilities of parents. Unfortunately, when some parents face difficulties and take their own lives, they take their children with them in death. Such behavior implies their desire to fulfill their parental responsibilities after death. Social workers and the government need to educate society about the importance of children's rights. Pong (1995) indicates that the Taiwanese child welfare policy seems to value the rights of the family and parents more than those of the child.

The maxims "People should show kindness and compassion for relatives and neighbors who are poor or in distress" and "Clan members with much should help those with little" indicate that clan members (people who share the same family name) are responsible for the welfare of those in their clan. Thus people in Taiwan are often reluctant to seek help from outsiders. To clients, professional helpers, including social workers, are outsiders. They may doubt why someone would help anyone outside their own clan. Social connections are particularly important to Taiwanese people. There is an old saying, "If you can make connections with someone special in a certain situation, everything should be okay. Everything matters." This maxim implies that who you know is more important than what you know. Therefore social workers often need to find ways to connect with clients in order to serve them more effectively. However, when done unskillfully, this may result in problems of transference and may even threaten professional relationships.

People in Taiwan value saving face and have a firm belief in the maxim, "Don't wash your dirty linens in public." They tend to put up with problems and dare not tell relatives or friends about them. Because of their strong defense mechanisms and concern about people's opinions, the likelihood of their seeking assistance from social workers is relatively slim. Thus respect for clients and confidentiality are two important principles of the professional relationship in Taiwan. Even social workers work to keep positive impressions of themselves in the eyes of their clients. Thus they may not be straightforward about clients' problems and prognosis at times. In some cases when social workers successfully help clients solve their problems, clients wish to express their gratitude through money or gifts. But social workers represent the agency they serve. Although refusing the gift may violate the cultural norms of connection in relationships, accepting it may infringe on the social work Code of Ethics.

Lastly, in the collectivist culture of Taiwan, people often put family benefits before personal goals, which may challenge client self-determination and affect their choice to seek help outside the family. It is common for Taiwanese families to share a household budget, which means that the possessions, incomes, and expenses of all family members are combined. When people make decisions, they often take the entire family's best interests into consideration, and they may even expect decisions to be a family rather than an individual responsibility. Thus when working with Taiwanese clients, social workers may need to identify key persons in their families regardless of the age and socioeconomic status of the clients because those key persons often have the final say as to whether the clients will continue the service.

There were only 191,310 newborns in 2009, with a crude birthrate of 0.829 percent. Compared with the previous year, the crude birthrate decreased by 0.035 percent (Ministry of the Interior 2010). The declining marriage rate in Taiwan is one of the main reasons for the decreasing birthrate. The Bureau of Health Promotion in the Department of Health conducted a telephone survey in 2005 regarding reasons for people not getting married, and the major concern seemed to be inadequate economic conditions. Traditionally in Taiwan child rearing was viewed as an investment to ensure reciprocal care in one's old age, but currently parents are worried about the high cost of raising a child. Since many married couples plan to have only one child, and the Taiwanese culture values boys over girls to enable continuation of the family name, couples may utilize technology to screen seminal fluid to ensure they can have a baby boy. Most parents living in the countryside who have a girl first will still raise her but will have a second child with hopes that this child is a male. However, urban parents seem more likely to choose to have only one child, regardless of its gender, or even no child at all.

The declining birthrate has a great impact on Taiwanese society in several ways. It threatens all levels of education, from kindergarten through university. All schools are struggling with enrollment difficulties, some teachers are facing severance, and some schools are facing closure. These conditions have forced authorities to adjust educational resources. Eventually this gender imbalance will also affect military service and bride availability. Furthermore, the declining birthrate will have an impact on the labor force, the elderly dependency ratio, and the government tax base (Hsueh 2003; Huang 2007).

The Aging Population

The birthrate decline, prolonged life expectancy, and an increase in the older population have put Taiwan into the aging society category since 1993. In December 2009 the population 65 years or older made up 10.6 percent of the total population in Taiwan. The index of aging—the number of people aged 65 or over per 100 youths under the age of 15—was 65.1. The Council for Economic Planning and Development of the Executive Branch estimates that in 2024 the older population will reach 20 percent of the total as people who were born during the demographic post–Chinese Civil War baby boom enter old age (Ministry of the Interior 2010). An aging society is a challenge to the country because of expenses for medical services, long-term care, financial security, and quality-of-life maintenance (Hsueh 2003).

In the past women were the main caregivers for children and older family members. As employment has increased among women, however, their time for family care functions has decreased. The social welfare policy toward the older generation in Taiwan must be revised in accordance with the societal and population structure trends. Old-age pensions, long-term care, medical services, and elderly housing and leisure should be addressed.

The Arrival of New Immigrants

Since the early 1990s new immigrants from economically developing Southeast Asian countries have been immigrating to Taiwan through cross-cultural marriages and as foreign laborers. Many immigrants are hoping to improve their economic condition and quality of life by marrying a Taiwanese citizen or working in Taiwan. New female immigrants tend to marry older men of low socioeconomic status who live in rural and remote areas (Chen 2008). Many of those marriages are arranged by marriage agencies working across countries. According to the Ministry of the Interior (2009c), of the 413,421 foreign spouses in Taiwan, about 66.3 percent are from mainland China, the rest coming from Vietnam, Indonesia, Thailand, and the Philippines.

The rate of cross-cultural marriages has been increasing annually since the early 1990s. Some foreign brides are valued mostly for their ability to procreate and are expected to bear sons to carry on the family name. They face common problems, such as a weak marital relationship, poor family economic conditions, a low status in the home, and a lack of social support networks (Control Yuan of ROC 2008). These foreign spouses usually try to build social support networks within their close society, with people from their home country, or with foreign spouses and laborers from other countries.

Most of the foreign spouses tend to have a low level of education; for example, only about 80 percent of new Vietnamese immigrants have received even nine years of education. They often feel challenged and helpless when tutoring their children in schoolwork. Consequently their children often face learning difficulties and are more likely to be teased and rejected by their schoolmates (Mo & Lai 2004). Additionally, children of an immigrant have a tendency to experience developmental delays in language. However, this usually improves once they have reached a certain developmental stage (Ministry of Education of ROC 2005).

The concept of a foreign bride in Taiwan often implies some kind of human-trading interaction. Some men are known to pay to marry a woman selected from a marriage agency's photo album. A family built on such a marriage may confuse the children, and they may face psychological contradictions and conflicts (Yang 2003). The second generation of immigrants is now rooted in Taiwan. They were raised and educated on the island, and they have become important in the development of the country. However, they still encounter many cultural adaptation issues, partly because of their parents.

Because of cultural differences and racial prejudices, new immigrants face deprivation, oppression, discrimination, and rejection. Employers often pay immigrants the lowest wages simply because of their ethnicity. Many are treated as contract workers, which means they do not qualify for any benefits, including labor insurance. Thus, promoting cultural adaptation and racial tolerance is an important social welfare imperative.

Members of families in poverty face financial crises and often experience depression, low self-image, and poor quality of life. Children from such families often work part-time while going to school, while others drop out of school, thereby decreasing their future competitive power in the employment market (Li & Lai 2004).

Government and NGO Responses to Social Welfare Issues

Declining Birthrate

A comprehensive family policy that promotes family functions, reduces child-raising costs, and increases the birthrate needs to be constructed. The government's Population Policy Protocol (Ministry of the Interior 2008a) offers the following suggestions.

Gender equality in employment. The Gender Equality in Employment Act of 2001 mandates that employers grant female employees a maternity leave before and after childbirth for a combined period of eight weeks. In the case of a miscarriage, the female employee is granted maternity leave for five days to four weeks, depending on the length of her pregnancy. The computation of wages during the maternity period is made pursuant to the related statutes and administrative regulations. Employers must grant two paid days off to employees whose spouses are in labor. Employers with more than thirty employees may grant parental leave without pay to employees with a minimum of one year of service before any of their children reaches the age of three years. The maximum period is limited to two years. During the period of parental leave without pay, employees may still participate in their original social insurance program, such as Labor

Insurance and Government Employee Insurance. Premiums originally paid by the employers are exempted, and premiums originally paid by the employees may be postponed for three consecutive years.

Aid for child care and preschool education. Child-care services are provided by public and private nurseries as well as kindergartens. The government has started a nanny system that promotes nanny training, licensure, job matching, and on-the-job training. By the end of 2008, twenty-four county or city governments had already set up local nanny systems (Ministry of the Interior 2009a). The government also offers preschool education vouchers to financially support families with children attending private nurseries or kindergartens. The value of vouchers varies by location because of the living standards of the area and the financial conditions of the local government. All government voucher payments are means-tested, the total in savings must be less than U.S.$4,688 (NT$150,000), and the value of real estate must be less than U.S.$203,125 (NT$6,500,000). The Support Pre-School Education for the 5-Year-Old Disadvantaged Children Program of 2007 provides financial subsidies for preschool education for disadvantaged children from age 5 until they attend elementary school.

Financial assistance to ease child-raising burdens. Four types of financial assistance are available to ease the burden of child raising: (a) the Financial Aid to Medium-Low or Low-Income Families Program offers families a monthly living allowance of about U.S.$44 to U.S.$222 (NT$1,400–NT$7,100) per child; (b) the insured person who is on parental leave without pay and has accumulated at least one year of insurance enrollment qualifies for Employment Insurance Act benefits; (c) childbirth subsidies are available to low-income families; and (d) county and city governments offer various amounts of childbirth allowance to promote the population policy. For example, citizens of Hsinchu City receive about U.S.$470 (NT$15,000) for their first child, U.S.$625 (NT$20,000) for their second child, U.S.$781 (NT$25,000) for their third child, U.S.$1,563 (NT$50,000) for twins, and about U.S.$3,125 (NT$100,000) for triplets.

NGOs play a cooperative role in improving the declining birthrate by implementing projects contracted to them by the government. For example, the city or county Social Affairs Department often contracts with the Taiwan Fund for Children and Families for nanny training. Because there is an insufficient number of public nurseries and kindergartens, the government contracts with private facilities to help implement the Support Pre-School Education for the 5-Year-Old Disadvantaged Children Program.

The Older Population

Older people in Taiwan are facing several immediate needs, such as economic demands, medical care, long-term care, and protection from elderly abuse. The Ministry of the Interior has planned the following services to meet their needs.

Health maintenance. According to the Senior Citizens Welfare Act of 2009, the relevant health authorities are to develop, promote, and supervise plans for elderly preventive, mental health, medical, recovery, and consecutive care. Authorities at all levels of government provide regular health checks, health care services, and follow-up. Low-income senior citizens 65 to 69 years of age receive subsidies through National Health Insurance. Furthermore, the government offers denture subsidies for older people from low-income families. Those who receive living or special-care subsidies or who live in residential facilities through government installment qualify for low-priced dentures. The government also offers low-income elders subsidies for hospital care. The 10-Year Plan for Long-Term Care of 2007 provides home care, day care, respite, community care stations, meals-on-wheels, assistive devices, and home improvements to promote a barrier-free environment.

Financial security. Living subsidies, special-care subsidies, and an annuity are provided by the central and local governments. Medium- to low-income older people who do not receive government installments may apply for living subsidies. Special-care subsidies may be issued to the care providers of elders with serious disabilities. Qualified individuals receive about U.S.$94 (NT$3,000) to U.S.$188 (NT$6,000) per month. The Special Care Allowance for Medium- or Low-Income Senior Citizens of 2008 is for disadvantaged elderly people with severe disabilities who do not receive home-care services, have no personal nursing aide, and do not receive day-care service subsidies. County or city governments provide monthly special-care subsidies of about U.S.$156 (NT$5,000) to the caregiver to compensate for financial loss due to care giving. The National Pension Insurance of 2007 was designed for people age 25–64 who are not qualified for labor insurance, government employee insurance, farmer insurance, or military insurance. In this program, as long as the insured pays the premiums on time, he or she can claim pension benefits on a monthly basis in the event of severe disability or once over 65 years of age. Survivors and dependants can claim pensions and funeral benefits in the case of death.

The program is sufficiently comprehensive to guarantee national basic economic security (Presidential Decree 2007).

Protection from elderly abuse. The Senior Citizen Welfare Act mandates the city or county government to provide short-term protection and settlement for older people who encounter difficulty or danger to their lives, bodies, health, or freedom due to inadvertence, mistreatment, or desertion by family members or contractual supporters. Local governments must assist older people in filing a lawsuit or demanding compensation from relatives or contractual supporters.

The medical staff, social workers, village heads, village officers, police officers, judicatory officers, and other personnel who execute welfare business for elderly people are required to report to the city or county government any suspicious case of elder neglect or abuse. Emergency relief and life-rescue networks against abuse and neglect are available for those living alone. The life-rescue networks evolved through collaboration among medical systems, the fire and police departments, and NGOs. In addition, there are missing-elders centers to help those with dementia return home.

Home-care services. Home-care providers assist people with home care such as laundry, living environment, food services, errands, and hospital trips. They also help take care of basic daily needs: showering, changing clothes, eating, taking medicine, and doing simple rehab activities.

Day-care services. Senior citizens are picked up in the morning and taken home in the evening by the agency shuttle bus. Group life and planned activities held in the day-care center may help people remain active and healthy longer. For family members, day-care services allow them to concentrate on their work during the day and enjoy being with their elderly family members in the evening.

Food services. Old Five Old Foundation seems to be the only NGO that provides meals-on-wheels and dinners on Chinese New Year's Eve for low-income people living alone.

Telephone greeting services. NGOs train volunteers to provide sustained care for elders living alone. Volunteers often plan activities for them on public holidays and special occasions to increase their social participation. Through phone greeting services, trained volunteers regularly communicate with those living alone to ensure their safety. For those who are in poor health, in-home or home-care services are arranged immediately.

Lifeguard system services. NGOs and some community centers equip emergency communication devices in homes of elderly people living alone and those with disabilities. In the case of accidents, an older person presses emergency notification buttons and the agency immediately notifies an emergency contact person to handle the accident. This service protects the life and safety of those in remote areas.

Leisure, culture, and game services. NGOs are often equipped with simple leisure facilities to entertain older people. Favorite activities include karaoke, dance, chess, mahjong, and handicrafts. Golden schools for elderly people promote their quality of life. Course content includes history, language, art, health care, science, technology, and socioeconomic studies.

Simulation education. Old Five Old Foundation has designed a set of simulation aids to help people experience the inconveniences that older people encounter daily. The intent is that through the simulation aids, people will have more patience and empathy for elderly people, help them maintain their dignity, and create for them a friendly environment.

New Immigrants

The Implementation of Foreign Spouses Orientation and Counseling Services of 2003 delegates related agencies to implement welfare activities to promote multicultural fusion and adaptation, including supportive services, language and cultural education, and cultural orientation for foreign spouses, as well as preschool education for children born to foreign spouses. The government also financially supports public and private sectors to provide counseling services on birth control, child raising, and associated services.

The Taipei city government has established the New Immigrant Hall, under the Department of Civil Affairs, to help new immigrants receive information about their country of origin as well as about Taiwan. The intent is that new immigrants become aware of available resources and general sentiments. The government also contracts with an NGO to operate the Taipei Yongle Women's Service Center, which serves foreign spouses in Taipei through casework, group work, hotline, and community programs to resolve problems associated with employment, marriage, parenting, and social skills.

The Taipei county government has established a cross-cultural marriage and family service center that provides legal advice, resource linkages and referrals, employment counseling, and subsidy applications. Courses on

Taiwanese culture, cross-cultural children tutelage, and motor scooter driving are available for foreign spouses to help them adapt to their new environment. Additionally, the Taiwanese government has relaxed the requirements for their naturalization. The rule that foreign spouses applying for naturalization must carry proof of financial means was abolished in 2008, making the naturalization process smoother.

TransAsia Sisters Association in Taiwan, the Pearl S. Buck Foundation, and Rerum Novarum Center are highly regarded NGOs that serve new immigrants. Their missions are to help foreign spouses cope with isolation and eventually become proactive social participants. Their services include the following:

- Living adaptation—providing training in language (in Chinese), parenting, and translation (training foreign spouses to be translators for new immigrants, especially when domestic violence or other legal issues occur). They also help form mutual support groups and encounter groups to rebuild their social support networks; offer financial aid and emergency relief; and provide hotlines and bilingual volunteer translators.
- Cultural education—planning and implementing cultural activities to raise local people's awareness of and respect for Southeast Asian cultures
- Advocacy for laws and policies—actively advocating for the rights of new immigrants and their citizenship (particularly by TransAsia Sisters Association in Taiwan)

Unemployment and New Poverty

The Taiwanese government offers the following assistance to people who are involuntarily unemployed.

Multi-Employment Development Program of 2002. The Council of Labor Affairs of the Executive Branch implemented this program and collaborated with enterprises to create both economic-development and social-service job opportunities. The economic-development opportunities come from private enterprises that develop industrial projects based on the unique local culture and ecological system and then hire involuntarily unemployed and older unemployed people. Wage subsidies for up to three years are available. Social-service job opportunities are a result of the local government sponsoring six-star community health or other projects to promote employment opportunities. These projects are designed to employ disadvantaged and long-term unemployed people. This temporary employment may last up to twelve months (Council of Labor Affairs 2002).

Unemployment benefits. The Employment Insurance Act of 2003 grants people who are involuntarily unemployed unemployment benefits, early reemployment incentives, a vocational training living allowance, and National Health Insurance subsidies. Insurance benefits are designed to maintain the basic livelihood of the unemployed and help them regain employment as soon as possible.

Public Service Employment Program of 2003. The government created new, temporary, supplemental public-service jobs that did not previously exist in the labor market. The purpose of this program was to reduce dependence on unemployment benefits and to increase the employment rate (Ministry of the Interior 2003).

Immediate Care for Emergency Relief of 2008. Needy families who lose their wage earners because of death, absence, severe illness or injury, unemployment, or other reasons that cause an inability to work are granted emergency relief. Based on their needs, emergency relief funds of about U.S.$313 (NT$10,000) to U.S.$937 (NT$30,000) are issued (Ministry of the Interior 2008c).

Reviving Economy Program of 2008. The global financial crisis caused industries in Taiwan to face problems of excess employees and inventory. To prevent the vicious cycle and chain reactions of enterprise closure and mass unemployment, the Reviving Economy Program was announced in 2008. To maintain the local economy and stabilize employment, a voucher of about U.S.$113 (NT$3,600), which was good from January to September 2009, was issued to each Taiwanese citizen (Ministry of the Interior 2008b).

Start Working Immediately Program of 2009. The Start Working Immediately Program urges private enterprises to create job openings and hire unemployed people. Employers who participate in this program receive a subsidy of about U.S.$313 (NT$10,000) per month for a six-month period after hiring an unemployed person (Council of Labor Affairs 2008).

NGOs promote employment opportunities for people both with and without disabilities. Employment services for people with disabilities are provided by the Chinese Deaf Association, Association of the Deaf, Syin-Lu

Social Welfare Foundation, Maria Social Welfare Foundation, Children Are Us Foundation, and Eden Social Welfare Foundation. Employment services for people without disabilities are mainly provided by 104 Job Bank and 111 Job Bank.

The Social Work Profession

In 1971 the Executive Branch planned the first phase of a social support system for the Republic of China by establishing a social work system and setting the social worker quota for provincial and city governments. The ratio of social workers to clients should be 1:200 in residential facilities. Every 500 low-income households should have one social worker. In 1973 Keelung, Taichung, Tainan, and Kaohsiung cities started hiring social workers. In 1975, with the support of the governor of Taiwan province, Tung-min Shieh, the city and county governments promoted the social work systems. By 1980, seventeen counties and cities had established social work systems.

The Taipei city government established a Department of Social Work under the Bureau of Social Affairs in 1978. The following year the Taiwan provincial government and the Kaohsiung city government also formed a Department of Social Work. The Taiwan province Systematic Social Workers Implementation Plan of 1979 describes social workers' responsibilities as (a) promoting family functions and preventing family problems, (b) counseling young people and serving older adults, (c) inspiring social awareness and improving community development, and (d) assisting in various social welfare services.

Professional social workers may have first appeared in hospitals. Liang-shao Liu, who worked at the Department of Social Service at the former Taiwan Provincial Taipei Hospital (currently the Taipei Municipal Chung Hsing Hospital) in 1949, may be the first social worker in Taiwan, followed by Yu-chieh Zou, who worked at the Department of Social Services at National Taiwan University Hospital in 1951. The Taiwan Fund for Children and Families was the first nongovernmental organization to hire social workers, in the 1950s.

Social workers were aware of the importance of establishing a professional system because of great pressure from social workers in the medical field. In 1983 the Medical Social Services Association ROC was established by medical social workers employed in hospitals. Some staff members of the social-services division in hospitals were not trained in social work. The official name of this association was changed to the Medical Social Work Association ROC in 1991, and its purpose is to provide training for medical social workers to improve their quality of services. Another professional organization, the ROC Association of Social Workers, was established on March 26, 1989. In 2000 its official name was changed to the Taiwan Association of Social Workers (TASW), and currently there are 1,030 full members, 20 student members, and 120 institution or group members. The purpose of the TASW is to unify the social workers in Taiwan, to enhance the professional growth and development of its members, to promote cooperation and collaboration among different fields of practice, and to improve the quality of social work services in Taiwan.

Almost fifty years after the first social worker appeared in Taiwan in 1949, the Social Worker Act was announced on April 2, 1997. Subsequently the social work licensure system was set up, and social work was recognized as a profession. Since then April 2 has become Social Work Day in Taiwan. On July 27, 1998, the Ministry of the Interior issued the Social Work Code of Ethics.

Shortly after the 921 Earthquake of 1999, local governments and NGOs in affected areas hired social workers to manage the reconstruction centers. Although many of them were trained in related fields such as sociology, psychology, or education, the social work profession was gradually being recognized by the people of Taiwan. Social workers function in hospitals, social agencies, and government agencies. Immediately following Typhoon Morakot (also known as the 8-8 Floods) of 2009, many social workers from the public and private sectors participated in relief work as both paid workers and volunteers. Because Taiwan is located in an area prone to environmental disasters, disaster social work seems to be the new proclivity in Taiwan.

Social work was advanced further when the Ministry of the Interior developed the Regulations on Specialty Certifications for Licensed Social Workers and Continuing Education (Ministry of the Interior 2009b), which was enacted on July 13, 2009. The third article of the regulation categorizes specialty social workers as (a) medical social workers, (b) social workers in mental health, (c) certified children, youth, women, and family social workers, (d) social workers in gerontology, and (e) certified social workers for people with disabilities. To maintain valid certificates, specialty social workers are required to complete at least 240 continuing education hours in six years by attending conferences or workshops organized by social work professional organizations in professional courses, professional regulations, professional ethics, and professional quality. The intent of professional development is to promote the quality of services in the five specialized fields of practice above.

The social work profession is continuing to gain recognition and status in Taiwan. As the following aspects of social work in Taiwan continue to develop and mature, the social work profession will also advance and be better able to empower clients on all levels and in all fields of practice: (a) the establishment of a social work licensure system, (b) the development of the Taiwan Association of Social Workers, (c) the unification of social work courses across universities, (d) the recognition of Social Work Day, (e) the promotion of collaboration between NGOs and the government, (f) the establishment of a specialty certification system for licensed social workers, and (g) the enhancement of continuing social work education.

The first formal social work education effort in Taiwan may be traced back to September 1950, when the Taiwan Provincial Junior College of Administration established the Department of Social Administration. In 1958 the department was divided into two tracks: sociology theory and social administration (later changed to social work). In July 1961 the department merged with the Provincial Taichung College of Agriculture, which then changed its name to the Taiwan Provincial Chung Hsing University, the first university to have a social work education department. A great demand for social administration workers encouraged universities such as Tunghai University and National Taiwan University to establish a Department of Sociology and offer social work courses. However, owing to an insufficient numbers of qualified teachers, the number of courses offered was limited. In 1963 the first Department of Social Work was established at the night school of Chinese Culture University.

In December 1964 the first social work education conference was held in Taipei. Its agenda consisted of group discussions on basic social science, social statistics and research methods, social administration, and an introduction to social work, casework, group work, and community work. Dorothy Moses, a delegate of the U.N. Economic Commission for Asia and the Far East, was invited to lead the discussions. The conference's main purpose was to examine and develop the course plan for social work education in Taiwan. The second social work education conference was organized by the Department of Social Affairs of the Ministry of the Interior in July 1969. Moses was invited again to help with the improvement of social work education in Taiwan (Mo & Lai 2004).

In 1973 the Chinese Culture University established the Department of Youth and Child Welfare, while Shih Chien College of Home Economics changed its Department of Early Childhood Care and Education to the Department of Social Work.

More than thirty faculty members from various social work departments initiated the Chinese Council on Social Work Education on February 16, 1992. The council works to facilitate communication between the social work departments of different universities, improve social work course plans, promote social work education, and cultivate high-quality social workers. Its official name was changed to the Council on Social Work Education (CSWE) in Taiwan on June 17, 2000.

From 1997 to 2010, twenty-eight public and private universities established departments of social work, social welfare, or social policy, providing degrees at the bachelor's, master's, and doctoral levels. Currently four universities—National Chi Nan University, National Taipei University, National Chung Cheng University, and Tunghai University—offer doctoral programs in social work and social policy.

This quick expansion of social work departments prompted the need for quality social work education. CSWE in Taiwan is aware of several fundamental issues facing social work education. The majority of faculty members serving in departments of social work were trained in the fields of sociology, education, psychology, public health, economics, public administration, human development, national development, and so forth, rather than social work (Lin 2010). Another major concern is that core courses are determined by individual institutions, and course content varies from university to university. Lastly, multiculturalism courses are missing in many social work departments, and when present their content is heavily dependent on the location of the university and on educator availability. Until a basic social work education curriculum across all social work departments on all three educational levels is created, with core courses and content including a rigorous field practicum, less attention will be available to identify indigenous Taiwanese models for social work practice and education.

Before CSWE in Taiwan can focus on the aforementioned issues, it needs to resolve structural needs, such as securing an office and paid staff. Volunteers currently operate CSWE in Taiwan. Recently social work education institutions have grown rapidly in Taiwan, and social work education now needs to have a greater vision and focus as well.

Future Perspectives

Social work, a relatively young profession in Taiwan, is addressing a number of major social issues. It does not appear that the issues of low birthrate, a large elderly population, and increasing numbers of new immigrants and those newly in poverty will be resolved in the near future. Social workers need to advocate for more government acts that protect the vulnerable and for a refinement of current laws that have ineffective policies.

It is not uncommon for a young social work profession to initially be directed by another entity, in this case the government, until the profession matures and participates fully in government decisions, and to struggle with a social welfare system that uses temporary, short-term crisis intervention.

The social work profession will grow in status and influence as the Taiwan Association of Social Workers develops and presents evidence of professionalism, such as (a) a robust membership that is actively engaged not only in practice, advocacy, research, and education but also in political parties, ministries, and departments; (b) a professional, research-based social work journal specific to the needs of Taiwan; (c) an annual or semiannual professional social work conference for the sharing of knowledge; (d) a continued presence and participation in international and regional social welfare associations; and (e) a fund for students and social work practitioners and administrators to study locally or abroad for graduate degrees in social work. TASW members need to be well trained in social work education to be effective as direct and indirect social work practitioners.

Social work education will become more mature as academics take a more active role in CSWE in Taiwan. A robust CSWE could assure that all social work programs provide not only the knowledge, values, skills, and ethics required for social work practice on many levels but also the faculty members trained in social work education.

As the social work profession, led by the Medical Social Work Association ROC, the TASW, and CSWE in Taiwan, grows and matures and trained social workers have more input in their profession and education, clients and society will be the beneficiaries. There is much to do in the social work arena, but Taiwan is moving in the right direction.

References

Chen, Y. (2008). "A Study of the Cultural Identity, Social Adaptation and Social Network of New Immigrants in Taiwan." *Nation and Society* 4:43–100.

Control Yuan of Republic of China (2008). "The Study Report of Foreign Brides and Mainland Spouses Care and Adaptation Issues (II)." *Gazette of the Control Yuan* 2608:1–26.

Council of Labor Affairs (2002). "Multi-employment Development Program." *Gazette of the Executive Yuan* 2 (7): 3–8.

——— (2008). "Program of Start Working Immediately." *Gazette of the Executive Yuan* 14 (203): 30,391–30,398.

Directorate-General of Budget, Accounting and Statistics (2008). "The Statistics of Foreign Spouses." *Gazette of Ministry of the Interior*, week 3.

——— (2009). "Major Socio-economic Indicator." *Monthly Bulletin of Statistics* 522:2–27.

——— (2010a). *Statistics Bulletin* 127, July 7. Taipei: Author.

——— (2010b) *Statistics Bulletin* 128, July 8. Taipei: Author.

Executive Yuan of Republic of China (2003). "Public Service Interim Regulations on Employment Expansion." *Gazette of the Executive Yuan* 9 (7): 37–40.

Hsueh, C. (2003). "Demographical Trends and Traits in Taiwan: Implications for Social Welfare Policy in Taiwan." *National Policy Quarterly* 2 (4): 1–22.

Huang, H. (2007). "Policy to Respond to the Trend of Aging Society and Declining Birthrate." *Taiwan Education Review* 648:27–36.

Huang, S., C. Lin, & C. Lin (2003). "New Poverty and Social Welfare Policy—Science vs. Value and the Elite vs. the Proletariat. *National Policy Quarterly* 2 (4): 83–124.

Li, S. (2007). "New Poverty in Taiwan: The Phenomenon and Policies." *Soochow Journal of Social Work* 17:193–219.

Li, S., & L. Lai (2004). *A Study of Family Poverty and Related Policies*. Taipei: Ministry of the Interior.

Lin, W. (2006). *Contemporary Social Work: Theory and Methods*. Taipei: Wu-Nan.

——— (2010). "The Development of Social Work Education in Taiwan." Paper presented at the 2010 Social Work Conference, Taipei.

Lin, W., & S. Shen (2008). "The Academic Trend of Social Work and Social Welfare Since the 1980s in Taiwan." *Social Policy and Social Work* 12 (1): 219–80.

Ministry of Education of Republic of China (2005). *A Study Report of Learning and Living Conditions of Elementary School Children of Foreign Spouses.* Taipei: ROC Government Printing Office.

Ministry of the Interior of Republic of China (2003). "Public Service Interim Regulations on Employment Expansion." *Gazette of the Executive Yuan* 9 (7): 37–40.

———— (2008a). *Population Protocol: Policies for Declining Childbirth, Aging Society, and Mass New Immigrations.* Taipei: ROC Government Printing Office.

———— (2008b). "Regulations on Qualifications of Recipients and Delivery of Economic-Stimulus Shopping Vouchers." *Gazette of the Executive Yuan* 14 (250): 36,731–36,734.

———— (2008c). Operation Directions for Urgent Caring and Assistance Scheme." *Gazette of the Executive Yuan* 14 (157): 23,739–23,745.

———— (2009a). *2008 Policy Performance Report.* Taipei: ROC Government Printing Office.

———— (2009b). *Regulations on Specialty Certifications for Licensed Social Workers and Continuing Education.* Taipei: Author.

———— (2009c). *Statistics Reports.* Taipei: Author.

———— (2010). *Monthly Bulletin of Interior Statistics.* Taipei: ROC Government Printing Office.

Mo, L., & P. Lai (2004). "The Issue of Birthrate Decline and the Problems of Children of Foreign Brides in Taiwan." *Community Development Quarterly* 105:55–65.

Pong, S. (1995). "Analysis of Child Welfare Policy in Taiwan." *Community Development Quarterly* 72:25–40.

President Decree. (2002). "Regulations on Living Allowance for Medium or Low Income Senior Citizens." *Presidential Office Gazette* 6 (464): 15–17.

———— (2007). "National Pension Act." *Gazette of the Judicial Yuan* 49 (10): 69–81.

Rhythms Monthly (2006). *Charities in Taiwan in the Past 400 Years.* Taipei: Author.

Yang, A. (2003). "Taiwan: New Emigration Upsurge Changes Taiwan Population Composite." *Common Wealth* 271:95–99.

6

Social Welfare and Social Work in Thailand

JITTI MONGKOLNCHAIARUNYA AND NUANYAI WATTANAKOON

The Kingdom of Thailand, located in Southeast Asia, consists of 514,000 square kilometers (198,455 square miles) of land. In 2010 the population was 67 million, of which 94 percent was Buddhist. The Thai people continue to enjoy the richness of Thailand's natural resources, especially its forests, water, and flat and fertile soil. Thailand has served as a world food exporter, or "world kitchen," for centuries. Nevertheless, the "Gift from God" (a Thai proverb) is declining with time because of excessive exploitation and inappropriate cultivation of Thailand's resources. For example, the size of the national reserved forestry has been reduced from 53.3 percent of the total land in 1961 to 25.3 percent in 2000 (Thailand Development Research Institute 2005).

Major foreign currency income is derived from tourism and exports of textiles and footwear, fish products, rice, rubber, jewelry, automobiles, computers, and electrical appliances. Major imports include capital goods, intermediate goods and raw materials, consumer goods, and fuel (Economy Watch 2009).

The 2007 Human Development Index for Thailand was 0.783, or a rank of 87 out of 182 countries (UN Development Programme 2009). GDP per capita is U.S.$8,135 (268,455 baht), but the income gap in Thailand is quite high. The Gini coefficient rate was 0.418 in 2007, approaching the halfway mark of equal income distribution on a scale from 0 to 1. The lowest income group (among five quintiles) owned 4.4 percent of total income while the highest income group owned 54.9 percent (Office of the National Economic and Social Development Board 2008).

Although Thailand has never been colonized by a Western country, it has adopted some Western ideas in education, economic development, government administration, and social welfare delivery. During King Rama IV's regime (1851–1868), royal family members and high-ranking officials who were sent abroad brought back modern development concepts that partially created the nation-state for King Rama V's regime (1868–1910) (Kosaiyawattna 2003).

Thailand's ruling system was changed from a monarchical to a democratic government in 1932. However, the king remains the leader of the nation and receives the highest respect and loyalty from citizens. King Bhumipol (Rama IX) has demonstrated for decades his concern and dedication to improving and enhancing the lives of the Thai people. He has initiated more than three thousand development projects (Thammasat University 2008), including the famous "sufficiency economy" concept. The executive (cabinet), legislative (national assembly), and judicial components of the government exercise their power on behalf of the king. High-ranking officers, members of Parliament, and judges are officially appointed by the king.

The central government (ministries and departments) makes national policy and macro plans, and the provincial administration ensures that the national policies and plans are completely and appropriately implemented in the provincial jurisdictions. The provincial governor is appointed by the Ministry of Interior, and the chiefs of provincial functionary offices are appointed by the ministries concerned. Local administrations have their own autonomy; the leaders or mayors are elected locally and can initiate local policy and action plans for the betterment of people within their jurisdiction (Puangngarm 2007).

Although development infrastructure standards in health, education, housing, and other public facilities different from those in Western countries, they are well established. Health care services, especially those operated by the private sector, seem to be the most developed. The government has a policy to make Thailand a medical hub of Asia. Public health services in public hospitals are free in most cases. These services also cover free medicine for 125,772 HIV patients (Population and Social Research Institute 2009). The quality of health care is better in urban than in rural areas.

Thai students enjoy fifteen years of free education. Approximately 41,326 persons with disabilities also receive educational opportunities (National Statistics Office of Thailand 2007). Those who want to study at the university level may apply for an education loan from the government and repay it after graduation. Although public schools operate in all subdistrict and district towns and provincial cities, the quality is uneven. Some large public and private schools and universities in Bangkok and other big cities have better reputations, but students must compete for seats in these select primary and secondary schools and universities. Many students have tutors to help them score high on entrance examinations.

History of Social Welfare in Thailand

Social welfare implies people attaining an adequate quality of life by using programs that are made available by multiple stakeholders. Nonetheless most Thai people perceive social welfare as government-support programs (Nontapattamadul 2007). The National Social Welfare Promotion Committee, chaired by the prime minister and established by the National Social Welfare Promotion Law, has defined social welfare as consisting of seven categories of services that Thai citizens are entitled to receive: education, health, housing and environment, recreation, secured employment and sufficient income, fair juridical treatment, and social services and assistance (National Social Welfare Promotion Committee 2006).

Khamhom (2006) has classified Thai social welfare history into three stages: the early stage (before 1956), the national development era (1957–91), and the present stage (1992–present); however, we have modified this classification as follows.

Conventional Stage (1200–1931)

During this time, the country adopted the monarchical administration system, whereby the king had absolute power in ruling the country and looking after his subjects. Slaveholders also provided minimum care and security for their slaves through a patron-client relationship. As Buddhists, all Thai kings have been taught to employ the ten Buddhist commandments as part of their daily lives. Two commandments that are relevant to social welfare service providers are to give (assets, love, and care to others) and to sacrifice personal happiness for the common good (Wattanasiritham 2007). The quality of welfare services depended on the competence and commitment of the ruler. For example, King Ramkhamhaeng (r. 1279–98) treated his subjects as if they were his children. He promoted tax-free trade, constructed irrigation dykes, invented the Thai alphabet, and ensured that every person's problems would be heard (Na Nakhon 2001). Anyone could voice a grievance by ringing the bell at the city front gate, and cases were fairly settled. King Chulalongkorn (Rama V, r. 1868–1910) abolished slavery in Thailand in 1905 and introduced new modern developments, such as communication and transportation infrastructure, a banking system, and bureaucratic reform. He also promoted education for the Thai people, especially public servants.

The first charitable organization in Thailand was Unalom Daeng, renamed Sapa Kachard, or the Red Cross Organization, in 1893 (Khamhom 2006). The main objective of the Red Cross Organization was to treat injured and sick Thai soldiers. King Mongkut (Rama VI) upgraded the Red Cross health facility, and when it became the first public hospital in 1914 it was called Chulalongkorn, after his father.

Buddhist temples and family were indigenous social service providers that gave food, health care, education, and other basics to those in need and their family members. In the agriculture-based society, extended families were formed, and family and community ties were quite strong. Elders and parents were taken care of by their children or other relatives. Mutual support among neighborhoods was available, especially in rural areas. This practice has continued to the present time.

Modernization Stage (1932–96)

In 1932 the revolution that transformed the national ruling system from a monarchy to a democracy occurred. Members of the military and public servants who had been trained in Western countries sought the change. Since then, democracy has been rooted in Thai soil. Immediately following the revolution, a few bright leaders following the socialist model tried to provide maximum socioeconomic opportunities to all citizens, but they failed. The government lacked not only resources but also support from many key government figures who feared that socialism would lead to communism.

From 1940 to 1957 the Pibulsongkram government made a major effort to modernize Thailand in many ways, one of which was to develop public social welfare and social work programs. The new Department of Public Welfare (now the Ministry of Social Development and Human Security) was established under the Prime Minister's Office in 1940 to ensure that Thai people had food, shelter, clothing, employment, and a decent lifestyle in accordance with government guidelines. In 1954 the Social Security Act was issued. More social services were founded, such as hospitals, homes for older people, residential facilities for juveniles, a foundation for people with disabilities, the Ministry of Public Health, and a social work education program at Thammasat University.

Meanwhile the country developed the first five-year National Economic and Social Development Plan in 1961. The purpose of this plan was to indicate the development direction for the country and major programs the government would implement. Before 1997 the plans emphasized economic development and yielded considerable success, such that economic growth was higher than 7 percent per annum. Owing to poor distribution of wealth, however, a number of social problems became widespread, including rural poverty, urban migration, slum expansion, poor health conditions, unemployment, and low education. Poor distribution of wealth was considered to be the root cause for political conflict among the haves and have-nots.

Although social infrastructure was established, including schools, hospitals, and social-assistance programs by public and nonprofit organizations, social services could help only part of the population. Thus equitability and quality issues needed to be addressed further. The YMCA and YWCA, international nonprofit organizations that provided hostel services for travelers and small community development projects, were established in 1932 and 1947, respectively. The Christian Children Fund began in Thailand in 1975. A year later the Holt Saha Thai Foundation, which aimed to help neglected children with food, education, and foster care, was established (Khamhom 2006). Earlier the Por Tek Teung Foundation had been founded by wealthy local Chinese residents in 1909 to help poor people by providing funeral services, food, and clothes. The foundation expanded its services to health care and higher education in 1941 and 1990, respectively (Pohtectung Foundation, Huachiew Hospital, and Huachiew Chalermprakiat University 2009). Many small local charitable foundations were founded to provide social assistance to needy people in the foundations' respective geographic areas. The Social Work Council of Thailand, under the king's patronage, was founded in 1960 to coordinate and promote social welfare services provided by charitable organizations. The government also launched rural employment projects during dry seasons to provide job opportunities for the rural poor.

One important milestone in Thai social security history was the enactment of the Social Insurance Bill in 1990. According to this bill, employers, employees, and the government would contribute funds to a common pool that would be used for paying employees when they were hospitalized, gave birth, became unemployed, or retired.

Reform Stage (1997–Present)

Democracy in Thailand has been growing slowly. The 1997 and 2007 constitutions acknowledged more human rights than any other former constitutions. For instance, according to former constitutions, Thai people could neither sue a public agency nor have access to public information without agency approval. This changed under the new constitutions, and these changes, along with others, promoted human rights, citizen rights for social welfare, and popular participation, and also dictated the content of future laws.

The economic crisis of 1996–97 resulted in the government applying for U.S.$83.3 million (2.75 billion baht) in loans from the International Monetary Fund, the Asian Development Bank, and the Japan Bank for International Cooperation to establish a social safety net and social protection programs (Techaatik 2002:1). Most projects were initiated by and implemented in local communities and employed the community development approach. The scope of the projects covered income generation, cultural preservation and development, natural resources and environmental management, local network strengthening, and community-based social welfare services for disadvantaged groups. The focal point of the eighth and ninth five-year development plans shifted from economic advancement to people-centered development.

In 1999 Parliament issued the administration's Decentralization Act, and the roles of social welfare planner, implementer, and evaluator would be gradually moved from the central government to local administration organizations (LAOs). It is anticipated that LAOs will be responsible for all services for their residents in the near future. At present some strong LAOs administer schools, health centers, occupation development programs, and social assistance programs, such as living allowances for elderly people and people with disabilities in their jurisdiction.

It must be noted that social welfare laws issued after 1997 have been more liberal and open to public participation. Major laws that have passed include (Mutual) Funeral Management Laws B.E. 2545 (2002), Child Protection Laws B.E. 2546 (2003), Elderly (support) Laws B.E. 2546 (2003), Social Welfare Promotion Laws B.E. 2546 (2003, revised in 2007), revised National Housing Laws B.E. 2550 (2007), Domestic Violence Laws B.E. 2550 (2007), Child and Youth Development Laws B.E. 2550 (2007), Promotion of Quality of Life of Disabled B.E. 2550 (2007), Human Trafficking Control Laws B.E. 2551 (2008), Education for Disabled Laws B.E. 2551 (2008), and Mental Health (Mental Patient Protection) Laws B.E. 2551 (2008). These laws define the beneficiaries, protect their rights, specify kinds of services, and clarify the role of relevant stakeholders, particularly the government, in the prevention, care, development, and rehabilitation of respective target groups (Ministry of Social Development and Human Security 2010).

According to the Strategic Plan for the Promotion of Social Welfare in Thailand (2007–11), welfare services are to be pluralistic in nature. This means that not only the government (central and local levels) but also the private sector, nonprofit organizations, civic society, and the local community should provide services.

There has been a trend for deinstitutionalization of social welfare services and the promotion of community-based welfare service schemes due to the inefficiency and ineffectiveness of the government bureaucracy in coping with alarming and complicated social problems (Ministry of Social Development and Human Security 2005). However, government budgetary constraints shorten the transition process. Community saving and borrowing groups have been organized widely among the people. The profits drawn from money lending are used to sponsor educational scholarships, health care subsidies, community development projects, and so forth.

The number of community-based organizations has expanded from 42,199 in 2004 to 64,952 in 2008 (Community Organizations Development Institute 2010). These organizations operate on sustainable natural resource management and utilization objectives (watershed management, community forestry, and small fishery groups); on cultural and local wisdom practices (self-help welfare services, saving and lending groups, mutual caring groups for elderly and disabled communities); or on problem-solving issues (community housing arrangement groups, credit unions, community businesses, self-help health insurance). Most community-based organizations do not have legal status but operate on mutual trust, common goals, and cooperation. Scope of service, management styles, and rules of operation are adapted to suit local contexts, and local leaders play a crucial role in the development of community welfare schemes. The total membership in these organizations in 2008 reached 16.65 million individuals, and the organizations had acquired U.S.$478.5 million (15.79 billion baht) in savings.

Current Social Welfare Issues

Population Change: The Elderly Society

Improved living conditions and health services have increased the life expectancy of the Thai people. Since 2005 Thailand has been an elderly society, as the number of people over 60 years of age has exceeded 10.7 percent of the population (National Statistics Office of Thailand 2008). These seniors have moved from active engagement in the workforce to being dependent on the family. Most of these older people are poor and reside in rural areas with their young grandchildren, whose parents work in Bangkok and other cities for low wages in the industrial and service sectors. While it seems that grandparents and grandchildren may benefit from each other, in reality most elderly people cannot cope with the lifestyle of the younger generation.

Gradually the gap between the generations is widening. Elderly parents of middle-income families living in cities are also confronted with depression, as their adult children, pressured with work and travel challenges, spend less time with the family. In addition, most working adults cannot share their work experiences with their parents because current conditions are totally different from what the parents are familiar with (Foundation for Thai Elderly Research and Development Institute 2007). Government expenditures for elderly living allowances rise as the number of elderly people increases, but government revenue from income taxes declines as older people retire from work.

Capitalism, Consumerism, and Adolescents

Capitalism and consumerism are growing in Thailand. Consumerism has been promoted strongly by business enterprises and the government to boost the national economy. The younger generation is bombarded with advertisements and the media encouraging them to purchase modern technologies such as cell phones, motorcycles, fashionable clothing, and fast food. Families who have the income and can provide guidance to their children are able to adjust to this new phenomenon; however, with many parents living and working in the city and separated from their teenage children, the circumstances back home may be problematic. Common problems in rural areas include unsupervised adolescents playing games at commercial Internet shops, loitering and roaming around in gangs, and engaging in promiscuous behavior, often leading to more serious problems such as pregnant teenagers, school dropouts, single parents, and early marriages. Problems with adolescents also are becoming more visible. The number of juvenile delinquents has increased about 12 percent per annum from 2003 to 2007 (Department of Juvenile Observation and Protection 2008).

A tangential but serious potential problem related to capitalism and consumerism is how adolescents might act in order to acquire a large amount of money for major purchases. Also, the more money that is required for a costly and unaffordable purchase, the greater the possibility of young girls, and some young boys, becoming engaged and trapped in prostitution.

Undocumented Foreign Laborers

High socioeconomic conditions entice laborers from surrounding countries to immigrate to Thailand. It is believed that more than two million foreign laborers are working in Thailand, particularly along the border and in large cities such as Bangkok and Chiang Mai. In 2006 there were 705,293 registered foreign workers, but it was estimated that 970,903 transnational migrant laborers were undocumented (Nontapattamadul & Cheecharoen 2008). Illegal laborers frequently work and live in poor conditions, are underpaid, and fear being captured and returned home. This situation can lead to human-trafficking issues due to the existence of corruption and the inefficiency of the immigration officer-in-charge. To handle the illegal labor issue, and immigration police officer is assigned to work closely with local police and officers from the Ministries of Labor, Interior, and Justice. The Thai government recognizes the shortage of domestic laborers and their refusal to accept the less-preferred jobs available in the fishery and construction fields. There is a policy that welcomes foreign laborers whose employers register them for security and development purposes, but compliance is far from usual. Illegal laborers are cheaper for small- and medium-size employers as businesses can avoid paying their taxes and registration fees.

Drugs

Geographically Thailand is located in a drug-sensitive area. Myanmar, Laos, and Thailand comprise the "golden triangle" for manufacturing drugs, in particular amphetamine. In addition, the northern part of Thailand is mountainous, with an environment optimal for growing opium. Every year drug-suppression reports describe smugglers and dealers who have been arrested or killed. The number of drug users increased from 575,312 in 2007 to 605,095 in 2008. The numbers of both drug users and dealers have increased over time (Office of the Narcotics Control Board 2009). There are indications as well that the number of new drug dealers is increasing. Of arrested drug dealers, 70 percent are new dealers. Drug dealers are often addicted themselves and demand more money to purchase drugs for their own use. A recent policy considers drug users as patients to be cured in public hospitals rather than treated as criminals. Drug dealers, however, may still be given the death sentence.

Wealth and Political Power: The Fragmented Society

Thailand is currently undergoing extreme political unrest. There is an underlying threat that a civil war will occur in the future owing to an economically divided country and misuse of power by high government leaders. There is a large lower class, a smaller middle class, and an even smaller upper class in Thailand. It seems that opposing politicians have enticed either the rural poor or urban middle- and upper-class people to their political party. The former and ousted prime minister Thaksin Shinawatra and his successors, Samak Suntarawech and Somchai Wongsawad, leaders of the Pua Thai Party, ambiguously provided financial support to the red shirt United Front for Democracy Against Dictatorship (UDD) political movement. The three former prime ministers were linked to malpractice, misbehavior, and vote buying, respectively, and were removed from office. The UDD movement is aligned with the lower class, especially farmers in rural areas. Meanwhile, outgoing prime minister Abhisit Vejjajiva, who led the Democrat Party since 2006, also indirectly supported the yellow shirt People's Alliance for Democracy (PAD) movement and was preferred by the middle and upper classes.

From mid-March to May 2010 the UDD, in its attempt to regain control of the government, organized a nationwide rally in Bangkok and some provincial cities in the northern and northeastern regions. The largest demonstration, initially peaceful, occurred in Bangkok, where UDD leaders announced that the rally would continue until Prime Minister Abhisit Vejjajiva dissolved Parliament and allowed for a new election to occur. However, gradually the rally turned into a riot that resulted in 88 deaths and 1,885 injured (Erawan Emergency Medical Service Center 2010).

The UDD's 2010 rally was well planned and organized. Villagers in the northern and northeastern regions went through a political sensitizing process. Issues of democracy, the unequal treatment of rich and poor, the double-standard law-enforcement services for Thaksin and his party, and the inability of the government to solve the poverty problem were emphasized. Many rallies that supported the one in Bangkok were organized in other provinces. UDD's supporters were mixed among those who were in favor for Thaksin's administration, those who preferred a political change that would gradually lead to socialism, and a few terrorists who mingled with the protesters and sporadically attacked officers (Anonymous 2010a).

In Bangkok the mob blocked almost all junctions or intersections on Rajadamneren Avenue, the location of many ministerial offices and not far from the government house and Parliament since March 2010. The government accused some prominent supporters of the red shirt UDD of plotting against the monarchy.

In April 2010 the government made an attempt to dissolve the rally at Kok Wua junction and Phan Fah junction but failed because of strong opposition from the protestors and some unidentified gunmen. As a result, 21 civilians and 5 soldiers died and 864 people were injured (Anonymous 2010b). Then the riot moved to Rajprasong junction, considered by many to be the commercial heart of Bangkok. Large hotels, department stores, and other businesses immediately closed, but damage later was estimated to be in the billions of baht (a few hundred million U.S. dollars).

After civilians and officers were ambushed in a few places in Bangkok, the government decided to crack down on the mob; from May 13 to 19, 2010, more people died. In counterattack, people rioted in northern and northeastern provinces such as Chiang Mai, Ubolrathjathani, and Khon Kaen. Protestors set fire to scores of buildings, and four provincial administration offices were completely burned in the northeastern regions of Khon Kaen, Ubolrathjathani, Udornthani, and Mukdaharn (Anonymous 2010c). The government declared a state of emergency in various provinces, including Bangkok. Violence ceased by the end of May 2010, but there was no assurance that the red shirt pro-Thaksin movement would stop its operations in local communities.

While most political clashes in recent decades were generated by politicians and the army and were of less interest to everyday citizens, there were some clashes that involved students and everyday citizens where blood was shed, including in 1973, 1976, and 1992 (Special Report 2010). However, each incident lasted no longer than a few days, and no private businesses were affected directly.

The longest political rally, which occurred in 2007, was organized by the PAD movement and attempted to oust Prime Minister Thaksin Shinawatra for corruption and misuse of his authority to benefit his family and friends. The 193-day rally, which started at Rajadamnern Avenue, eventually occupied the government house and employed nonviolent civil disobedience strategies against the pro-Thaksin Samak and Somchai governments. Some PAD demonstrators were killed by unidentified gunmen and grenades as the demonstrators attempted to surround Parliament while it was in session. The PAD did not riot in business or residential districts.

In April 2009 the UDD pro-Thaksin movement organized a rally to press for the removal of the chair and some privy council members who were accused of unlawful political intervention. The protestors also accused Prime Minister Abhisit of being incapable of ruling the country. When the UDD surrounded the government house for a month and later blocked a main road junction to paralyze Bangkok traffic, the government responded by using troops to free both locations. The mob was dispersed in two days.

The spring 2010 riots were more violent and extensive, and deaths, injuries, and business and government losses were far more serious than in any other political conflict or demonstration in recent history. This grave unrest created wounds in people's minds and fragmented relationships among neighbors and regions. The red shirt pro-Thaksin movement gained millions of followers as did the yellow shirt PAD movement. The two movements had their own communication channels but refrained from communicating with each other. The huge division in Thai society between the red and yellow shirts presents an ominous threat of civil war if reconciliation is not forthcoming.

The Response of Government and Nongovernmental Organizations

National Government Response

In Thailand the role of the national government is extensive and significant. Several departments and agencies are directly involved in the provision of social welfare services. The Ministry of Social Development and Human Security (MSDHS) has social welfare agencies throughout Thailand. There are agencies to care for babies, children, people with disabilities, elderly people, at-risk women, survivors of domestic violence and sexual harassment, and homeless people. The local government is supposed to be responsible for these agencies, but budgetary and professional constraints make this decentralization difficult. In addition, there are national committees that oversee various welfare services to target groups such as seniors and people with disabilities. Funds to support income-generating and other welfare projects are also available. Two other agencies under the purview of the MSDHS are the state enterprise National Housing Authority, which provides low-cost housing, and the Community Organizations Development Institute, which promotes the establishment and empowerment of self-help community organizations and self-reliant welfare services.

The national government policy to invite the private sector and community to participate in the delivery of social welfare services is enhanced by a tax incentive. Recently the tax incentive was extended to the employment scheme for people with disabilities. In 1998 the corporate social responsibility concept was introduced, as well as a code of ethics for business operations. In addition, the Stock Exchange of Thailand established the Social Responsibility Network to promote and monitor ethical practices among registered public companies (Stock Exchange of Thailand 2006). The private sector can file a tax reduction claim for making social welfare expenditures such as donations for educational purposes or expenditures on managing a firm's child-care center.

An anti–human trafficking law was enacted in 2008. This law clearly describes human-trafficking incidents, the officers in charge and their powers, the procedures to follow, and the operational fund. A multidisciplinary team to address human trafficking consists of a health officer, a social worker, a police officer, a labor welfare officer, an NGO representative, teachers, and a few others at the provincial level. All seem to work quite well together. The campaign against human trafficking is widespread, and Buddhists feel empathetic toward the survivors; however, many Thai people consider prostitution as a personal life decision rather than a social issue.

The Office of the Narcotics Control Board is the main agency that oversees drug issues. The police and military work to suppress the drug problem while hospitals are expected to provide curative measures for addicts who are there either voluntarily or involuntarily. The government policy is to promote community-based prevention and curative and rehabilitative interventions. Some Buddhist temples provide drug rehabilitation programs. At Wat Tham Krabok, the most famous drug treatment temple, the abbot uses herbs to detoxify the chemical substance, and then patients remain in the temple for a few days to regain their mental health before returning home.

In addition, there are several occupational training programs for the needy under the auspices of the Ministries of Agriculture, Education, Interior, Labor, and Social Development and Human Security. Loan schemes are also available for small- and medium-sized enterprises. Villagers have access to various kinds of government-funded revolving funds.

The 2010 semi–civil war among the Thai people warned everybody that structural problems such as poverty, unequal income distribution, and unequal justice need to be tackled immediately. While the national government needs to take its share of responsibility for this division of the people, all stakeholders, such as political parties, and all citizens should collaborate for the harmony, integrity, and development of the nation.

Many governments have tried to solve these problems, but the results have been far from successful. The sufficiency economy concept (National Economic and Social Development Board 2000) described at the beginning of this chapter has been praised by all ministries and is disseminated regularly, but it seems that even the trainers do not fully understand what it is and have not achieved much.

Local Government Response

Local government administrations are now mandated to provide care for older persons. Each month people over 60 years of age receive a U.S.$15 (500 baht) cash subsidy from their local government. A few local government administrations offer health care checkups, exercise programs, and entertainment programs for elderly people.

Local government administrations have received subsidies from the national government to build day-care centers and preschool centers in every subdistrict. Schools and the family are expected to be the mechanisms for youth development. Because parents have considerable income- and job-related stress, they rely on schoolteachers to help train their children; unfortunately, teachers have similar pressures, sometimes work overtime as tutors, and are unable to provide meaningful personal guidance outside the classroom. National and local government agencies have yet to deal with this problem effectively.

Nongovernmental Organization Response

Nongovernmental organizations include nonprofit organizations, community organizations, civic societies, charitable organizations, religious institutions, and institutions in the private sector that provide welfare programs to people.

Nonprofit organizations and some university projects have played a vital role in warning society of problems as well as recommending ideas to prevent or solve the problems. NGOs such as the Foundation for the Children, Christian Children Fund Foundation, and Holt Saha Thai Foundation have mobilized societal resources and used them to support child development programs, purchase food, and fund school expenses. A few NGOs work with street children. But it must be accepted that the existing NGOs cannot adequately serve the large number of youth and children in Thailand.

Thai people readily donate money to temples and then expect to have a good life or good luck in return. Most temples use these donations for temple infrastructure development; however, several temples utilize money to create a social safety net for poor people. Some temples provide not only religious education but also food, shelter, occupational training, and medical care (Mongkolnchaiarunya 2007). The Buddhist temple Wat Prabat Namphu has gained considerable recognition as an institution for helping hundreds of HIV/AIDS patients in their last stages of life. The abbot of this temple utilizes the large sums of money donated to pay for all costs incurred in the temple. Some patients may use both modern medicine and herbs to prolong their lives, while others feel more confident using meditation to control their sickness. The temple also provides food, shelter, and education for orphans whose parent(s) have died from HIV/AIDS.

A community-based welfare scheme supported by community leaders and by government agencies in charge of community-development affairs and social security is well known throughout the country. In this scheme, local people save their money together and use it to pay for welfare expenditures. The type of welfare service (compensation for medical care, funeral donations, scholarships for children, top-up age pensions, etc.) and degree of coverage (amount of compensation, qualification of clients) depend on the affordability of each scheme. Since January 2010 the government has been matching the community-based welfare fund up to U.S.$11.06 (365 baht) per annum per member (Community Organization Development Institute 2010).

Some NGOs have introduced community-based programs for older people. Elderly people are encouraged to offer their expertise in the areas of occupational skills as well as cultural dances with the community. These programs provide teaching opportunities and physical exercise for elderly people and have the additional benefit of making them proud of their accomplishments.

The Social Work Profession

Most professional social workers in Thailand work in the various agencies in the Ministry of Social Development and Human Security; in hospitals and health centers under the Ministry of Public Health; in the Department of Corrections and Homes of Juvenile Delinquents under the Ministry of Justice; in the police hospital and Child Delinquency Unit under the National Police Bureau; in the Ministry of Labor; and in local administration authorities, including the Bangkok Metropolitan Administration under the Ministry of Interior.

Other social workers are employed by NGOs. These practitioners work with those in need or at risk and cover all demographic ranges and health conditions. Most social workers are engaged in clinical casework and group work, but there are a few who work at macro level in community development and planning and in conducting research, analyzing policy, and teaching social work.

The social work profession is sometimes misunderstood in Thailand. Even the Thai word *sang khom songkroh* means both "social work" and "charity work," a fact that has negatively affected the status of the social work profession. In addition, most professional social work positions are within the government structure, and some of these professionals are trained in other social sciences. The social work profession is a complex and comprehensive profession that requires its workers to be trained in social work specifically so that they can work directly with people, as individuals, as families, and as communities, or, indirectly, work in administration, research, policy formulation, higher education, and so forth.

Why do we allow social workers without training in social work to be hired? Perhaps the decision makers and general population are not fully cognizant of the specialization of social work education and social work practice. Perhaps more social workers trained in social work need to apply and promote their specialized social work knowledge, values, and skills so there is a clear distinction between their performance and that of their colleagues who use generic bureaucratic practices based on training in other disciplines.

The Thai bureaucracy is quite strong, and professionals may feel pressured to follow the official policies and bureaucratic systems of the administration; however, perhaps self-advocacy may be appropriate and warranted. Social work practice is a time-consuming process before success at the individual, group, family, or community levels may be observed. Some fiscal policies and financial regulations are actually more burdensome than supportive to the social work treatment process. Social work practitioners should not simply follow rules for the sake of convenience but should instead try to explain their position and challenge the administration to make further reforms.

Despite the above situation, social workers are well respected for the work they perform. Social workers who work in the mental health field under the Ministry of Public Health or those who work with target groups such as elderly people and those with disabilities have been recognized by their colleagues. Capable social workers in other fields of social work are also highly regarded.

Many politicians, high-ranking officers who do not work closely with professional social workers, do not fully recognize the worth of these social workers. However, there is a trend to increase the number of social workers at the local administration level. More universities are also incorporating social work courses into their existing curricula because social welfare issues have received much public attention.

Thailand celebrates National Social Work Day on October 21, the date on which the present king's mother passed away. She was highly respected and seen as one who devoted herself to bettering the quality of life of the Thai people.

The Thailand Social Work Association, the Thammasat University Social Work Alumni Association, and the Ministry of Social Development and Human Security collaborated to advocate for a bill that recognizes social work professionals as akin to medical doctors, dentists, scientists, nurses, and lawyers. The Nursing Board, fearing competition, was one of the bodies most resistant to this bill, claiming that family and community work were already part of their professional tasks. Opposition also came from bureaucrats fearful that the proposed (and likely to be enacted) social work licensing system would discourage volunteerism and the role of the royal family in helping the poor. Currently the number of voluntary social welfare providers far surpasses the approximately 1,600 professional state social workers and about 200 professional social workers employed by NGOs (Nontapattamadul & Cheecharoen 2008). Social work licensing and registration are not yet available in Thailand.

Social Work Education

Social work education is taught at five universities in Thailand. The Faculty of Social Administration at Thammasat University (TU) was established in 1954 as the first to offer a social work curriculum, and TU the only state university to ever do so. TU provides all levels of social work education: a bachelor's degree in social work, two master's degrees (in social work and in social welfare policy and administration), and a doctoral degree, with an emphasis in social administration. The Faculty of Social Work and Social Welfare at the private Huachiew Chalermprakiat University (HCU) opened its social work program in 1990. HCU also offers all levels: a bachelor's degree in social work, a master's degree in social welfare policy, and a Ph.D. degree in social welfare policy and administration, which is set to begin in 2012. The Faculty of Liberal Arts School of Social Welfare at Krik University (KrU) started its social work education program the following year, in 1991. KrU offers only a bachelor's degree in social work and social development. (Mongkolnchaiarunya, 2009). The Faculty of Social Sciences at Mahachulalongkornrajavidyalaya University Chaingmai Campus (MCU) began offering a bachelor of arts in Social Work in 2001(Mahachulalongkornrajavidyalaya University 2008). The curriculum integrates Buddhism with social work practice. TU, HCU, KrU, and MCU are quality schools accredited by the Commission on Higher Education under the Ministry of Education.

Finally, the Faculty of Humanities and Social Sciences at Prince of Songkla University, Pattani Campus (PSU), is set to begin offering the bachelor's degree in social work in 2012 with a curriculum designed to meet the needs of the southern situations and the Islamic base in that region.

The bachelor's degree program is important for professional social work training comprises 130 to 144 credit hours of courses, including social work principles, values, ethics, methodology and tools (casework, group work, community work, research, empowerment process, etc.), and vulnerable groups. Selective psychology, sociology, anthropology, economics, and law courses are also required for completion of the degree. The program provides students with the opportunity to learn about social change, social problems, social justice, social welfare system management, and the systems approach. Some faculty members also emphasize critical theory, postmodern concepts, and indigenous knowledge in their classes. Students are taught and challenged to consider how to apply local culture and wisdom in social work intervention.

Most important, field practicum is compulsory for all social work students. The number of credit hours required in each university's program varies slightly and can be divided into separate categories: (1) the casework and group work skills used in social welfare agencies when dealing with specific target groups, and (2) the community work skills used when working in either urban or rural communities. Because of a shortage of social workers, some community work field supervisors are not social workers; however, they do supervise students because they are experienced in working in the particular community. TU faculty members visit students at their sites four times throughout the practicum, while HCU faculty take turns staying with groups of students in the community. Each practicum requires at least 270 hours.

All social work courses in Thailand are conducted in the traditional classroom format. An online program has not yet materialized, although some subjects taught at TU at the undergraduate level use a complementary online system.

The number of undergraduate student enrollments in TU, HCU, and KrU is 300, 120, and 15, respectively. TU also enrolls about 80 master's degree students annually, and 20–30 apply for the master's degree program at HCU. Two to three doctoral students are accepted annually to study at TU. The undergraduate and doctoral programs at TU are competitive; however, the master's degrees at TU and social work programs at other universities are not as competitive.

Since a social work curriculum was initiated in Thailand in 1954, it has been importing social work know-how from England, Canada, and the United States. Thai society places much importance on obtaining a formal degree from higher education institutions, especially from abroad or from the few famous national universities, including TU. While a considerable number of students in various fields have obtained theoretical knowledge and limited skills to perform their jobs, in social work the standard of attainment of book knowledge by students is decreasing.

Gradually Thai social work education has moved from having a broad perspective to becoming tailored to meet local problems and demands. As all schools of social work employ the basic problem-solving approach, Thai bio-psycho-social assessment tools have been developed. Local problems are emphasized, and local wisdom is utilized to solve those problems. Indigenous tools and techniques for community empowerment have been satisfactorily developed by local wise people, some reality-based scholars, and some practitioners. When concentrating on clinical social work, we still recognize the importance of community strengths that can be used for the development of our domestic social welfare system. Currently indigenous clinical social work knowledge is less developed. The local community social welfare system is taught extensively, and students integrate and apply this during field practicum in the community.

While Thai social work education still uses a lot of imported knowledge, it does not totally depend on it. Nevertheless, Western knowledge has its uses. Some techniques are specifically applicable in Thai society, such as the faith-based model (or Sattha). One research study found that a community-based mental health rehabilitation program led by a local monk was far more effective in terms of cost and recovery than a similar program provided by the professional health officer (Koomsapanant 2008). The mental health clients who stay at the temple and are counseled by the monk can be rehabilitated quicker and more cost-effectively than those who stay with their family and are helped by the health officer.

Social welfare and social work in Thailand in the socioeconomic context are well aware of government and civil organizations. Historically the king has played a major role in providing social welfare assistance for the people along with Buddhist temples and the family. When Thailand became a democracy and modernized, the constitution acknowledged more human rights and the social welfare system began to promote human rights and citizen rights for social welfare services. At present government social welfare policies encourage all partners (local government, NGOs, communities, and the business sector) to provide social welfare services. Furthermore, these stakeholders are encouraged to uphold social welfare laws regarding social welfare promotion, child protection, domestic violence, quality of life for those with disabilities, human trafficking, etc. as protective tools for social welfare rights.

However several current social welfare issues, such as the aging society, capitalism, consumerism, adolescents, undocumented foreign laborers, drugs, wealth, and political power, have produced a fragmented society. There is an increasing need for the social work profession and social work practitioners to work with people affected by these issues and to help them access social welfare programs and services. Most social workers are engaged in clinical practice and group work, but there are a few who work on the macro level.

Thailand is not able to produce enough professional social workers, and many politicians and high-ranking officials do not recognize the worth of professional social workers. Thus more social workers are trained in social sciences other than social work. Five universities in Thailand offer social work programs in an effort to strengthen the social work profession and enable clients to be serviced by trained social workers; however, these programs are not able to meet the needs of the population, and the government has yet to recognize the full strength and power of the social work profession.

Future Perspectives

The social work profession in Thailand is currently undergoing major changes. For decades the Thai government has tried to increase social welfare services for its citizens, but this effort continues to occur in a piecemeal fashion. Services such as free education, free health care, and free short-term training, as well as many grant projects, are attractive to voters, whether or not these services or projects are worthy and sustainable. Recently the government declared a national agenda for creating a welfare society that integrates the input and contributions of the private sector, civic society, community sector, and general public. In time there will be an increase in the number of bills passed related to social welfare, human rights, and social justice, and the role of social workers will be emphasized and more recognized.

Politicians, economists, and health-related experts now track social welfare issues and increasingly intervene in the day-to-day responsibilities of the relevant agencies. If professional social workers and social welfare providers do not insist on and fight for their professional positions, this may result in the demise of the social work profession. On the other hand, if social workers can demonstrate their capability and value, the social work profession will have a prosperous future, and micro, mezzo, and macro populations will benefit.

In time the social work credential bill acknowledging the social work profession will be approved. Social work licensure benefits clients, increasing the educational standardization and the capability of practitioners and eventually benefiting the country as a whole. Social workers should prepare themselves now with the knowledge, skills, and experience for the time when they will be called on to demonstrate their best practices for service quality to sustain the evolving social welfare system in Thailand.

Government resources may diminish and social welfare will require more contributions (such as health insurance) from its beneficiaries, including the business sector in its various forms. The local governmental and community sectors will also need to take a more active role in providing social welfare services. There is room for social welfare system improvement, and the system will always need professional social workers and other professionals to intervene.

References

Anonymous (2010a). "Keeping an Eye on the Government & Military Signal on Tactical Artifice to Close the Game." *Matichon Weekly Bulletin*, April 23–29.

—— (2010b). "Historical Inscription of Red Shirt Demonstration Crackdown on April 10, 2010, at Kok Wua Junction and the Success Factor Depends on the Role of the Pro Red Shirt Soldiers." *Matichon Weekly Bulletin*, April 16–22.

—— (2010c). "67 Days of Red Shirt United Front for Democracy Against Dictatorship End—a Problem Doesn't End, Expand (Territory), War, and the Riot Spreads Nationwide." *Matichon Weekly Bulletin*, May 21–27.

Community Organizations Development Institute (2010). "Report on 10 Years Achievement of CODI During 2000–2010." Bangkok: CODI Public Organization.

Department of Juvenile Observation and Protection, Bureau of Justice System Development for Child and Youth (2008). "Annual Statistic Report 25006." Retrieved April 16, 2011, from http://www.djop.moj.go.th/stat/show_stat.php.

Economy Watch (2009). *Thailand Trade, Exports and Imports*. Retrieved March, 16, 2011, from http://www.economywatch.com/world_economy/thailand/export-import.html.

Erawan Bangkok Emergency Medical Service Center (2010). "Report on Situation of the Red Shirt United Front for Democracy Against Dictatorship." *Matichon Newspaper*, June.

Foundation for Thai Elderly Research and Development Institute (2007). *Situation of the Thai Elderly in 2006*. Bangkok, October.

Khamhom, R. (2006). *Social Welfare and Thai Society*. Bangkok: Prikwan Graphic.

Koomsapanant, S. (2008). "Management of Community Mental Health Network: Case Study of Choomchon Wat Bangrahong and Choomchon Wat Raukbangsi-thong, Nonthaburi Province." Ph.D. dissertation, Thammasat University.

Kosaiyawattna, S.(2003). *The National Development in the Reign of King Rama IV: The Basic Plan for Upgrading Traditional Society to Modern Society of Siam*. Retrieved November 16, 2011, from http:// www.edu.buu.ac.th/journal/Journal%20Edu/Link_Jounal%20edu_16_1_3.pdf.

Mahachulalongkornrajavidyaya University (2008). *Curriculm of Mahachulalongkorn-rajavidyaya University*. Retrieved November, 7, 2011, http://www.mac.ac.th/site/curriculm.php.

Ministry of Social Development and Human Security (2005). *Report on the Study of Trends and Models of the Thai Social Welfare System.* Bangkok: Author.

—— (2010). *Laws on Duties of Ministry of Social Development and Human Security.* Bangkok: Kanarutamontree and rachakitjanubecksa.

Mongkolnchaiarunya, J. (2007). "Relationship Between Buddhism and Social Welfare in Thailand." Lecture delivered at the special international conference held to commemorate the retirement of Prof. Hagiwara, Department of Social Work, Taisho University, Tokyo, Japan, November 4.

—— (2009). "Social Work Education and Profession in Thailand: Sunrise or Sunset." *Proceedings of the Seoul International Social Work Conference,* Social Work Education and Practice Development in Asia Pacific Region, by Asia Pacific Association for Social Work Education (APASWE), Korean Council on Social Welfare Education (KCSWE), and Korean Association of Social Workers (KASW). Seoul, April.

Na Nakhon, P. (2001). "King Ramkamhaeng the Great." *Thai Encyclopedia, 25.* Bangkok: Sahamitr Printing.

National Economic and Social Development Board (2000). *What Is Sufficiency Economy?* Bangkok: National Statistics Office.

National Social Welfare Promotion Committee (2007). *First Five Years Strategic Plan for Thai Social Welfare and Action Plan for Social Welfare System Development 2007–2011.* Bangkok: Ministry of Social Welfare and Human Security.

National Statistics Office of Thailand (2007). *Summary of the Findings of the 2007 Disabilities Survey.* Retrieved April 15, 2011, from http://www.mict.go.th/download/static/deformed-50.pdf.

—— (2008). *Report on the 2007 Survey of Older Persons in Thailand.* Bangkok: Thana Press.

Nontapattamadul, K. (2007). *Social Welfare for Neglected Groups: Well-being and Rights' Policy.* Bangkok: Edison Press.

Nontapattamadul, K., & C. Cheecharoen (2008). "Country Paper: Thailand." Paper presented to the Planning Workshop to Develop an Asian Consortium of Schools of Social Work and Practices, Manila, Philippines.

Office of the Narcotics Control Board (2009). *Report on the Situation of Narcotics in 2009 and Its Trend.* Retrieved April 16, 2011, http://www. nccd.go.th/upload/content/situationtrendin 2009(published).pdf.

Office of the National Economic and Social Development Board (2008). *Statistics/ Indicators of Poverty and Income Distribution 1988–2007.* Retrieved August 16, 2011, http://www.nesdb.go.th/portals/0/tasks/eco_crowd52531–2550.pdf.

Pohtectung Foundation, Huachiew Hospital, and Huachiew Chalermprakiat University (2009). *Huachiew Chalermprakiat University History.* Bangkok: Rongangsamutsairoung.

Population and Social Research Institute (2009). *Health of Thai People in 2009.* Nakhonpathom: Amarin.

Puangngarm, K. (2007). *Theories, Concepts and Principles Related to Local Government.* Bangkok: Expernet.

Special Report (2010). "The Encirclement of Rajprasong Junction to Revoke the Area, by Abhisit Vejjajiva Government. *Matichon Weely Bulletin,* May 21–27.

Stock Exchange of Thailand (2006). *Guideline for Corporate Social Responsibility.* Bangkok: Stock Exchange of Thailand.

Techaatik, S. (2002). *Social Investment Fund.* Retrieved October 13, 2002, from http://www.thaioctober.com/smf/index.php?topic=205.0.

Thailand Research and Development Institute (2005). *Prioritizing the Importance of Natural Resources and Environmental Problems.* Retrieved April 16, 2011, from http://www.thaienvimonitor.net/Concept/order.htm.

Thammasat University (2008). *His Majesty the King's Roles and Concepts in Royalty-Initiated Urban, Community and Architecture Development.* Bangkok: JBP Center.

United Nations Development Program (2009). "2007 Thailand Country Profiles of Human Development Indicators." In *The Human Development Report 2009.* Retrieved March 16, 2011, from http://hdrstats.undp.org/en/countries/country_fact_sheets/cty_fs_THA.html.

Wattanasiritham, P. (2007). *Goodness Mapping.* Bangkok: Matichon Press.

7

Social Welfare and Social Work in Indonesia

ADI FAHRUDIN

Indonesia is an archipelagic country of 17,508 islands (more than 6,000 of which are inhabited) that stretch along the equator in Southeast Asia. The five major islands are Sumatra, Kalimantan, Java, Sulawesi, and Papua. The country's strategic sea-lane position has fostered interisland and international trade. Indonesia is divided into two regions, Java and the Outer Islands (Geertz 1963). Based on the National Census 2010, the population of Indonesia is 237.6 million, many of whom are descendants of people from various migrations, creating a diversity of cultures, religions, ethnicities, and languages. The official language of Indonesia is Indonesian (Bahasa Indonesia). It is the language that unifies Indonesia, with its 350 ethnic groups and 750 native languages and dialects. The archipelago's landforms and climate have significantly influenced agriculture, trade, and the formation of the state. Indonesia is divided administratively into provinces and districts. Between 2001 and 2010 the number of provinces expanded from 27 to 33. Each province is subdivided into municipalities, cities, and the decentralized administrative unit. In 2010 there were 398 districts, 93 cities, and 6 administrative units in Indonesia (Ministry of Domestic Affairs 2010).

Indonesia proclaimed independence from Japanese colonial rule on August 17, 1945. Since then the country has experienced several profound political developments. Indonesia's founder, President Soekarno, was succeeded by President Soeharto in 1966. A "new order" government was established in 1967, and it was oriented toward direct overall development. A period of uninterrupted economic growth was experienced from 1968 to

1996, when per capita income increased sharply from about U.S.$50 (IDR 439,000) to U.S.$385 (IDR 423,000) in 1986 to U.S.$1,124 (IDR 12,364 billion) in 1996. The national economy expanded at an annual average rate of nearly 5 percent. This situation was abruptly reversed by the 1997 economic crisis that affected Southeast Asia.

In 1997 and 1998 Indonesia went through its worst economic crisis since independence. Economic growth reversed to negative 13 percent (CBS 2003). After more than three decades in power, President Soeharto resigned in 1998. The political situation underwent rapid transition. Soeharto's last vice president, B. J. Habibie, succeeded him as president from 1998 to 1999, and he was followed by Abdurrahman Wahid from 1999 to 2001 and Megawati Soekarnoputri, daughter of President Soekarno, from 2001 to 2004. A historic direct presidential election took place for the first time in October 2004, when President Susilo Bambang Yudoyono came into office and was subsequently reelected for a second term, 2009–2014.

History of Social Welfare in Indonesia

Information about social welfare activities during the Dutch and Japanese colonial era is limited. According to Praptokoesoemo (1982), social welfare as a service activity started before Indonesia gained independence from the Japanese in 1945. During the colonial period, poverty affairs were included in the Department of Justice. Certain Statsblad regulations provided care for poor people under the domestic affairs departments in Java, Madura, and other regions outside Java. Based on these regulations, the Dutch colonial government was not directly involved in social welfare service for poor people. Instead, informal organizations, including religious and community groups, provided decentralized services. However, the colonial government did establish a residential facility for children (Byblad no. 2853, in Praptokoesoemo 1982).

During Japanese colonialism (1942–45), Gunsikanbu Naimubu (Department of Domestic Affairs) included the Koseikai (social affairs unit) and Komukyoku (labor office), which were basically inactive. Japan merely continued the Dutch practice of giving subsidies to social agencies through municipal and city governments. The Komukyoku exploited the people of Java and Sumatra and forced them into repressive work for the Japanese military, in addition to sending many to Thailand and other countries (Praptokoesoemo 1982).

Social welfare was started formally when the Department of Social Affairs was established on August 19, 1945, after Indonesia gained independence. The Department of Social Affairs had no predecessor during the Dutch colonial era. Short-term services for poor people and neglected children were established as a result of Article 34 of the 1945 Basic Constitution. In the early stages, social welfare efforts were focused primarily on providing assistance to refugees and war victims, including former forced laborers who survived World War II, and helping repatriate Indonesian people from Australia, Holland, and other countries.

President Soekarno confronted major challenges during the early years of independence and nation formation, from 1945 to 1965, including a stagnant economy, an unstable government, political riots, communist conspiracy, and military and civil rebellion. Finally, in 1965, President Soekarno was overtaken by General Soeharto, who was formally appointed president in March 1968. President Soeharto's new-order administration garnered economic support and investments from the West, helping contribute to three decades of economic growth for Indonesia. During President Soeharto's administration, the government and community organizations openly gave intensive attention to social welfare programs and the development of social welfare (Fahrudin 1997). The Department of Social Affairs established offices in every province, city, and municipality. Social work education and the social work profession began to appear in senior high schools, colleges, and universities; however, in mid-1997 Indonesia fell into an economic, social, and political crisis. Unstable political and economy conditions have had both direct and indirect impacts on the social well-being of the people of Indonesia. The collapse of the economy led to various short- and long-term social and economic problems, such as increased unemployment, declining real income, and a lower quality of social services (Fahrudin 1999).

In 1999 the new president, Abdurrahman Wahid, dismantled the Ministry of Social Welfare and replaced it with the National Social Welfare Board. The board provided little direction and guidance to maintain social welfare activities in provinces and districts, and this led to the collapse of the social welfare system. In 2001 a political uproar occurred when President Abdurrahman Wahid was dismissed by the People's Consultative Assembly. He was replaced by Vice President Megawati Soekarnoputri, the daughter of the first president, Soekarno, and she served as president from 2001 to 2004. President Megawati reactivated the Ministry of Social Affairs. The Reformation Era following President Soeharto's resignation in 1998 led to a strengthening of the democratic process, including a regional autonomy program and the first direct presidential election in 2004. However, history and insufficient preparation for reformation have led to religious and racial conflict, violence, acute corruption, and political and economic instability (Fahrudin 2005).

It has been many years since Indonesia was hit by the economic crisis of 1997–98. Despite the government's claim that the Indonesian economy has recovered and that the country now enjoys a stable exchange rate, increasing economic growth, and a decreasing budget deficit, Indonesia rank low in terms of most social indicators, including life expectancy, literacy, education, and standard of living. For example, the 2011 *Human Development Report* shows the Indonesian Human Development Index rank at 124, which is in the Medium Human Development level (UNDP 2011). The Human Development Index rank measures life expectancy, literacy, education and standards of living for countries worldwide.

Natural disasters, terrorism, and health problems have also slowed progress in Indonesia recently. The massive 2004 earthquake and tsunami disaster in Aceh and other parts of Indonesia devastated the country and brought more death, missing and injured persons, and hunger and homelessness to an already struggling people (Fahrudin 2005). Terrorism, riots, violence, and religious conflict also have negatively affected social development. Despite commendable efforts by the government to reduce unemployment and poverty, the people of Indonesia continue to battle against massive unemployment and deteriorating infrastructure as well as outbreaks of dengue fever, avian flu, and tuberculosis. Indeed, many obstacles keep the government and nongovernmental organizations from addressing social issues in the varying regions and subregions within the country, such as rural areas, uninhabited islands, indigenous people, and the separatist movement in Papua.

Major Social Problems

Indonesia is plagued with a number of fundamental social problems, described below.

Poverty and Malnutrition

Poverty is a huge social issue in Indonesia that affects as much as 48 percent of the population. Accompanying the problem of poverty are malnutrition, illness, poor housing, inadequate clothing, substandard medical facilities, and impure water. The World Bank's Jakarta office, in its outstanding report, "Making the New Indonesia Work for The Poor" (2006), makes an urgent case for programs to drastically reduce *problems such as* malnutrition among a quarter of all children below the age of 5; high maternal mortality rates (307 deaths in 1,000 births); weak education outcomes (among 16 to 18 year olds from the poorest quintile, only 55 percent completed junior high school); and impure water (access to safe and clean water is limited, at 43 percent in rural areas and 78 percent in urban areas for the lowest quintile). In 2007, 23.6 million rural Indonesians were living below the national poverty line, one million less than in 1996. Poor people represent 20 percent of the rural population and 11 percent of the total population. But the overall national poverty rate masks the large number of near-poor people who live just above the poverty line and are at risk of sliding below that line into poverty. In November 2010 there still were 32.5 million poor people in Indonesia subsisting on less than U.S.$2 (IDR 20,000) per day (CBS 2010). Poverty-reduction strategies need to focus on increasing the income of both poor and near-poor people.

Hunger and malnutrition remain devastating problems facing the majority of Indonesians, especially the poor. Despite general improvements in food availability and health and social services, the problems of hunger and malnutrition (*gizi buruk*) exist in some form in almost every district in Indonesia. At present, about half the population is iron deficient, and one-third is at risk of iodine deficiency disorders. Vitamin A deficiency disorders still affect approximately ten million children (Atmarita 2005).

Unemployment and the Workforce

The unemployment rate in Indonesia tends to decrease from time to time. In August 2009 the unemployment rate was 7.87 percent, which was lower than the 8.39 percent in August 2008 and 8.14 percent in February 2009 (CBS 2009). The Indonesian workforce accounts for 49 percent of the country's population of 231 million. The workforce in Indonesia increased from 104 million in February 2008 to 112 million just six months later. About 52 percent of the workforce, or 55.2 million people, have an education level below elementary school. The main problem regarding the workforce is that while the number of workers entering the workforce annually is growing rapidly, the rate of job creation is only slightly above the rate of labor force growth. The government's goal to drop unemployment to 5.1 percent in 2009 was far from being achieved. Policies to send women overseas to work as domestic helpers and decrease unemployment instead resulted in new social problems, such as human trafficking. Many Indonesian women and children are trafficked for sexual and labor exploitation in Malaysia, Singapore, Brunei, Taiwan, Japan, Hong Kong, and the Middle East (UNICEF 2000).

Children's Issues

Children in Indonesia are confronted with many difficult situations that preclude them from being educated and having a healthy lifestyle. Data indicate that there are 3,488,309 neglected children, 1,178,824 neglected babies and young children under 5 years of age, and 10,322,674 neglect-prone children; there are also 193,155 adolescents with disabilities and 367,520 children with disabilities (Ministry of Social Affairs 2009). There were 94,674 street children in 2002, according to the National Socioeconomic Survey (SUSENAS) results in cooperation with the Central Bureau of Statistics (CBS) and Center for Data and Information Social Welfare, an increase of more than 100 percent from 1998.

According to CBS data, there were 2.3 million street children over the age of 10 in August 2000. The International Programme on the Elimination of Child Labour, International Labour Organization (IPEC/ILO) estimates there are about 8 million child workers under the age of 15 in Indonesia. From 1995 to 1999, there were 11.7 million children who had dropped out of school. Between 40,000 and 70,000 children under the age of 18 are being sexually exploited in child prostitution, and some of them are involved in child trafficking to foreign countries. In 1997 and 1998, there were 75,106 hidden or registered brothels, wherein approximately 30 percent of the occupants were under 18 years of age (UNICEF

2000). Problems of sexual abuse and sexual exploitation of children have increased each year since 1995 (Farid 1999).

In Indonesia a juvenile delinquent is a child under the age of 18 who violates any criminal law. Juvenile delinquency problems have become more diverse and have been increasing in the last few years. There were a total of 198,578 juvenile delinquency cases in 2008 (Ministry of Social Affairs 2009). CBS data indicate that more than 4,000 law violations are committed by children under the age of 16 each year. Criminal statistics also show that in 2009 there were 5,789 children who violated the law, an increase from the 3,084 in 2001 (Directorate General of Correctional Institution 2009; Supeno 2010).

Drug Abuse

Another serious social problem in Indonesia is illicit drugs and drug abuse. According to the drug abuse survey conducted in 2008 by the National Narcotics Board (NNB) in cooperation with the Center for Research on Health of the University of Indonesia, 3.1–3.6 million people, or 1.5 percent of the population, are drug abusers, 26 percent are experimental users, 27 percent are regular users, 40 percent are nonintravenous drug users (IDU), and 7 percent are IDU, or addicts. Survey results also showed that 60 percent are nonstudent abusers, 40 percent are student abusers, 88 percent are male abusers, and 12 percent are female abusers. Of the new drug users, 90 percent are students, while most regular users and addicts are nonstudents. The most abused or popular drugs are cannabis (92 percent), shabu-shabu, or methamphetamine (64 percent), ecstasy (54 percent), tranquilizers (52 percent), and heroin (32 percent). The pattern of abuse is poly- and multidrug (National Narcotics Board 2009). A study by the International Labour Organization office in Indonesia reported that approximately 4 percent of illicit drug users in the country are children under the age of 17. Two out of ten users are involved in illicit trafficking. According to the NNB (2009), some teenagers become involved in producing and trafficking narcotics (*narkoba*) between the ages of 13 and 15. Drug abuse has also contributed to the increase of HIV/AIDS patients in Indonesia through the use of unsterile needles. Indonesia could have as many as one million intravenous drug users.

HIV/AIDS

The first case of AIDS in Indonesia was reported in 1987. Since then, 3,614 HIV/AIDS patients have been recorded; 332 of these have died. The threat of HIV/AIDS in Indonesia could be more devastating than in Africa because the disease multiplies more rapidly when drug addicts use contaminated syringes. In 1995 only 2 percent of new HIV/AIDS infections nationwide were due to drug use, but by 2001 this had risen to 20 percent. From January 1987 to September 2010, the number of people with AIDS in Indonesia was 22,726; of these, 4,249 died (Ministry of Health 2010). At the beginning of 2004, the six provinces of Jakarta, Papua, Bali, East Java, West Java, and Riau were designated priority provinces because of their high numbers of people with HIV/AIDS, and by the end of that same year, six others joined the priority category: West Kalimantan, North Sumatra, North Sulawesi, Central Java, Jogjakarta, and Banten. According to the NNB (2009), the key means by which the HIV virus is transmitted is drug needles, sexual intercourse, blood transfusion, and perinatal transmission. The percentage of risk factors for HIV/AIDS infection in 2007 for heterosexual intercourse was 4,664 persons, or 41.9 percent; IDU was 5,555 persons, or 49.8 percent; homosexual or bisexual intercourse was 434 persons, or 3.9 percent; perinatal transmission was 189 persons, or 1.7 percent; blood transfusion was 10 persons, or 0.1 percent; and unknown was 289 persons, or 2.6 percent.

Approximately 40 percent of people with HIV/AIDS are young people ages 10 to 24. In 2010 it was estimated that there were 90,000 to 130,000 people with HIV/AIDS in Indonesia (Ministry of Health 2002). In 2007 Indonesia was ranked 99th in the world by prevalence rate, but because of the lack of understanding of the disease symptoms and the high social stigma attached to it, only 5–10 percent of people with HIV/AIDS actually get diagnosed and treated. Therefore, the United Nations Program on AIDS (UNAIDS) declared that Indonesia is one of Asia's fastest growing HIV epidemic countries. Indonesia has already moved from being a low-prevalence HIV/AIDS country to a concentrated HIV/AIDS country (Ministry of Health 2002). The rapid growth rate of HIV/AIDS is due in part to better statistics, the growing availability of voluntary counseling and testing services, and the actual rapid spread of infection among injecting drug users, female and male sex workers and their clients, and transvestites.

Older People

According to the CBS, 7.6 percent of people in Indonesia, or 16,522,311, are over age 60, constituting the seventh largest elderly population in the world today (Ministry of Social Affairs 2010). CBS data predict that the percentage of Indonesians over 60 will rise to 11.3 percent in 2020. Comparable shifts in Europe took fifty years in the case of Britain and more than a century in France. Not only is the speed of change remarkable, but also the scale of the Indonesian situation is mind-boggling. Owing to a rapidly growing national population, in absolute terms the numbers of older people will increase by 300–400 percent. Large numbers of these people are not being taken care of: 15 percent, or 2,426,190 persons, are neglected, and 28 percent, or 4,658,280 persons, are prone to neglect. It is projected that in 2020 the number of neglected elderly persons will be approximately 28,822,879 (CBS, 2010).

Government and NGO Responses to Social Welfare Problems

The government must cooperate with nongovernmental organizations in responding to social problems. In Indonesia NGOs play a key role in supporting the national government in the development of social welfare and delivery of social services.

NGOs' Presence in Indonesia

Despite the government's dominance in many areas of social action, NGOs, most of which are homegrown, have a rich history in Indonesia. Many NGOs focus on social welfare and include family planning, rural health, mutual aid, legal aid, and workers' rights. NGOs in Indonesia are based on religious and nonreligious groups. Muslim and Christian organizations have been active in education, community education, social services, and health care since the early twentieth century. Besides the government, religious organizations play an important role in meeting the needs of the poor. Many Islamic organizations in Indonesia, such as Muhammadiyah and Nahdlatul Ulama, were active in the development and provision of social services. The Muhammadiyah organization was founded in 1912 by Ahmad Dahlan in the city of Yogyakarta as a reformist socioreligious movement (Peacock 1978). Muhammadiyah has many universities, schools, hospitals, and child-care centers for both Muslims and non-Muslims.

The Christian organization PELKESI (Indonesian Christian Association for Health Services) offers a hospitalization program that provides aid for health tools, equipment, and capacity building for all Christian hospitals. It also provides primary health care for the poor and disaster services throughout Indonesia.

Government-Provided Social Services

The responsibility for most formal public health and social welfare programs rests primarily with the government and secondarily with private and religious organizations. Social welfare programs to benefit the poor are minimal compared to the need, and rural economic development activities are modest compared with those in cities. Indonesian national development requires the harnessing of its capital and human and natural resources to meet the demands of its population as comprehensively as possible.

Poverty, unemployment, and malnutrition. The government has programs that combat poverty, unemployment, and malnutrition, such as the National Health Insurance for Poor People (Askeskin), Hopeful Family Program (PKH), National Public Empowerment Program (PNPM), and People's Credit Scheme (KUR). The purpose of the Askeskin 2007 scheme is to resolve poverty and health problems, especially in rural areas. The Askeskin health insurance program was introduced to expand social security to the informal sector, aiming at a target population of sixty million people. The insurance includes basic outpatient care, third-class hospital care in grade A–D hospitals, an obstetric service package, mobile health services and special services for remote areas and islands, immunization programs, and medications. Hospitals can submit claims for services delivered to Askeskin beneficiaries based on a fee for services, while primary health centers are compensated on a per capita basis. Although Askeskin insurance was initially intended to cover private health services as well, only a third of private health care providers accept it. Resources and risk were pooled at the district *(kabupaten)* level, with monthly premiums of U.S.$0.56 (IDR 5,000) being fully subsidized by the government. The total annual budget for 2005 was set at approximately U.S.$400 million (IDR 3.9 trillion) and was initially financed through energy subsidy reductions (Aran 2007; ILO 2008).

The government's Medium Term Development Program *(Rencana Pembangunan Jangka Menengah,* or RPJM) aimed to reduce the poverty head count from 18.2 percent in 2004 to roughly 8.4 percent by 2009. When the plan was announced in the first cabinet meeting in October 2004, no one foresaw the various domestic and international crises that would severely affect the trajectory of the poverty reduction program.

The Indonesian government plans to allocate approximately U.S.$3 million (IDR 270 trillion) in funds for its poverty eradication program from 2010 to 2014 (Bappenas 2010). The government also intends to adopt a poverty eradication policy and program consisting of three clusters: to provide protection and assistance for poor families and communities, to boost poor people's empowerment to improve their welfare, and to empower micro- and small-scale businesses.

The government also will improve the quality of the three clusters by implementing family-based social protection programs, by improving the quality of the National Program for Community Empowerment (PNPM Mandiri) in an integrated way, and by improving the implementation of the People's Credit Scheme (KUR). Another program under the coordination of the Ministry of Social Affairs, the Hopeful Family Program (PKH), will empower poor people by focusing on education for children and health for children and mothers. The PKH program deals with several aspects of development simultaneously. In addition to school attendance and health visits, gender is an important issue for consideration in the impact studies of such programs. Indeed, the PKH provides a viable means of analyzing the role of women in social protection or development programs in general. Although its aim is to increase human investment for the next generation, rather than target women, the PKH places women in a unique position as the allowance recipients (Hutagalung, Arif, & Suharyo 2009).

In the Social Welfare Law No. 11 Year 2009 and Poverty Alleviation Law No. 13 Year 2011, the Indonesian government recognized that to be a socially inclusive nation, all Indonesians must have the opportunity to secure a job, access services, connect with family, friends, and the community, deal with personal crises, be free from discrimination, and have their voices heard. The government also committed to achieving these aims by partnering with provinces and local governments and the not-for-profit and private sectors, and by delivering targeted and tailored interventions that address localized systemic disadvantage through unconditional cash transfer (Bantuan Langsung Tunai, or BLT) and conditional cash transfer (Program Keluarga Harapan, or PKH). The program goal is to counter the impact of increasing poverty as a result of the increase of gasoline prices.

Both cash transfers help the poorest households and poor households with pregnant mothers and children of elementary school age. Community cash transfer, or PNPM Generasi, provides assistance for better health and education services through the community empowerment process. Another program that reduces poverty is Social Welfare Insurance (Askesos), which is a form of social security for independent worker groups and those that work in the informal sector. This program is expected to maintain a stable income for citizens and so prevent the advent of poverty. In addition, the Community Health Care Security Program (Jaminan Kesehatan Masyarakat) is a continuation of preceding social programs that were established to overcome the multidimensional crises endured by all people. This program started with the development of the social safety net.

Children's issues. The Indonesian government has established a coordinating body to address violence against women and children in addition to establishing a national plan of action. Indonesia also has a national health care network that offers treatment either free of charge or for a nominal cost through several types of medical facilities for mothers and children. District medical centers, the most comprehensive of which combine general medical clinics with maternal- and child-health centers, provide services in family planning, school health, nutrition, communicable disease control, health statistics, environmental health, health education, dental health, and public-health nursing. The district centers also supervise the community and village health centers, or *puskesmas*, which are the primary health providers in rural areas. A third type of public medical facility is the *posyandu*, an integrated health service for children at the local community level.

The government also has launched the National Action Plan for Disabled People to ensure that children with disabilities have the same opportunities and supports as everyone else in the community. This policy protects people with disabilities from discrimination (Fahrudin 2007b).

Drug abuse and HIV/AIDS. The Narcotics Law No. 35 Year 2009 is the foundation on which the government and NGOs collaborate to prevent and combat drug abuse and HIV/AIDS. Since the NNB's inception in 2002, it and the national drug control programs have gained strong political support from the legislature, the president, and the ministries.

Indonesia established a National AIDS Commission (Komisi Penanggulangan AIDS Indonesia) in 1994 to focus on preventing the spread of HIV, addressing the needs of people living with HIV/AIDS, and coordinating the efforts of the government, NGOs, the private sector, and community activities. The government of Indonesia signified its continued commitment to fighting HIV/AIDS in 2005 when it budgeted U.S.$13 million (IDR 1.3 billion) to HIV/AIDS programs, an increase of 40 percent over the amount disbursed in 2004. However, the national budget for HIV/AIDS has since been stagnant. A 2006 presidential regulation stressed the role of prevention as the core of Indonesia's HIV/AIDS program and recognized the urgent need to revitalize and enhance treatment, care, and support services. The AIDS national strategy emphasized the importance of conducting proper HIV/AIDS and sexually transmitted infection surveillance; carrying out operational research; creating an enabling environment through legislation, advocacy, capacity building, and antidiscrimination efforts; and promoting sustainability. Building on this framework, the National AIDS Strategy for 2007–2010 added several priority targets: reaching 80 percent of the most-at-risk people with comprehensive prevention programs; influencing 60 percent of the most-at-risk people to change their behaviors; and providing antiretroviral therapy to 80 percent of those in need.

The needs of older people. The *Elderly Social Welfare Law No. 13 Year 1998* promotes age-friendly communities by clearly stating that discrimination on the basis of a person's age is unlawful (Fahrudin 2008b). Government and NGOs have worked actively to enhance the quality of life for elderly people (Fahrudin 2007a). The National Commission of Elderly People (Komnas Lanjut Usia) is a semigovernmental organization that has played an important role in raising awareness and educating the community about age discrimination and helping to foster age-friendly communities. HelpAge Indonesia (Yayasan Emong Lansia) is a foundation that works with the Indonesian government and the community to create an environment where elderly people can live with dignity. The mission of this foundation is to improve policies, programs, and facilities that enhance the quality of life for elderly people.

The government implementation of the Social Welfare Law No. 11 Year 2009 through the Elderly Social Insurance Program (Jaminan Sosial Lanjut Usia) cares for bedridden, poor, and neglected older people. Since 2007 the government has been rolling out U.S.$33.09 (IDR 300,000) per person per month, and today there is coverage in 28 provinces, 138 districts/ cities, 286 subdistricts, and 864 villages. This program currently includes 3,500 elderly people, but the target of 39,132 elderly persons includes all older people throughout Indonesia.

Indonesian Culture and Social Welfare

Indonesia is a multicultural country. The Indonesian coat of arms enshrines the motto of Bhineka Tunggal Ika (Unity in Diversity), written on a banner held in an eagle's talons. *Pancasila* is the official philosophical foundation of the Indonesian state. It consists of two Sanskrit words, *panca*, meaning five, and *sila*, meaning principles. It comprises five principles: belief in the one and only God (Ketuhanan Yang Maha Esa), just and civilized humanity (Kemanusiaan Yang Adil dan Beradab), the unity of Indonesia (Persatuan Indonesia), democracy guided by the inner wisdom in the unanimity arising out of deliberations amongst representatives (Kerakyatan yang dimpimpin oleh Hikmat Kebijaksanaan dalam Permusyawaratan dan Perwakilan), and social justice for all the people of Indonesia (Keadilan Sosial Bagi Seluruh Rakyat Indonesia). It is believed the Pancasila should be practiced and implemented in all aspects of life, including in social welfare.

The Indonesian culture strongly encourages the spirit of the value *gotong royong*, or communal self-help. Gotong royong is a very familiar social concept in many parts of Indonesia and forms one of the core tenets of Indonesian philosophy. Geertz (1983) describes the importance of gotong royong in Indonesian life as an enormous inventory of highly specific and often quite intricate institutions for effecting cooperation in work, politics, and personal relations alike. Gotong royong means *rukun*, or mutual adjustment, while *tolong-menolong*, another common value, means reciprocal assistance. These values are needed to complete a wide range of village community tasks and activities, such as maintaining rural roads and irrigation facilities, coping with emergencies in natural disasters, providing mutual help for house construction and daily agricultural operations, and contributing labor or financial support for important ceremonies.

These traditional types of cooperative relationships have developed naturally over extended periods of time. Some of these daily interactions enable economic and social survival by sharing the burden to accomplish tasks. Gotong royong activities also can organize people into a collective action group anxious to improve access to services and overall family welfare (Suyono 2008). Cooperation in relationships in local community associations may well be more important than the specific functions of the associations. Social welfare programs must be based on the cultural values in the local community, especially gotong royong, which is an important source of social capital in the development of social welfare.

The Social Work Profession

Some people believe the situation for the social work profession is bleak in Indonesia because the government has neither established the profession as an independent profession nor valued social work training (Fahrudin 2004a). While trained social workers are hired by the Social Welfare Department, these employees are relegated to lower-midrange job positions. In addition, only untrained, rather than trained, social workers are eligible to compete for the national excellent social worker award, which is sponsored by the Ministry of Social Affairs. The possibility of engaging in private social work practice is almost nonexistent. Volunteer workers, religious leaders, government officials, and political activists who also call themselves social workers seem to be more valued than trained social workers.

People of other professions and lay people also do not have a high regard for the social work profession. Doctors, nurses, teachers, and psychiatrists are better known as professional and are better regarded than social workers (Fahrudin 1999). Doctors and psychiatrists are particularly respected since they may prescribe medications, while professional social workers cannot prescribe anything. In addition, there are a number of lay people, such as local leaders and religious leaders, who readily provide assistance and counsel. Clients are happier discussing their personal problems with indigenous healers, astrologers, priests, healing men (*dukuns*), and clever men (*orang pintar*) because they offer mantras, flowers, prayers, water with prayers (*air jampi-jampi*), and so on, and they are said to possess charismatic powers capable of healing all problems. Clients do not hesitate to pay lay people in hopes of solutions to their problems.

Currently there is a semigovernment licensing system under the Ministry of Manpower and Transmigration for the Professional Certification

National Board for professional workers, including professional social workers; however, the absence of a licensing system specifically for social work practitioners in Indonesia results in an uncertain quality of social work services. It is also very difficult for practitioners to work in other countries (Fahrudin 2004b) because there is no standard for the quality and competence of Indonesian social workers.

While the above conditions seem to be dismal for the profession, Indonesia has established four social welfare organizations that collaborate with the government and NGOs on common issues, such as higher-quality social services throughout Indonesia; improved quality of social work practice; and indigenous social work education relevant to Indonesians. The first is the Indonesian Association of Social Workers, or Himpunan Pekerja Sosial Indonesia (HIPSI), which was established in 1987 by Siti Hardiyanti Rukmana, the oldest daughter of President Soeharto. Members of this organization are professional social workers and volunteer workers. The second organization is the Indonesian Association of Professional Social Workers, or Ikatan Pekerja Sosial Professional Indonesia (IPSPI), which was established on August 19, 1998. This organization includes professional social workers exclusively. The third organization is the Indonesian Association for Social Work Education, or Ikatan Pendidikan Pekerjaan Sosial Indonesia (IPPSI), which was established in 1985. The fourth organization is the Indonesian National Council on Social Welfare, or Dewan National Indonesia Untuk Kesejahteraan Sosial (DNIKS), which was established in 1982. Ongoing political and financial problems make it difficult for these four organizations to sponsor significant activities that promote social development, social work practice, and social work education in Indonesia. Therefore members of these four organizations should consider increasing their participation in international social work associations to ensure that social workers in Indonesia are always kept abreast of the progress in international social work.

Indigenous Social Work Education

The most fundamental social work education issue in Indonesia today is the need to indigenize social work curricula and social work programs (Midgley 1981). Indonesian social work, according to Coulshed (1993), needs to create and develop appropriate curriculum design, while Hammoud (1988) advises that Indonesia needs to develop indigenous social work education models that are more relevant to social work practice in the Indonesian context.

Indigenization of course content and teaching methods is a viable way to teach students social work that is directly related to Indonesia's development and culture. In 1987, after the Asian and Pacific Association of Social Work Education–International Federation of Social Work Asia Conference in Jakarta, the Indonesian Association for Social Work Education organized the first national workshop, the National Social Work Education Curriculum Standard, in Bandung (Sulaiman 1985). The result of this workshop was a new indigenous curriculum that was implemented in all social work education programs.

Important progress has been made in indigenizing social work education by integrating social work with religious studies and the local culture (Fahrudin 2009). In 2004 the State Islamic University in Yogyakarta collaborated with McGill University and Canada International Development Agency (CIDA) to establish a postgraduate program in Indonesia. The master of arts in Interdisciplinary Islamic Studies with a major in Social Work combines the Islamic and secular perspective of social welfare and social work (Fahrudin 2008). In addition, the Bandung College of Social Welfare initiated an indigenous social work curriculum and fieldwork. The curriculum was developed for the Diploma IV Program with a concentration in social rehabilitation and community social development. The fieldwork emphasizes a community-based service model that enhances the social work student's skills and competencies in macro systems.

While there has been a general development of indigenous social work education, further work remains. Teaching materials, reference books, and fieldwork models from the United States still need to be refined and transformed into indigenous social work education for Indonesia (Brigham 1982). Since the tsunami disaster in Aceh in 2004 and the earthquake in Yogyakarta in 2006, social work education and practice in Indonesia have been influenced by international professional social workers, international volunteers, and international humanitarian organizations (Fahrudin 2008a, 2009). For example, after the 2004 tsunami the professional social worker organization, IPSPI, in collaboration with Families and Survivors of Tsunami (FAST Project) and supported by the International Federation of Social Workers (IFSW) and the Commonwealth Organization for Social Work (COSW), trained child protection workers (Tiong & Rowlands 2006).

Social work education and practice in Indonesia should adopt international trends while also being indigenous and following the direction of the Indonesian Association of Social Workers and the Indonesian Association for Social Work Education. The change in the global social work environment, particularly in relation to multicultural, global, and sustainable development, affects social work education and practice in Indonesia. However, since the adaptations universities and colleges make depend on their perception and interest, the development and expansion of the areas of social work can be slow, and the expansion is very limited in disaster social work, domestic violence, women and child trafficking, child abuse, conflicts and mediation, and international social work (Fahrudin, 2009).

Other social work education issues include curriculum standards, research, and accreditation. Indonesia needs to review, develop, and submit a national standard for social work education related to the International Association of Schools of Social Work (IASSW) policy standard and guidelines. Some factors that need to be taken into consideration in remodeling the multilevel curricula are the conceptual and operational design of fieldwork and the nature of field instruction, the examination system, field extension services, and research (Fahrudin 2002, 2009). There is also a need for indigenous literature in the national languages that can be used in social work education and training. It is also important to incorporate in instruction Indonesian thought that reflects Pancasila (Five Pillars) in social work values and ethics.

Research needs to be conducted in multicultural social work, good practice evidence, and indigenization. Funding is needed to ensure that Indonesian social workers are scientists-practitioners moving toward the further development of indigenous social work through research. Very little research on social work practice has been published in international social welfare journals. Social work educators should conduct research based on their own teaching and fieldwork supervision experiences. Similarly, social work students should engage in research about fieldwork placement and produce small projects that document indigenization.

Lastly, social work education can promote competent social workers in social welfare and social service delivery by establishing a system to accredit social work programs and a means by which to prepare social workers for social work licensure. Accreditation can help to ensure an appropriate social work education in a supportive academic environment. Social work education programs that are accredited are recognized as meeting minimum standards for social work education and training as proclaimed by an independent organization. Graduates from accredited social work education programs are qualified to pursue generalist social work practice. In 2010 most social workers who graduated from social work programs in Indonesia practiced under the authority of the Ministry of Social Affairs. In the near future the government will be able to enforce Social Welfare Law No. 11 Year 2009, which prevents unqualified professionals from practicing social work.

Indonesia is strapped with major social welfare problems, such as poverty, unemployment, drugs, HIV/AIDS, and issues regarding children and elderly people, that are very complex and require many organizations to resolve. Both universities and colleges with social work education programs and the social work professional organizations, including the Indonesian Association of Social Workers, the Indonesian Association for Social Work Education, and the National Council on Social Welfare, play a vital role in the development of social welfare and the delivery of social services. In addition, many stakeholders must give their support to promote and improve the quality of indigenous social work education and practice in Indonesia for the benefit of clients and society.

References

Aran, M. (2007). *Pro-poor Yargeting and the Effectiveness of Indonesia's Fuel Subsidy Reallocation Programs.* Jakarta: World Bank.

Atmarita (2005). *"Nutrition Problems in Indonesia."* Paper presented at the Integrated International Seminar and Workshop on Lifestyle-Related Diseases, Gajah Mada University, Yogyakarta, March.

Bappenas (Badan Perencanaan Pembangunan Nasional) (2010). *Rencana Pembangunan Jangkah Menengah Nasional 2010–2014.* Book 1: *National Priorities.* Jakarta: Bappenas.

Brigham, T. M. (1982). "Social Work Education Pattern in Five Developing Countries: Relevance of U.S. Microsystems Model." *Journal of Education for Social Work* 18 (12): 21–26.

Central Bureau of Statistics (2009a). *Number and Percentage of Poor People, Poverty Line, Poverty Gap Index, Poverty Severity Index by Province.* Jakarta: CBS.

——— (2009b). *National Labour Force Survey 2009.* Jakarta: CBS.

————— (2010). *National Population Census Report*. Jakarta: CBS

Coulshed, V. (1993). "Adult Learning: Implications for Teaching in Social Work Education." *British Journal of Social Work* 23:1–13.

Directorate General of Correctional Institution (2009). "Evaluation of Child Protection Task Force." Paper presented at Bappenas-UNICEF workshop, Bogor, November.

Fahrudin, A. (1996). "The Effect of Social Work Intervention in the Dynamic of Poor Community Group: The Case of Poverty Eradication Programme in West Java, Indonesia." M.A. thesis, University of Science Malaysia.

————— (1997). "Social Work Higher Education: A History, Problems Agenda and Relevance with National Development." Paper presented at Annual Scientific Conference. Indonesian Students Association in Malaysia. Penang, May.

————— (1999). "Professional Commitment Among Social Work Students in Indonesia." Ph.D. dissertation, Universiti Sains Malaysia.

————— (2002). "Direction for Social Work Education." Paper presented at National Workshop on Social Work Education. School of Psychology and Social Work, Universiti Malaysia Sabah, Sabah, August.

————— (2004a). "Social Work Education–Based Competence Training." Paper presented at National Workshop on Social Work Education, Bandung College of Social Welfare, Bandung, April.

————— (2004b). "Global Standard in Social Work Education and Critic to Social Work Education Curriculum Indonesia." Paper presented at International Seminar on Social Work Education Curriculum Development, Bandung College of Social Welfare, Bandung, November.

————— (2005). "Mainstreaming Social Development in National Policy and Program." International Conference on Social Development, State Islamic University, Jakarta, May.

————— (2007a). "Social Welfare Circumstances and Policy of the Aged in Indonesia and International Cooperation for Improving the Quality of Their Life." In *Proceeding of EURASIA Workshop and Symposium on Improving Quality of Life of the Aged and Disabled Persons*, ed. Soung Yee Kim. APPLE Project and Korean Association of Social Workers, Daegu, South Korea, November.

————— (2007b). "Current Situation Persons with Disabilities in Indonesia: Policy and Quality of Life." In *Proceeding of EURASIA Workshop and Symposium on Improving Quality of Life of the Aged and Disabled Persons*, ed. Soung Yee Kim. APPLE Project and Korean Association of Social Workers, Daegu, South Korea, November.

————— (2008a). "Improving Quality of Life with Information Technology in Meeting the Care Needs of Elderly in Long Term Residential Institutions in Indonesia." In *Proceedings of International Conference for Information Society and the*

Elderly: Global Perspectives, ed. Jae Son Choi et al. Symposium organized by the Center for Social Welfare Research, Department of Social Work, Yonsei University, Seoul, February.

———— (2008b). "Islamic Value and Philosophy in Social Work Theory and Practice." Paper presented at International Conference on Integration of Islamic Thought in Social Work, College of Social Work and Community Development, University of the Philippines, Western Mindanao State University, and Japan Foundation, Zamboanga City, Philippines, October.

———— (2009). "Future Challenges and Direction of Social Work Education and Practice in Indonesia." Paper presented at Seoul International Conference on Social Work (Deans Conference), Social Work Education and Practice Development in the Asia and Pacific Region, Korean Association of Social Workers, Korean Council on Social Welfare Education, and APASWE, Seoul, April.

Farid, M. (1999). *Situation Analysis on Sexual Abuse, Sexual Exploitation, and Commercial Exploitation of Children in Indonesia*. Jakarta: UNICEF Indonesia.

Geertz, C. (1963). *Peddlers and Princes: Social Change and Economic Modernization in Two Indonesian Towns*. Chicago: University of Chicago Press.

———— (1983). "Local Knowledge: Fact and Law in Comparative Perspective." In *Local Knowledge: Further Essays in Interpretive Anthropology*, ed. C. Geertz, 167–234. New York: Basic Books.

———— (1967). "Indonesian Cultures and Communities." In *Indonesia*, ed. R. McVey. New Haven: HRAF Press.

Hammoud, H. R. (1988). "Social Work Education in Developing Countries: Issues and Problems in Undergraduate Curricula." *International Social Work* 31 (3): 195–210.

Hutagalung, S. A., S. Arif, & W. I. Suharyo (2009). *Problems and Challenges for the Indonesian Conditional-Cash Transfer Programme*. Jakarta: Social Protection Asia.

International Labour Organization (2008). *Social Security in Indonesia: Advancing the Development Agenda*. Jakarta: International Labour Organization.

Midgley, J. (1981). *Professional Imperialism: Social Work in the Third World*. London: Heineman.

Ministry of Domestic Affairs (2010). *List of Provinces, Districts, Cities, and Subdistricts in Indonesia*. Retrieved June 10, 2010, from http://www.depdagri.go.id/media/filemanager/2010/01/29/0//0.induk kec.pdf.

Ministry of Health (2002). *Cases of HIV/AIDS in Indonesia Reported Through September 2002*. Jakarta: Directorate General of Direct Communicable Disease Control & Environmental Health.

———— (2010). *Cases of HIV/AIDS in Indonesia Reported Through September 2010*. Jakarta: Directorate General of Direct Communicable Disease Control & Environmental Health.

Ministry of Social Affairs (2009). *Info Care Bulletin.* Jakarta: Directorate General of Social Services and Rehabilitation.

———— (2010). *Practical Guidelines of Social Care for Elderly: Home Care.* Jakarta: Directorate General of Social Services and Rehabilitation.

National Narcotics Board (2009). "Country Report of Indonesia." Paper prepared for tThe Sixth Meeting of the AIPA Fact-Finding Committee (AIFOCOM) to Combat the Drug Menace, Chiang Rai, Thailand, May.

Peacock, J. L. (1978). *Purifying the Faith: The Muhammadijah Movement in Indonesian Islam.* Menlo Park, Calif.: Benjamin/Cummings.

Praptokoesoemo, S. (1982). "History of Social Welfare Service in Indonesia." In *The Summary View of Social Welfare Service.* Jakarta: Regional Office of Social Department.

Sparrow, R., A. Suryahadi, & W. Widyanti (2010). *Social Health Insurance for the Poor: Targeting and Impact of Indonesia's Askeskin Program.* Retrieved July 11, 2011, from http://www.smeru.or.id/report/workpaper/askeskin/askeskin_eng.pdf.

Sulaiman, H. (1985). *Promotion and Development of Direction of Social Work Eeducation in Indonesia.* Bandung: Bandung College of Social Welfare.

Supeno, H. (2010). *The Criminalization of Children: Bids Radical Ideas Without Criminalization of Juvenile Justice.* Jakarta: Gramedia.

Suyono, H. (2008). "Empowering the Community as an Effort to Revive the Culture of Self-reliance in Community Social Security." Paper presented at 33rd Global Conference of International Council on Social Welfare, Tours, France, July.

Tiong, T. T., & A. Rowlands, A. (2006). "Report of FAST (Families and Survivors of Tsunami)." Project Report to IFSW General Meeting 2006.

United Nations Development Program (2011). *Human Development Report: The Real Wealth of Nations: Pathways to Human Development.* New York: UNDP.

UNICEF (2000). *Women and Children Situation—Indonesia Reports.* Jakarta: UNICEF.

8

The Dynamics of Social Welfare

The Malaysian Experience

AZLINDA AZMAN AND SHARIMA RUWAIDA ABBAS

Malaysia is a small, multiethnic and multireligious Southeast Asian country located between Thailand in the north, Indonesia in the west, and Singapore in the south. It comprises two land masses: the peninsula, with
eleven states, and Borneo Island, with two states, usually referred to as East
Malaysia. Initially known as the Federation of Malaya (or Malaya) when it
achieved independence from Great Britain in 1957, it was later known as
the Federation of Malaysia (or Malaysia) beginning in 1963 when Sabah,
Sarawak, and Singapore joined the federation. In 1965 Singapore left Malaysia to become an independent city-state.

The main ethnic groups are the Malays, Chinese, and Indians. Before
Sabah and Sarawak joined Malaysia in 1963, the new grouping Bumiputera
was introduced to replace the Malay ethnic group. The Bumiputera grouping includes all Malays (born Muslims) and all Muslim and non-Muslim
indigenous people in the country, the majority of whom are from Sabah
and Sarawak. Bumiputeras, which literally means "the sons of the soil," enjoy the same constitutional privileges as Malays since they are the natives
of the country. Bumiputeras constitute 67 percent; Chinese, 24.3 percent;
Indians, 7.4 percent; and others, 1.3 percent of the twenty-eight million
people who live in Malaysia (Economic Planning Unit 2010).

Although Islam is the official religion of Malaysia, the Malaysian con-
stitution provides for freedom to practice other religions. Each faith largely
correlates with a specific ethnic group; for example, Malays are Muslims,
Chinese are predominantly Buddhist and Taoist, and Indians are mainly
Hindus. Christianity has made inroads into the country, attracting mainly
Indians, Chinese, and the indigenous people. Most Malaysians speak Ma-

lay, the official language, although every ethnic population also speaks its own mother tongue. English is also spoken widely and is regarded as an important language for commercial reasons.

The Malaysian culture has tended to work with the many ethnic groups despite their different ethnic and religious affiliations. For example, Malaysians celebrate each other's festivals. This cooperation between ethnic groups has developed over the years and has created respect, support, and tolerance among the groups. This cultural orientation has meant that Malaysian welfare services serve those most in need regardless of their ethnic background and religion. This cooperation has been possible because in the years prior to independence from Britain the population was smaller and the society less complex.

Since then the country has grown to be a developed nation in the region. Many successive development policies have been implemented with the ultimate aim of improving the quality of life for the population. The New Economic Policy (1971–90) was aimed at eradicating poverty and restructuring the society. The National Development Policy (1991–2000) endeavored to create a balance between economic growth and equity, while the overriding objective of the National Vision Policy (2001–10) was to achieve national unity.

With rapid industrialization and urbanization in the 1970s and 1980s, Malaysia has undergone a dramatic economic transformation, from a large dependence on the agricultural sector to a dependence mainly on the industrial sector. This economic progress and development has somewhat transformed Malaysian society in that the traditional lifestyle has become more modern and complex and, as a result, more beset with a variety of social problems. Some of the new social phenomena facing modern Malaysia are the abuse, neglect, and abandonment of children, teen pregnancy, the loosening roles of extended families, and issues facing migrants. These new phenomena continuously challenge Malaysia in its efforts to offer quality social welfare services for the well-being of its people.

Culture and Welfare Services in a Multiethnic Population

Because Malaysia is a multiracial nation, it must provide culturally sensitive welfare services to the people. Of course, all ethnic groups are unique. However, the ethnic groups in Malaysia also adhere to certain general values, such as showing respect for one another. Both the younger and older generations address one another with respect, for example, calling a more senior person "uncle," "auntie," or "*encik*" or "*puan*" (Malay words for "mister" and "madam"). Addressing people with respect enables helping professionals such as social workers to readily build meaningful relationships in an effort to provide effective social services to different ethnic groups.

The languages of the ethnic groups need to be considered when providing social services. Malay, Cantonese, Mandarin, Hokkien, and Tamil are the main languages spoken in Malaysia. Each language has many regional dialects with which social workers need to be familiar. Being able to speak the dialect of the region can help a social worker be more readily accepted and connected to the community. Being culturally sensitive can facilitate enhanced intervention and services.

Another factor that contributes to the complexity of Malaysian culture is the variety of religions practiced in Malaysia. The Malay way of life is guided by the teachings of Islam, but Hindus, Buddhists, and Christians also hold on to their faiths in their daily lives. It is essential for social workers to have some understanding of and respect for the various teachings of the main religions in the country. Understanding the religious and cultural differences in the country, and being sensitive to those differences, will enhance the ability of helping professionals to serve the populations they are tasked with helping (Wing Sue 2006).

History of Social Welfare in Malaysia

In the early years before colonization, the locals, mainly the Malay population, led a less complex lifestyle in which the various communities helped each other. These communities played a major role in lending support through collective activities known as gotong royong. This practice encourages society to work together to help those in need. Services in these early years were mostly based on charitable, paternalistic, and humanitarian approaches (Shaffie 2005; Awang 1992).

When the British came to Malaya, they developed the rubber and tin mining industries and brought immigrants from China and India to work in the tin mines and rubber plantations, respectively. This immigration marked the beginning of Malaya as a diverse ethnic society and changed Malaya from a simple society wherein local communities were able to provide assistance to each other to a more complex society that needed more than just gotong royong to meet its social needs.

In 1912 the British introduced more formal social welfare to help improve the well-being of migrant laborers by establishing the Social Services Department (Baba 1992). Because of financial constraints, this department was abolished during the Depression of the 1930s. It was not until 1937 that a separate Social Service Department was created within the Colonial Office to provide social services to the communities, and this signified the beginning of a more structured social welfare system in Malaya (Mair 1944).

Social welfare services in Malaya during those times primarily focused on labor, health, and education. The Colonial Office concentrated on the welfare of the migrant workers but also emphasized some aspects of the social development of the local community, particularly that of the Malays. Various organizations, such as the village councils, community associations, and cooperative societies, addressed issues related to poverty, housing, youth services, and home industries (Mair 1944). Prison services were under the purview of the Colonial Office during that time. These programs ultimately led to the beginning of a more systematic and formalized social service system in the country.

The Japanese occupation (1942–45) of Malaya during World War II changed the course of the country's development. Poverty and poor health increased tremendously, and health services were curtailed. Many of the nongovernmental institutions that had been established since 1914 were unable to play an active role in helping society, resulting in many deaths and trauma due to homelessness and a lack of food and basic health services.

The British returned after the Japanese surrendered in 1945, and they helped to minimize social dislocation, poverty, and illness while improving health services. A wide range of complex social problems existed in Malaya at this time (Awang 1992), and a few NGOs, such as the Relief Department and State Rural Welfare Office, were established to address these problems.

On May 23, 1946, the governor of the Malayan Union announced the establishment of the Central Welfare of Malaya. On June 10, 1946, the first Department of Social Welfare was established with the main objectives of addressing poverty, starvation, and poor health due to the effects of the war. In 1964 this department became the Ministry of Social Welfare

(Department of Social Welfare 2010), but in 1985 it was abolished and was returned to department status under the Ministry of National Unity and Community Development (DSW 2010; Baba, 1992) and renamed the Department of Social Welfare (DSW). The DSW was responsible not only to provide professional services but also to implement government policies on matters pertaining to social welfare. The social welfare services carried out by the DSW included casework, foster care and adoption, juvenile probation and parole, protective services for older people, youth correctional institutions, and child protection services (Shaffie 2005). These welfare policies and programs were influenced by the British philosophy of the time (Abdul Rahman 2005).

The development of social welfare services in Malaysia also proceeded in the hospital setting. In 1952 the Ministry of Health introduced medical social workers to local hospitals to help individuals regain good health and social well-being and to help prevent further ill health (Awang 1992). One of the earliest medical social work departments in Malaysia was established in 1964 at the University Hospital Kuala Lumpur.

Although there was a great need for medical social workers in many hospitals in Malaysia, not enough people were adequately trained as medical social workers. Instead, social welfare assistants who had no formal training or qualifications were taken from the Ministry of Welfare Services to fill the vacancies of medical social workers (Awang 1992). This development has somewhat contributed to the many semitrained medical social workers who are now giving services in the hospital setting. Also, the recruitment of untrained graduates was primarily due to the general public's misconception that social work does not require professional training and skills (DSW 2009).

In summary, welfare services in Malaysia were initially based on a charity model, and programs were implemented in an ad-hoc and uncoordinated manner because of a lack of appropriate government policies. With the help of the voluntary organizations, the government was ultimately able to implement and maintain programs for various target groups; however, the programs were limited merely to care and rehabilitation by way of financial assistance or institutional care. It was not until the late 1960s and early 1970s that the orientation of welfare programs became centered on developmental and preventive efforts.

Today welfare services and programs have changed significantly. Many of the social services offered by the DSW, ranging from services for children, the aged population, and people with disabilities to family and community development, have enhanced society's well-being. In addition, the support of NGOs has contributed to social welfare services throughout the country. Many NGOs have been very supportive in assisting both the national government and local communities in carrying out social services targeting older adults and those with disabilities and addressing various chronic social problems, including absolute and relative poverty, child abuse, marital breakdown, domestic violence, and mental illness. With new emerging social issues, the roles and responsibilities of the DSW, along with those of the NGOs, have increased in order to ensure the best services to enhance society's well-being.

Emerging Social Issues and Government and NGO Responses

As Malaysia's population has increased and the economy has moved from a traditional agricultural to a more sophisticated, modern economy, new and costly social issues and problems have emerged. Child abandonment, premarital sex and teen pregnancy, and undertrained social service providers currently challenge the DSW and NGOs.

Child Abandonment

While child abandonment, or "baby dumping," is one of the major emerging social issues (Fong 2010), it is not a recent phenomenon. Historically there were relatively few cases of child abandonment, and they were rarely reported, thus making it appear to not be a serious issue in the country. This has now changed as baby dumping is increasing and is often reported both in print and in electronic media. According to a Royal Malaysian Police report (2010), in 2004, 78 babies were abandoned. In 2005 the number was reduced to 67 babies, but it increased to 83 cases in 2006. In 2007, 2008, and 2009, the number of babies that were dumped was 76, 102, and 79, respectively, according to the same report.

By fall 2010 a total of 60 babies had already been reported as having been abandoned; of these, 25 were male and 21 were female, and the sex of 14 babies could not be determined owing to decomposition (Fong 2010; Abdul Hamid 2010; Mansor 2010).

The government and NGOs have combined efforts to address the serious developing problem of child abandonment, including providing care for abused and abandoned children and conducting campaigns (such as poster exhibitions in shopping malls and other public places) and road shows to create public awareness of the problem. The purpose of the road shows is to disseminate information to the public on the types of services available for unwed mothers or for those who do not want to care for their newborn babies. In addition, weekly campaigns in all mass media are carried out, urging the public to respond to the problem collectively.

The recently established Baby Hatch, a baby bank initiated by the NGO OrphanCARE, is the first in the country to care for abandoned babies (Ngah 2010), with the objective of preparing the children for possible adoption. The program has become an alternative to child abandonment, allowing unwed mothers to save their babies and simultaneously avoid possible prosecution. In addition, the government and NGOs are discussing how to upgrade the quality of child-care services—in particular, how to set up better-managed homes for abandoned and neglected children.

In an effort to decrease the incidents of child abandonment, the Ministry of Women, Family, and Community Development has proposed to classify child abandonment that results in the child's death as a crime warranting the death sentence. The intent of this proposal is to encourage people to have their babies legally adopted and is an indication of the serious effort made by the government and NGOs to address the issue of baby dumping (Foong 2010).

Premarital Sexual Activity and Teen Pregnancy

Premarital sexual activity and teen pregnancy are also social problems that need serious attention. Although these problems might appear to be independent of child abandonment, they are actually interrelated. Modernization and urbanization have made teenagers more exposed, and many get involved in premarital sexual activity with little knowledge about sex. Because Malaysia has no formal sex education, teenagers are presumably more likely to get pregnant and to acquire sexually transmitted diseases such as HIV/AIDS (Kam 2010; Loo 2010). Unwanted pregnancies can factor into teenagers' decisions to run away and then abandon their babies, for fear of their parents' censure and society's stigma (Fong 2010).

Data on teen pregnancy and on the premarital sexual activity of teenagers is unavailable for several reasons. For one thing, many cases are unreported because of social stigma. Even NGOs that provide help to unwed mothers do not report such cases in order to preserve the confidentiality of their clients. It is also unclear as to which agency is responsible for maintaining a database; thus, whatever data are available are probably not comprehensive or reflective of the actual situation. However, ad-hoc studies done by independent bodies have shown that Malaysian teenagers do engage in premarital sexual activity. According to a sexual attitudes and behaviors survey done in 2002 by Durex involving 2,500 Malaysian young adults, about 60 percent of those below the age of 18 reported they were sexually active and had sex at least 11 times a month, or on the average 135 times a year. Another source reported that among young urban Malaysians, 47 percent have had unsafe sex, and 42 percent of young people between the ages of 18 and 24 admitted to having had unprotected sex with different partners (*Star* 2002). Research conducted by the Ministry of Health through the Health and Lifestyles Survey of 1992 also found that 52 percent of the adolescents between the ages of 17 and 24 had more than one sex partner, while half of them had engaged in premarital sexual intercourse (UNESCO 2002).

The debate on sex education in schools is ongoing. While waiting for this issue to be resolved, the government and relevant NGOs have come up with various interim programs to educate teenagers about reproductive health. The National Population and Family Development Board has developed modules on reproductive health. Other efforts include the establishment of Café-at-Teen centers to help teenagers obtain accurate information about sex. To ensure a more effective program, teenagers are employed as peer educators to disseminate information on sex. Other NGOs organize talks, seminars, and workshops to help teenagers better understand reproductive health and the importance of taking care of their bodies and acquiring negotiating skills to postpone premarital sex and prevent unwanted pregnancies.

The government and NGOs have also established centers for unwed pregnant teenagers, although it remains a question whether teenagers and families will seek assistance, given that many may not want to be in the centers to avoid discrimination and labeling from society.

There is also a proposal to establish a special school for unwed pregnant teenagers. Such a school would give pregnant adolescents the opportunity to continue their education, which is currently not allowed by the education system. The proposal has received some criticism and, because it requires in-depth discussions with many relevant parties, is currently unresolved (Mansor 2010).

The Problem of Untrained Workers

With the various social problems facing the nation, it is critical for Malaysia to address the problem of untrained professional social workers. The majority of staff in professional social work positions in the DSW lack the skills and competencies of a trained social worker. NGOs employ volunteers to do tasks similar to those done by professional social workers, a fact that sometimes aggravates the social issues. Untrained social workers have also contributed to the misunderstanding about the respective roles of trained social workers and of volunteers, leading people to believe that volunteers are social workers, a fact that has made it more difficult to get the social work profession recognized as a helping profession.

The shortage of trained personnel in the DSW system is widespread (Awang 1992; Azman 2009; Baba 1992; DSW 2009). Graduates who are not trained in social work have been recruited to fill social work positions in the Public Services Department (Azman 2009), making it more difficult for the DSW to offer effective welfare services to the targeted populations. This is evidenced by a survey conducted by the Malaysian Association of Social Workers (MASW) in 2005, which revealed that while about 62 percent of the 433 respondents employed in social work settings have diplomas or degrees, only 14 percent have social work–related qualifications (DSW 2009). The study has prompted the DSW to rigorously train its personnel in social work positions. One immediate effort is to create minimum competency standards for staff giving direct services and intervention to the community.

Development of Social Work Education

Prior to 1975 the majority of social welfare workers in Malaysia received their social work training from the University of Malaya in Singapore, with some also being trained in the United Kingdom, Australia, the United States, the Philippines, and India.

In 1975 the UN Economic and Social Commission for Asia and the Pacific and the Ministry of Social Welfare encouraged Universiti Sains Malaysia to be the first institution to introduce formal social work education in the country (Azman 2009; Baba 1992; Desai 1991; Mas'ud, Ali, & Raja 2005; Yasas 1974). For the first four years, this social work program was developed exclusively to train the staff in social work positions in the Ministry of Social Welfare (Azman 2009; Baba 1992, 1998; DSW 2009; Yasas 1974).

During the 1980s and 1990s several developments highlighted the urgent need for more universities to train social workers to work in the relevant ministries, agencies, and NGOs. These developments included the campaign to create a caring and civil society; the formation of new human service organizations by NGOs; and emerging social problems such as the deterioration of the family, abuse and neglect, domestic violence, drug issues, and HIV/AIDS (Baba 1992; Sin & Salleh 1992).

The 1990s appear to have marked the beginning of crucial development in social work education in Malaysia. Between 1993 and 2002 seven public higher-education institutions in the country introduced some form of social work education. The rush to introduce social work programs may have stemmed from recognition of the need to better address the new and ongoing social problems and social development issues.

At present there are many more private institutions that want to offer social work education programs. Unfortunately, a number of these private institutions do not have enough faculty trained in social work. Some faculty members at private institutions erroneously believe that faculty trained in other disciplines are qualified to teach social work courses. This situation has led to misconceptions about required social work content and training, making a nationwide social work education standard essential.

In January 2002 the Universiti Sains Malaysia formed the National Joint Consultative Committee on Social Work Education (NJCCSWE) to address these social work academic issues. The committee comprises representatives from seven universities: Universiti Malaysia Sarawak, Universiti Utara Malaysia, Universiti Malaysia Sabah, Universiti Kebangsaan Malaysia, Universiti Malaya, and Universiti Putra Malaysia (Baba 2002). Its purpose is to ensure that higher-learning institutions have at least the minimal standards for social work education (Azman 2009; Baba 1998, 2002). The NJCCSWE continues to promote standardized social work education for the nation, but rigorous efforts are needed for social work curriculum standardization to be approved by the Ministry of Higher Education (Azman 2009).

There is an urgent need to set up an organization that may tentatively be called the Malaysian Social Work Council (MSWC), which would be tasked with setting and maintaining standards for social work education programs at the university level. The MSWC would also be responsible for social work education accreditation at higher-learning institutions based on the stipulated guidelines for core curriculum content, course duration, practicum hours, field supervision expectations, qualification and experience of social work educators, as well as the ratio of social work educators to students (NJCCSWE 2000–2009). The MSWC would serve as a gatekeeper to ensure that institutions offering or planning to offer social work education follow the minimal standards of a social work education program (Azman 2009). It would be responsible not only for accreditation functions but also for regulatory and social work licensing responsibilities. Monitoring the quality of social work education and practitioners in this way could improve the overall welfare services available to Malaysian society.

While there are ongoing efforts to produce a larger number of competent social workers in the country, the need for trained social work professionals is not being met. This shortage will probably continue for quite some time. However, if more private universities are able to offer quality social work programs, this will help ease the demand for social workers to address emerging social issues.

The Social Work Profession

The issue of social work professionalism has been debated in Malaysia for more than three decades. There has been a struggle to recognize the social work profession as on a par with similar helping professions, such as clinical psychology and counseling (Baginda 2005).

It was during the period of British influence that social work began to receive recognition as a discipline requiring a specific body of knowledge and skills (Mair 1944). At that time there was an awareness of the importance of sending social welfare officers to get proper training and qualifications in order to carry out effective social welfare functions or roles. The majority of social welfare officers were sent for social work certificates and diploma training in the United Kingdom, mainly in the areas of youth services, industrial welfare, and rural welfare (Mair 1944). It is these so-cial work pioneers who helped develop national welfare policies, programs, and delivery systems and who oversaw the beginning of the development of the social work profession in Malaysia.

The Malaysian Association of Social Workers, established in 1973, has been pushing to place the social work profession at the forefront of pro-viding relevant welfare services to those in need. Besides promoting and developing the standards of the social work profession in Malaysia, the MASW has made a significant contribution to alleviating various emerg-ing social issues, has made the public aware of social worker roles, and has provided support for improving society's well-being.

The DSW has also played a major role in positioning the social work profession as a means of alleviating social problems. In fact, to date, the DSW is still the primary government agency for social welfare and the larg-est employer of trained social workers in the country (Baba 2002, 2008; Abdul Rahman 2005). To better serve society, the DSW, with the help of the MASW, has been spearheading efforts to establish competency standards in social work practice in the country. The DSW continues to play a key role in advancing social welfare services in Malaysia as guided by the National Social Welfare Policy of 1990. The desire to formalize national standards on social work competencies is based on the firm belief that the national standardization of social work competencies is necessary to the provision of professional social welfare services in the country.

In spite of the efforts of the DSW and MASW, the position of social worker is not yet listed in the Public Services Department's category of jobs. Lacking proper guidelines, many government agencies end up re-cruiting non–social work graduates to fill vacancies. For example, as of 2010, although the Universiti Sains Malaysia has trained more than two thousand bachelor's, master's, and doctoral students, many social work graduates end up employed in non-welfare-related services, thus depriving them of the opportunity to serve society directly (Azman 2009).

Current efforts by the MASW, the DSW, and the NJCCSWE in pushing for a social worker's act are valued highly. Under the proposed act, trained social workers would be regarded in a more professional manner. The act would also place social workers in a higher position when compared to those who are not formally trained in the social work field. It is anticipated that when the proposed act is passed, human services organizations will hire only trained social workers. This would then help distinguish between competent and incompetent social workers in Malaysia. The proposed act would also encourage social workers to continue to enhance their practice in order to be able to give their best services to society.

The proposed social worker's act would give professional licensure to many trained social work practitioners. It is also hoped that the act would govern the social work activities carried out by semitrained and untrained social workers. This professional licensure would be best placed under the auspices of the MASW. The training or continuing education for those who are interested in upgrading themselves as trained social workers would then be handled by the social work educators at higher-learning institutions (Azman 2009; Mas'ud, Ali, & Raja 2001, 2005). In other words, social work educators would be responsible for devising a framework that would enable current practitioners to gain accredited skills relevant to their specific workplace. Many more practitioners can be trained as competent or professional social workers in Malaysia when the act is implemented.

The national social worker's act would also benefit the efforts of the NJCCSWE in coming up with standardized social work education to produce better-prepared social work practitioners. The act would further empower and recognize the role of the NJCCSWE in producing more qualified and competent social workers to address current social issues.

Future Perspectives

The future direction of social welfare services in Malaysia is directly linked to the development of the social work profession. To provide better social welfare services, there is a major need to train more professional social workers to help families and society deal with their current social problems. There are many issues that need to be addressed before Malaysia can offer the best services for the benefit of the client population. To promote changes in social work policy, all stakeholders, including social work educators, higher-learning institutions, the MASW, the DSW, the NJCCSWE, the Ministry of Higher Education, and other relevant agencies, must work closely together to achieve their mutual objectives.

A lack of understanding of the roles and functions of social workers is one of the major problems in promoting social work education in Malaysia. Many government organizations and NGOs have limited understanding of what trained social workers can do in promoting the well-being of individuals, families, and communities. The lack of knowledge and skills of untrained social workers has unintentionally tarnished the image of the social work profession itself. Under the proposed social worker's act, the Public Services Department would be directed to the critical need to employ graduates with a social work education background to provide effective human services to the client populations.

Currently there are many public and private higher-learning institutions that are seriously considering the establishment of social work programs without actually understanding the social work profession. Without trained social work educators, the general public will have greater misconceptions about the social work profession. There is an urgent need for these institutions to develop a standardized social work curriculum. With a professional body such as the MSWC, current and future social work programs could adhere to the same quality standards in social work education and minimize the misconceptions of professional social work practice and volunteer-based practice.

With no professional body to lend support and direction, the newer social work education programs may be at a disadvantage. Malaysia is therefore in urgent need of a proper professional body such as the MSWC and an accreditation body that can monitor the quality and standards for professional social work training. These bodies should serve as advisers to all relevant organizations that deal with social work (Azman 2009; Baba 2002, 2008; Mas'ud, Ali, & Raja 2000, 2005).

Relentless efforts have been carried out by the MASW, DSW, and NJCCSWE to look into the possibility of developing a professional body for social workers to monitor social work education and services carried out by the many trained and untrained social workers (Azman 2009; DSW 2009; Mas'ud, Ali, & Raja 2000). Such efforts are considered critical in order to offer effective services to individuals and communities.

On April 23, 2010, the Malaysian cabinet approved the development of national competency standards for social work practice in Malaysia to regulate and ensure the quality of social care and welfare (Ram 2010; Ram & Latiff 2010; Shari 2010). Approval of these standards will affect the future direction for the social work profession because the profession is now mandated to develop a social worker's act. A series of discussions with all parties is vital to ensure a more comprehensive act that takes into account matters related to licensing qualified social work practitioners and educators; employing trained social workers in relevant departments; standardizing social work education curricula at higher-learning institutions; developing relevant continuing education or training programs for social work practitioners; looking into those who have a social work role but not background; and seeking the opinions of the stakeholders to ensure the sustainability of the act.

Malaysia, a small, multiethnic and multireligious nation, has undergone a dramatic economic transformation from an agricultural to mainly an industrial state. This economic progress and development has transformed the traditional Malaysian lifestyle into a more modern and complex society. Consequently Malaysia is now being challenged with a variety of social problems. It is this new, emerging social phenomena that have continuously confronted Malaysia in its efforts to offer quality social welfare services for the well-being of its population.

This chapter has outlined the development of welfare services that were initially based on the charity model and then on a more formal social welfare model during the colonial era, and finally were transformed to the current welfare emphasis of ensuring the well-being of the population. The discussion also focused on the many emerging social problems, including child abandonment, premarital sexual activity and teen pregnancy, and the issue of untrained workers addressing the various social issues. Malaysian social workers now face the immense challenge of being recognized as professionals in particular because historically trained social workers and volunteers have both provided all forms of welfare services. The development of the national social worker's act, which will ultimately recognize social work as a profession; placement of competent social workers in welfare services; and the enhancement of a more standardized social work education at higher learning institutions are some of the main suggestions that can further strengthen the welfare services provided by the Malaysian government.

Malaysia is progressing rapidly. Since independence in 1957, social issues have moved from simple to complex, requiring more sophisticated responses. There is an urgent need for improved social welfare services. The future direction of welfare services in Malaysia is very much dependent on the development of the social work profession. The country needs more trained social workers to help tackle the current social problems.

There is a crucial need for full collaboration between the DSW, MASW, NJCCSWE (through the proposed MCSW), Public Services Department, and relevant ministries to hire competent social workers who can provide effective and efficient social welfare services in the country. The DSW, MASW, and NJCCSWE play significant roles in moving the social work profession to a higher level.

Having the social work policy and competency standards in place will further strengthen the welfare services provided by the Malaysian government. In addition, efforts to monitor the development of social work practice and education in Malaysia through the future establishment of the MSWC, for example, will enhance social welfare services in the country. Ultimately these efforts will contribute to recognizing the nation's social work practitioners and education programs as being equal to global social work standards. It is through cooperation from all stakeholders that Malaysia will be able to respond better to the emerging challenges and complex social problems.

References

Abdul Hamid, R. (2010). "Bayi perempuan dalam tong sampah." *Utusan Malaysia*, August 12, 3.

Abdul Rahman, S. M. (2005). "Pengurusan perkhidmatan kerja sosial ke arah kecemerlangan." In *Pengurusan perkhidmatan kerja sosial di Malaysia*, ed. Z. Jamaluddin, 11–15. Sintok, Kedah: Universiti Utara Malaysia.

Anonymous (2002). "Study: 47% of Youths Having Unsafe Sex." *Star*, November 27, p. 20.

Awang, Z. (1992). "A Caring Society in Malaysia: A Vision." In *Caring Society: Emerging Issues and Future Directions*, ed. C. K. Sin & I. M. Salleh, 3–17. Kuala Lumpur: ISIS.

Azman, A. (2009). "Proposal: Bachelor of Social Work at Universiti Sains Malaysia." Ms. Department of Social Work, Universiti Sains Malaysia, Penang.

———— (2009). "Strategizing Changes in Social Work Education Policy in Malaysia." Paper presented at the National Symposium on Social Work Competency, Pahang, Malaysia, August.

Baba, I. (1992). "Social Work: An Effort Towards Building a Caring Society. In *Caring Society: Emerging Issues and Future Directions*, ed. C. K. Sin & I. M. Salleh, 509–29. Kuala Lumpur: ISIS.

———— (1998). "The Need for Professionalism in Social Work: In the Case of Malaysia." Paper presented at the Advancing Social Work Education, Seminar and Planning Meeting, Kota Samarahan, Sarawak, November.

———— (2002). "A Report: The Establishment of a Council on Social Work education in Malaysia." Round-table Meeting at School of Social Sciences, Universiti Sains Malaysia, Penang January.

———— (2008). "Social Work in Malaysia: Issues of Social Work Practice and Education in Malaysia." Paper presented at International Counseling and Social Work Symposium, Penang, January 6–8.

Baginda, A. M. (2005). "Management of Social Work in Malaysia." In *Pengurusan perkhidmatan kerja sosial di Malaysia*, ed. Z. Jamaluddin, 3–10. Sintok, Kedah: Universiti Utara Malaysia.

Department of Social Welfare (2009). "Challenges and Opportunities in Competency Change." Paper presented at the National Symposium on Social Work Competency, Pahang, August.

———— (2010). *Statistics*. Retrieved August 20, 2010, from http://www.jkm.gov.my

Desai, A. S. (1991). *Report of the Academic Assessor to the Social Development and Administration Section*. Penang: Universiti Sains, School of Social Sciences, October–November.

Economic Planning Unit (2010). *Statistics*. Retrieved June 7, 2010, from http://www.epu.gov.my.

Fong, L. F. (2010). "Shelter Home: Get to Root Problem of Baby Dumping." *Star*, June 1, p. 2.

Foong, J. (2010). "Capital Punishment Not the Answer, Say NGOs." *Star*, August 13, p. 14.

Gong, L. F. (2010). "Murder Charge for Dumpers." *Star*, August 13, p. 12.

Kam, P. (2010). "Rethinking Sex Education." *Star*, April 22, p. 5.

Loo, T. E. (2010). "Too Much, too Young." *Star*, May 2, p. 11.

Mair, L. P. (1944). *Welfare in the British Colonies*. Great Britain: Broadwater Press.

Mansor, A. S. (2010). "Menghalusi idea sekolah remaja hamil." *Harian Metro*, August 9, p. 3.

Mas'ud, F., K. Ali, & G. Raja (2000). "Directions for Social Work Education." Paper presented at the National Conference on Social Work Management, Universiti Utara Malaysia, Sintok, Kedah, January.

———— (2005). "Directions for Social Work Education." In *Pengurusan perkhidmatan kerja sosial di Malaysia*, ed. Z. Jamaluddin, 97–111. Sintok, Kedah: Universiti Utara Malaysia.

National Joint Consultative Committee on Social Work Education at Higher Learning Institutions (2000–2009). *Educational Policy Standards for Social Work Education in Higher Learning Institutions, Malaysia*. Penang: Universiti Sains Malaysia.

Ngah, I. (2010). "Wujudkan lebih banyak kemudahan untuk perlindungan bayi: OrphanCARE." *Berita Harian*, August 20, p. 8.

Ram, S. (2010). "Shahrizat: Standards for Social Work Timely." *New Straits Times*, May 6, p. 14.

Ram, S., & R. Latiff (2010). "Six Steps to High Quality Social Work." *Star*, May 6, p. 4.

Royal Malaysia Police (2010). *Statistics*. Retrieved July 8, 2010, from http://www .rmp.gov.my.

Shaffie, F. (2005). "Satu tinjauan mengenai latar belakang kerja sosial di Malaysia." In *Pengurusan perkhidmatan kerja sosial di Malaysia*, ed. Z. Jamaluddin, 19–32. Sintok, Kedah: Universiti Utara Malaysia.

Shari, I. (2010). "Proposed Social Workers Act Gets the Government's Nod." *Star*, May 5, p. 15.

Sin, C. K., & I. M. Salleh (1992). *Caring Society: Emerging Issues and Future Directions*. Kuala Lumpur: ISIS.

United Nations Educational, Scientific and Cultural Organization (2002). *Case Studies—Malaysia: Adolescent Reproductive and Sexual Health*. Bangkok. Retrieved August 8, 2010, from http://www.unescobkk.org/ips/arh-webdemographics/ malaysia2.cfm.

Wing Sue, D. (2006). *Multicultural Social Work Practice*. New York: Wiley.

Yasas, F. M. (1974). "A Report to the Government of Malaysia on the Establishment of a Professional Course in Social Work and Community Development Training at the Bachelor's Level at the Universiti Sains Malaysia, Pulau Pinang." Ms. United Nations Economic Commission for Asia and the Far East and Department of Social Work, Universiti Sains Malaysia, Penang.

9

Social Work for a Sustainable Micronesian Region

VIVIAN DAMES, JOLIENE HASUGULAYAG, LISALINDA NATIVIDAD,
AND GERHARD SCHWAB

The region of Micronesia, a word derived from the Greek meaning "tiny islands," consists of more than two thousand islands north of the equator and east of the Philippines in the western Pacific. In this chapter we focus on the emergent sovereign island nations of the Republic of Palau, the Federated States of Micronesia, the Republic of the Marshall Islands, the U.S. unincorporated Territory of Guam, and the Commonwealth of the Northern Mariana Islands. The total population of these islands is approximately 300,000 and is dispersed in a combined land area of about 2,600 square kilometers (1,616 square miles) that span an expanse of the Pacific Ocean comparable to that of the continental United States. Although these islands and populations are small when compared with Asian countries, their global significance in terms of their natural ecology, cultural diversity, and role in the U.S. military empire is great.

Considerable debate continues about whether Micronesia is a coherent region and, if it is, how it should be defined. Geography and cultural practices "have always been at the heart of the issue" (Peterson 2009:13). The remarkable ecological diversity of the region, both physical and cultural, the people's responses to the difficulties of occupying these islands, and a succession of colonial powers have shaped Micronesian island societies. Today, while life on some islands is still much like the subsistence societies that have characterized the region for centuries, life on other islands, especially Guam, has become urbanized and cosmopolitan. Some islands now host growing numbers of immigrant and contract workers, some have become popular tourist destinations, some have served as a way station for refugees and asylum seekers, and some are duty stations and recreation stops for U.S. military personnel and their dependents.

The United States has been a military and colonial power in Asia and the Pacific for more than one hundred years. U.S. global ambitions began with the seizure of Hawaii, Samoa, the Philippines, and Guam in the late 1800s. After World War II the United Nations entrusted the war-devastated Micronesian islands, except Guam, to the United States with a mandate to lead these "trust territories" toward economic self-sufficiency and political self-determination (Hanlon 1998:2). Negotiations toward this end began in the 1960s and resulted in the creation of four new political entities: the Commonwealth of the Northern Mariana Islands, the Republic of the Marshall Islands, the Republic of Palau, and the Federated States of Micronesia, which includes the states of Pohnpei, Chuuk, Yap, and Kosrae.

In 1975 the people of the Northern Mariana Islands voted overwhelmingly for U.S. citizenship and commonwealth status in political union with the United States. People in the Marshall Islands (in 1979), the Federated States of Micronesia (in 1979), and the Republic of Palau (in 1981) voted for political independence. These three sovereign nations entered into the Compacts of Free Association with the United States. These agreements give the United States full authority and responsibility for defense and security matters for these island states and commonwealth. The United States provides certain welfare benefits and access to other federal programs; in return, these island states are mandated to conduct their foreign policies consistent with the national policy priorities of the United States. Citizens of associated states can freely enter the United States and its territories, lawfully engage in occupations, and establish residence anywhere in the United States.

Guam has the longest colonial history of any Pacific island. It was a Spanish colony for approximately three hundred years until the United States wrested it from Spain as a spoil of war in 1898. The people of Guam remained a ward of the U.S. Navy for half a century, except from 1941 to 1944, when the island was occupied by Japanese forces. Although the United States in 1950 designated Guam as an unincorporated territory and conferred U.S. citizenship on its inhabitants, the indigenous people of Guam, the Chamorros, are still denied their inalienable right of political self-determination. Guam remains on the UN list of Non-Self-Governing Territories of the world. Currently Guam is bracing for the largest military buildup since World War II in anticipation of the relocation of U.S. Marines from Okinawa in Japan to Guam.

This chapter describes social welfare in Micronesia as a contested site within the context of complex U.S. federal-territorial relations and the ongoing project of decolonization (Dames 1992, 2000). Social welfare issues are contested because of the fundamental questions that social welfare raises about dependency, sovereignty, and island sustainability. We provide an overview of the history of social welfare and discuss major cultural concerns, social issues and problems, and the interrelationship between social work education and the emergence of the social work profession. We conclude that social workers are both cultural workers and political workers.

History of Social Welfare in Micronesia

In traditional Micronesian societies, "it is the extraordinary webs or ties binding the individual populations of Micronesians that characterize social life" (Peterson 2009:10). While specific forms and practices may vary, it is through these webs and ties that social welfare is achieved. As Peterson (2009:2) has noted:

Micronesian societies are organized around interlocking lineages and clans. Lineages are relatively small groups, located within single communities. Each lineage is a segment of a larger clan, which in turn has numerous lineages dispersed among different communities and on many separate islands. It is the dispersed character of the clans that provides Micronesians with networks of support, but it is the lineages, with their patterns of face-to-face interaction, that typify daily life. The lineages possess land and control political titles, regulate marriages, provide the matrix within which child rearing takes place, and, in general, endow the individual Micronesian with a sense of personal identity. Micronesians draw upon their families' lands and the landscapes and seascapes of the home islands for some part of their sense of self, and they draw as well from their communities.

Reliance on these webs or ties has shifted during the past century—in some islands only slightly and in other islands dramatically—in response to the introduction of new social welfare institutions under different colonial

Table 9.1 Colonial Powers and Political Statuses in Micronesia

Year	Guama	CNMIb	FSMc, MId, Palau
1880	Spain	Spain	Spain
1900	United States	Germany	Germany
1920	United States	Japan	Japan
1943	Japan	Japan	Japan
1970	United States	UN Trust Territory under United States	UN Trust Territory under United States
2000	United States	Commonwealth under United States	Independence and free association with United States

[a] The political status of Guam has remained the same since it was annexed by the United States in 1898, except when occupied by Japan from 1941 to 1944.
[b] Commonwealth of Northern Mariana Islands
[c] Federated States of Micronesia (Yap, Chuuk, Pohnpei, and Kosrae)
[d] Marshall Islands

administrations. Mirroring the historical and social contexts of the time, social welfare in Micronesia has had the various goals of evangelization, Americanization, militarization, and decolonization. In other words, social welfare has been a means for political leaders at both the federal and local government levels to achieve different ends at different times.

In the centuries following the first contacts with the Western world, the Micronesian islands were colonized by four foreign administering powers: Spain, Germany, Japan, and the United States. Table 9.1 illustrates the similarities and differences brought about by the changes of colonial powers and political relations that framed the development of social welfare in the Micronesian islands.

These foreign powers brought with them religious ideologies and institutions with the intent of converting people and advancing social welfare. Examples in terms of the Catholic Church in Guam include the following: In 1927 the St. Vincent de Paul Society began to provide material goods to those in need; in 1970 a youth service organization called Sanctuary was established by Robert Phelps, a Catholic priest; in 1975 the Diocesan

Refugee Office oversaw the resettlement process of refugees from Vietnam; in 1979 Catholic Social Services was established and since then it has become the largest nonprofit human service organization in Guam (Dames 1998). In Pohnpei an organization called the Micronesian Seminar has gradually evolved from a Jesuit pastoral research institute into a nonprofit organization that now broadly facilitates critical public dialogue and public education on socioeconomic and political issues and developments in the Micronesian islands region.

In addition, military strategic interests and the presence of U.S. military bases have influenced the development of social welfare. While these military activities are of a humanitarian nature and include disaster relief and recovery efforts (Dodge 1991), they also serve a public-relations function. One of the oldest and possibly most symbolic examples of these activities is the U.S. Air Force Christmas Drop. Every Christmas since 1952, military planes have flown over remote Micronesian islands and parachuted packages of clothing, toys, fishing equipment, sporting goods, food items, and tools for the residents. Over time, the U.S. military has developed a broad spectrum of its own high-quality educational, health, and social services in Guam and other Micronesian islands exclusively for military personnel and their immediate dependents.

Simultaneous with the militarization of many Micronesian islands, the Americanization of indigenous social welfare systems has meant that these systems have been replaced or dramatically changed through education, health care, and public welfare assistance. This process began first in Guam in 1958 when the U.S. Congress extended the Social Security Act to Guam. In other Micronesian islands the program with the strongest imprinting effect was likely the Needy Family Feeding Program, which was first introduced in Chuuk. Beginning in the mid-1970s, the U.S. federal government began to feed needy families in Micronesia, starting with children in public schools and then extending to every woman, man, and child. As Hanlon (1998:174–75) describes, "Every Micronesian was to receive twenty pounds of rice, ten cans of evaporated milk, and a specific mix of other food items and canned goods designed to provide a balanced diet; these supplies were to be distributed every 60 days and were regarded as sufficient to provide three meals a day per person over the two month allotment period."

Overall, U.S. federal social welfare policies and programs served to Americanize the people of the Micronesian islands and to influence the political decolonization process. Some well-established U.S. domestic welfare programs, such as Social Security, Food Stamps, and the Supplemental Security Income Program, were selectively and in various forms extended to Guam and the Commonwealth of the Northern Mariana Islands. For example, the Supplemental Security Income Program is available to the people in the Commonwealth of the Northern Mariana Islands but not to the people in Guam. The Republics of Palau and the Marshall Islands and the Federated States of Micronesia now receive financial aid packages and participate in various U.S. federal grant programs as part of their Compacts of Free Association with the United States. The initial financial aid packages of the compacts for the Federated States of Micronesia and the Marshall Islands were in effect from 1986 to 2003, and the renewed and amended compacts are in effect from 2004 to 2023. The provisions of the compacts between Palau and the United States are in effect from 1994 to 2044.

Culture and Social Welfare

In this chapter we focus on Micronesian cultures in terms of the degree to which external forces have affected traditional practices related to three integral elements of traditional Micronesian cultures: the land-kin bond and identity; subsistence and sustainable living; and reciprocity.

On one end of the continuum are the cultures of Yap, which is one of the four states of the Federated States of Micronesia and considered the most traditional island group in Micronesia today (Ridgell 2006). On the opposite end is the Chamorro culture of Guam and the Northern Mariana Islands, where the impact on traditional cultures has been the most extensive.

Land and Identity

Land, surrounding waters, and reefs play a significant role within all the traditional cultures of the region (Hezel 2001). In contrast to common Western notions, land is viewed as a living thing that, when cared for and respected, provides everything needed for survival, including food, clothes, tools, materials for shelter and transportation, and medicine. In clan communities, rights to land are defined by clan membership. Micronesian clans are mostly matrilineal: one has rights to one's mother's clan lands (Miles 1991). To lose one's rights to land represents not only a loss of the means for survival, but also a loss of one's place within the kinship system and the community. In traditional Micronesian society, this loss of recognition can be equated to becoming a "nonperson" (Hezel 2001:35). The importance of land to cultural identity is also reflected in the Yapese term Refaluash, which means "The People of Our Lands," and in the Mariana Islands where the ancient Chamorros called themselves TaoTao Tano, which means "People of the Land."

In the Micronesian islands today, the role of land varies considerably, even among the islands of Yap. In the small atoll of Ulithi, in the outer islands of Yap, land is still perceived and used much the way it was centuries ago. Rights to the land are inherited through bloodlines, and these bloodlines are recorded in oral histories by the Palul Wolfulu, or "Land Navigator" (Ulithian language). While the elders may collectively control family land, there is no single owner, and land is never sold. In terms of social welfare, this system of collective ownership of land with culturally defined social responsibilities avoids oppressive problems concerning tenancy. It also has other benefits: it generates cooperation among clan members; it serves a welfare or social security function by providing a place where clan members can have housing and gardening regardless of their other wealth; it assures future generations similar security; it equalizes access to natural resources within the clan; it minimizes the fragmentation of land and boundary disputes; and (as a result of the foregoing) it preserves social harmony and group survival (Miles 1991).

Primarily because of the introduction of cash economies, most Micronesians now view land as something that can be bought, sold, traded, or condemned by anyone who has enough money or political control to do so. Hezel (2001:36) sums up this change of attitude toward land by quoting a Marshallese government official: "Once the people said that they belonged to the land; now they say the land belongs to them." Today "the land situation in Micronesia defies simple description; it is a mixture of the traditional and the new" (40). While the outer islands of Yap continue to observe traditional landownership, individual landownership has become the prevalent form of land tenure in Guam.

In addition to the above changes, the people of Guam and the Marshall Islands experienced significant and dramatic dispossessions of ancestral lands by the U.S. government for military purposes following World War II. Two examples are that nearly 60 percent of Guam land was designated for permanent U.S. military bases, and the entire atolls and lagoons of Bikini and Enewetak in the Marshall Islands were destroyed, forcing displacement and resettlement of all residents, when the U.S. military performed sixty-seven nuclear tests between 1946 and 1958. Today, after more than half a century and despite several relocations of these atoll communities, people's identities are still strongly tied to their lost land; these people have experienced a sense of forced homelessness, and many of them continue to fight legal battles against the United States to reclaim ownership of and access to their land.

Subsistence and Sustainable Living

Historically, all Micronesians ate what they could grow on the land or catch in the ocean while taking care not to deplete their natural resources. Certain types of fish and other marine life were caught only during the appropriate seasons to allow their offspring a chance to grow and reproduce. Select types of crops were planted and harvested seasonally as well. This respect for the land and marine resources is what has allowed many Micronesian island communities to maintain subsistence lifestyles and practices of sustainability into the present.

In the outer islands of Yap, for example, while canned goods, rice, and other foreign goods are brought in via ship, a sustainable, subsistence lifestyle is still evident. According to Ridgell (2006:131), "Yap State relies more on subsistence agriculture than any other FSM state." Islanders continue to obtain their food from the land and the surrounding waters, and all that is harvested and caught is shared with the clan.

Nowhere in the Micronesian islands has sustainable living been more compromised than in Guam. While some small-scale agriculture and fishing continues, the indigenous subsistence economy has been replaced by a cash economy and heavy reliance on imported food and consumer goods. The elimination of the traditional land tenure system by the Spanish, the introduction of dependency on the U.S. Navy for the provision of basic health and public health services in the first half of the twentieth century, and, after 1950, the gradual introduction of U.S. federal social welfare programs have created a dramatically different context for survival and social care in Guam. For many, this has meant more economic uncertainties and new types of socioeconomic problems.

Reciprocity

After Western contact, throughout the Micronesian islands region the close family and clan linkages were supplemented by a pervasive custom of mandatory obligations between unrelated individuals. The complementary kinship practices of reciprocity, cooperation, and shared responsibility among biological and social "kin" are the backbone of traditional Micronesian cultures and represent not only a way of life but also the means for physical and cultural survival.

In the Chamorro culture, the principal expression of such obligations is chenchule', "a support system of exchange in which families express their care and concern for each other, as well as a sense of obligation to each other while working together to help each family meet its needs" (Guampedia 2011). As one Chamorro woman was quoted by Iyechad (1998:178): "[Hu] nisisita-hao. [Un] nisisita-yo"—"I need you, you need me." Chenchule' can take the form of food, money, labor, or other gifts or assistance, and it continues to play a significant role as an informal source of social support in helping to meet the needs of family members.

The transition from a subsistence society to a cash economy has provided a new means of survival and lessened the interdependence within families, resulting in lasting changes from the extended to the nuclear family structures. Though the extended familial safety net still exists, it is weaker and less involved. Concomitantly, while reciprocity practices still exist, they also have changed over time.

Although the traditional cultures in the Micronesian islands are based on many similar values and practices, one can now see the varying degrees of changes that have occurred, as well as the coexistence of two opposing and sometimes conflicting value sets: the traditional cultures of the region and the foreign cultures introduced by various occupiers. Wright (1947:23) best sums up this difference in values and standards of living: "If civilization were measured by flush toilets, ice cubes, machine guns, and sewing machines, then Micronesians were indeed savages. If, however, civilization meant an economic system in which there was no relative poverty, but rather adequate food, shelter, physical security, and a social system in which all participate equally and actively in the material and aesthetic standards of community life, then the people of Micronesia were indeed civilized and had much to teach the rest of the world."

In the next section we discuss some of the social issues and problems that have arisen from the weakening or loss of these social safety nets once so tightly woven together by traditional land tenure systems, subsistence and sustainable living, and reciprocal practices of exchange.

Current Social Issues and Problems

The Social Work Program at the University of Guam developed a regional list of social problems in which stakeholders in the field of social welfare had an interest. These included family disorganization; dislocations of identity growing out of the movement from traditional to acquisitive societies; dependency arising from the provision by external or internal governments; lack of a self-development approach; economic insufficiency; inadequate care for children of working mothers; child neglect and children without homes; idle youth and youth who leave school early; juvenile delinquency; adult crime; excessive underage drinking; use of intoxicants and inhalants; adults and children with disabilities; rapid population growth; unemployment and underemployment; the needs of older adults; and, as a general matter, a failure to identify community needs and to press for appropriate services (Manis 1981).

Manis (1981) interviewed eighty key informants on social welfare issues throughout the Micronesian region, from Palau to the west to the Marshall Islands to the east. When asked, "What are your social problems?" the first participant responded, "The dependence of the people" (8). Many others pointed to newly created dependencies on U.S. aid programs as well: "Dependency attitudes are everywhere. This has gradually been built into the lives of the people who now think 'Uncle Sam provides.' Individually, the people under the Americans have been given the freedom to do what they wanted but United States government subsidies have produced widespread dependency" (8–9).

Today, several decades later, we still see diverse indigenous cultures with varying degrees of change and adaptations to external influences. From a regional point of view, we notice sets of common patterns of societal changes that frame and constitute three main current social welfare issues and problems: the fragmentation and transformation of indigenous kinship and familial structures, public and environmental health problems, and unprecedented demographic changes in Micronesian communities.

Fragmentation and Transformation of Indigenous Kinship and Familial Structures

Despite the great cultural diversity and variations in how men and women define their gender roles, we can generalize that Micronesian island societies have strong matrilineal histories, with women being central to sustaining functional family and kin structures. In general, gender roles have evolved over the centuries to be complementary to optimize the utilization of available natural and social resources. Men and women were part of social, economic, and political structures that ensured the well-being, safety, and respect for all men and women, young and old. For example, although men tend to be the ones with public leadership and liaison roles, women are clearly the ones in charge of planning, implementing, and overseeing household and familial affairs (Kihleng 1996). This is why women enjoy a high degree of personal safety and protection that is assured not only by their fathers and brothers but also by their uncles, male cousins, and male social peers.

However, these Micronesian gender arrangements have experienced tremendous stress and have undergone dramatic changes. The imported ideal of the nuclear family with men as "heads of households" became the norm that was promoted and enforced by colonial administrations, churches, and the new economic structures of capitalist cash economies, as well as by modern mass media primarily produced in the United States. The above have contributed to the dramatic fragmentation and nuclearization of kinship structures, with more independence for nuclear families and less interference and support from kin. Less kin involvement has resulted in more uncertainties and stressors for individual men and women. This has also meant that women have lost much of their protective network of male kin, resulting in an increase of domestic violence and child abuse and neglect within Micronesian families. According to verbal reports of key informants, women are now attempting suicide at much higher rates than previous years in several Micronesian islands. Additionally, suicide rates among men in Micronesia have been among the highest in the world for decades (Hezel 1989; Rubinstein 1983).

Gendered social orders that evolved in agricultural subsistence communities poorly equip young couples for the challenges of earning their livelihoods and raising their children in modern cash economies away from their home islands. Living in urbanized Micronesian islands leads most young people to want to attain the comforts of the lifestyles that they see in consumer-oriented mass media. Although many young people succeed and become significant economic contributors in modern urban island economies, many others end up in no-win situations: no matter how hard and how much they work, their professional skill levels within the available income-opportunity structures in urbanized Micronesian centers, such as Guam and the Northern Mariana Islands, often do not allow them to earn enough money to afford the lifestyle they desire. Affected people respond to this economic situation in various ways. While many continue their search for better economic opportunities and move to Hawaii and the mainland United States, many others adapt to being part of the working poor in urbanized islands. For example, in June 2010 about 21 percent of the population of Guam, or 37,432 people, received food stamp benefits. While some groups return to their home islands and reenter their communities with subsistence economies (sometimes after periods of desperate and criminal ways of meeting their human needs), a growing number of young men and women join the U.S. military for economic advancement. The per capita rate of young men and women of the Federated States of Micronesia enlisting in the U.S. military is twice the per capita rate of U.S. citizens (Davies 2008). These high enlistment rates also result in the need for communities to learn how to address the physical and mental health problems that military veterans bring home after being stationed in war zones around the world.

Public and Environmental Health Problems

Throughout their colonial histories, people in the Micronesian islands have struggled to cope with and survive imported diseases, in particular, diphtheria, typhus, and sexually transmitted diseases (Hezel 2001; Rogers 1995).

While traditional lifestyles were characterized by activity and healthy diets, the newly introduced Westernized lifestyles are characterized by little or no physical activity and unhealthy imported foods such as Spam, a canned meat low in nutrients and high in fat. This development has helped create new and widespread public health problems (Hezel 2004). Trend statistics in Micronesia clearly evidence that noncommunicable diseases such as diabetes, heart disease, and stroke are now the top three causes of death in the Micronesian islands (Hezel 2009). These killer diseases, as Hezel (2009:4) notes, "didn't instantaneously appear in the islands like a sudden epidemic; they were growing all the while, especially during the 1960s and 1970s, the age of new prosperity in the islands, thanks to the increase in cash and the rise of imported foods and the ease of transportation." Obesity associated with these lifestyle changes has become a major contributor to the current epidemic of noncommunicable diseases. A recent study of Pohnpei reported that 83 percent of Pohnpeian women and 64 percent of Pohnpeian men are overweight (Federated States of Micronesia Government and World Health Organization 2008:40).

Since Europeans brought sexually transmitted diseases to the Micronesian islands, these diseases have been and continue to be serious public health problems. For example, in 2008 in Guam, the rate of infection for syphilis was 25.9 persons per 100,000 persons, which is significantly higher than the U.S. national rate of 15.3 the same year (Centers for Disease Control and Prevention 2009:110). Although official infection rates for AIDS in Guam (3.1 in 2008) and the Northern Mariana Islands (1.9 in 2008) are significantly lower than U.S. national rates for AIDS (12.3 in 2008) (Centers for Disease Control and Prevention 2010:117), high-risk sexual activities and the cultural stigma associated with HIV/AIDS testing give reason to be concerned that a rising number of people in Guam and other Micronesian islands do not know that they are infected.

The U.S. military carried out one of the largest ecological disasters in the world when it detonated sixty-seven nuclear bombs in the Marshall Islands from 1946 to 1958. Along with this nuclear testing, the environmental toxicity resulting from the continuous U.S. military presence has rendered the use of land and sea dangerous, especially in the Marshall Islands, Guam, and the Northern Mariana Islands. Cancer and other illnesses are associated with these military activities and the military presence. In the Marshall Islands, for example, nuclear fallout accounts for the 330 percent increase in thyroid cancer among Marshall Island inhabitants and for 10 percent of the increase of all cancers in 2004 and in future years (Mabuchi 2005). In Guam between 2003 and 2007, "there has been an 18% increase in the annual, age-adjusted incidence rates [of cancer], and a minor increase in mortality rates per 100,000 population" (Government of

Guam, Department of Public Health and Social Services and the University of Guam 2009:A-3).

As in earlier colonial times, people in the Micronesian islands continue to suffer and die from diseases associated with the continuous toxic polluting of island environments caused by foreign economic and military powers.

Demographic Changes

Changing population demographics illustrate the magnitude of external influences on the small populations of the Micronesian islands. These population changes, in particular migration and aging patterns, are unprecedented and create new social phenomena and problems.

Growing numbers of Micronesians leave their home islands for better educational and economic opportunities. While small remote islands have the greatest net outflows of people, Micronesian communities in Guam, Hawaii, and the mainland United States continue to grow (Hayes 2010). Having no control over in- and out-migration of their island, indigenous Chamorros in Guam have gradually become a minority on their home island. The Chamorros constituted 91 percent, or 20,177 residents, in 1940 (U.S. Government Printing Office 1941:4), but in 2000 they made up only 37 percent (57,297 people) of Guam's total population of 154,805 people (U.S. Census Bureau 2004:1). At the same time, the 58,240 Chamorros who migrated to the mainland United States are more than the Chamorros who lived in Guam in 2000. The number of migrants from other Micronesian islands residing in Guam and in the mainland United States has also significantly increased. Between 1980 and 2000 the number of Micronesians other than Chamorros in the United States has increased by 759 percent, from 2,983 individuals in 1980 to 22,636 in 2000. "This trend will likely continue for Micronesians in the years to come as economic and political conditions continue to destabilize the islands" (Untalan 2009).

As much of the world's population undergoes a profound aging transformation, the trend in Guam is amplified, in part because of the migration patterns and the disproportionate rates of cancer and other noncommunicable diseases described above. The analysis of census data, especially from 1990 and 2000, shows unprecedented trends of an aging population in Guam. While young people have been leaving Guam, older people have been arriving. This unique trend is explained primarily by the brief period of demilitarization of Guam during the early 1990s and the economic downturns subsequent to several typhoons during the same decade. For example, between 1990 and 2000, the number of young adults 20–24 years of age decreased by 16.6 percent, from 14,379 to 11,989. During the same time period, the age group of people age 75–84 increased by 70.9 percent, from 1,170 to 2,000 individuals. Because of the disproportionately high cancer rates and unique migration patterns in Guam, the number of people 65 years or older has increased from 3.9 percent to 5.3 percent of Guam's population, or from 5,230 individuals in 1990 to 8,215 in 2000 (Guam Department of Commerce 2002:6).

The most dramatic and still forthcoming population change is associated with the current military buildup in Guam. According to U.S. military plans, Guam's population was expected to increase by 79,178 between 2010 and 2014 because of an influx of people associated with the military buildup (U.S. Department of the Navy 2010). Depending on estimates of the current population, this influx would have created a population explosion of 30–40 percent within four years. Due to local protests and national U.S. policy reconsiderations, the current U.S. military buildup in Guam has been delayed, but it is certain to occur in a yet to be determined scope and time frame.

Government and NGO Responses

Current government structures in the Micronesian islands are built in part on particular sets of colonial administrative structures, and also on the indigenous and culturally rooted governing bodies. These government structures are very young bureaucratic institutions and are still developing the ways and means to govern their island communities under the complex and dynamic political and institutional environments that currently exist.

In general, governments have instituted and legitimized the use of taxes for the purpose of providing social services and public benefits to their citizens as part of broader public welfare policies. This is the dominant approach in countries with histories of strong democratic and socialist influences. In addition to government funding, philanthropic organizations have also assumed significant roles in generating resources for the provision of social services and benefits. This approach has been emphasized in countries with strong capitalistic influences. The emergence of social work as a profession of "welfare managers" has been contingent on societies' ability to generate and allocate the necessary resources to develop and maintain particular institutional welfare structures.

In the case of young Micronesian governments, they have neither a broad base of taxpayers nor economies that generate fiscal surpluses that can be channeled into philanthropic civil organizations for social welfare purposes. At the same time, Micronesian societies have been exposed to and at times forced into globalizing processes that have dramatically changed their societal infrastructures. These changes weakened indigenous capacities of communities to care for their members and created new and unprecedented social issues and problems. For example, children in all the Micronesian islands know about and follow cartoons and entertainment, sports, and fashion trends as featured in international and, primarily, U.S. mass media. As a result, these children idealize the lifestyles they see on television and their computer monitors. For Micronesian parents, these "American dreams" of their children result in impossible expectations that the parents cannot fulfill. For governments, these "American dreams" create administrative and political dilemmas for which there are no manuals or policies to follow. Recognizing these unique conditions for the governance of social welfare in Micronesian island societies, below we outline the major approaches of both government and nongovernmental groups in response to these changing familial and kinship structures, public health and environmental problems, and future demographic challenges.

Governmental Responses

Symptoms of fragmenting and rapidly changing familial and kinship structures in the form of increasing child abuse, domestic violence, substance abuse, and suicide can be observed throughout the Micronesian region. We contend that governments tend to focus on dealing with these symptomatic social problems but allocate relatively few resources to the exploration of the causes of these problems as they relate to the changing underlying social structures. The Western ideal of the nuclear family as the foundation of society has been adopted by governments in most Micronesian islands.

While extended familial and kinship structures are informally recognized, valued, and utilized, they receive little or no public resource allocations for their maintenance.

The political status of Guam and the Northern Mariana Islands has allowed these two island governments to access U.S. federal welfare programs. Through U.S. congressional acts, the people in Guam (in 1950) and the Northern Mariana Islands (in 1986) became U.S. citizens and hence eligible for most major U.S. federal welfare programs. The Social Security Act was the first major U.S. domestic welfare program to be extended to Guam (in 1960) and to the Northern Mariana Islands (in 1978). Medicare and Medicaid, food stamps (the Supplemental Nutrition Assistance Program), Pell Grants, the Special Supplemental Nutrition Program for Women, Infants, and Children, and other social welfare programs followed.

Currently entire departmental structures of the local governments of Guam and the Northern Mariana Islands mirror funding structures of the U.S. federal government. For example, the Department of Mental Health and Substance Abuse and the Department of Public Health and Social Services (with divisions of Child Protective Services, Adult Protective Services, and Senior Citizens) of the government of Guam depend in varying forms and degrees on financial subsidies and grants from the U.S. federal government. Because these programs are largely funded by the U.S. government, the local governments are in turn required to accept and meet U.S. national quality and accreditation standards for health and human services. In situations where departments do not meet quality and accounting standards, the U.S. federal government assumes control by appointing federal receivers, who then temporarily take charge of the local departments.

The Republics of Palau and the Marshall Islands and the Federated States of Micronesia have differences and similarities in their governmental welfare programs. These island nations are sovereign countries and full members of the global community in the United Nations. They have bilateral relations with many countries, and, as noted above, they have entered into compacts with the United States. As part of these compacts relations, the United States gains military access to the islands and in return assumes defense responsibilities and provides time-limited financial aid packages. In the absence of revenue-generating economies and a broad base of taxpayers, compacts monies and financial aid from other international donors are the primary sources for the funding of social welfare programs in these Micronesian sovereign nations. Through these programs, local governments are also able to create institutional bases to gain indirect access to some additional U.S. federal welfare programs. For example, U.S. federal agencies like the Substance Abuse and Mental Health Services Administration have become significant funders for programs addressing serious substance abuse problems throughout the region.

After reviewing the first fifteen years (1986–2001) of compacts relations with the Federated States of Micronesia and the Marshall Islands, the U.S. federal government assumed more control over the allocation and administration of current and future compacts aid packages. In the newly amended compacts with the Federated States of Micronesia and the Marshall Islands, in effect from 2004 to 2023, the U.S. Congress determined the funding sectors and established the Joint Economic Management and Financial Accountability Committee to control the allocation and management of compacts funds. Three out of five members, including the committee chair, are appointed by the U.S. Congress.

In summary, governments in the Micronesian region seek to provide Westernized social welfare programs and health care with primary funding from the U.S. federal government, which is gradually exerting more control over the management of its financial aid packages.

Regarding the regional migration flows and the associated population decreases and increases, we see that Micronesian governments have very limited and only indirect powers to influence these trends. The political statuses and relations among the islands' political entities allow people to move freely back and forth between their islands and the United States. Regarding the military buildup in Guam, we see the government of Guam supporting the military buildup while at the same time trying to slow it down by extending decision and implementation deadlines to address the many social and environmental problems raised by opponents of the buildup.

Nongovernmental Responses

The NGO actors in the fields of social welfare in the Micronesian islands are churches, civic organizations, businesses, and familial and kinship systems.

During the past few decades churches have become strong social welfare providers by making available social services through their affiliated nonprofit organizations, such as Catholic Social Services and the Salvation Army. Their nonprofit status permits them access to local, national, and international funding sources. The religious affiliation of these NGOs also provides them access to local social networks and gives them the public legitimacy needed in the struggle for organizational survival. Nonprofit social service organizations that are not affiliated with a church are much more likely to have relatively short life spans, and those that are able to provide continuous social services for longer periods of time are the rare exceptions. In recent years there have been renewed efforts to strengthen the nonprofit sector by creating supportive umbrella organizations such as the Micronesian Youth Services Network and the Payu-Ta.

Some U.S.-based and international health care businesses, such as the FHP Corporation (originally the Family Health Program, a nonprofit organization based in Los Angeles) and Bumrungrad International (which operates one the world's best hospitals in Bangkok and treats patients from more than 190 countries), have discovered in the Micronesian islands a new market to attract wealthy people for medical treatment in their affiliated hospitals in Manila, Bangkok, Honolulu, and Los Angeles. At the same time, public hospitals and health services in the Micronesian islands region are in general underfunded and cannot fully meet the health care needs of their citizenries. There has been an increase in the number of families organizing fund-raisers along roads of busy intersections or selling parts of their family land to be able to afford much-needed medical treatment at facilities located abroad.

In summary, nonprofit organizations and businesses that provide social services and health care in Micronesia are tightly linked with and depend directly or indirectly on national and international resources and institutional networks. The collective experience of the nongovernmental social and health services sector in Micronesia demonstrates that the chances of NGOs surviving in the turbulent Micronesian economic, social, and political environments increase significantly if organizations are able to draw from more stable national and international resource pools such as U.S. federal and U.N. grant programs.

The strongest and most stable and competent providers of social welfare in Micronesia remain the familial and kinship networks. Despite the many societal changes and many problems, the connectedness of people with the land, their ways of sustainable island living, and the maintenance of networks of reciprocal relationships are still the cardinal principles that generate the means and meaning for everyday living for most people in the Micronesian islands. These traditional social structures and processes give people their identities, allow them to redistribute wealth and resources, and include people in the maintenance and reshaping of families, kin, and communities.

Many men and women from small island communities who have earned college degrees now work in international businesses or have joined the U.S. military; they are building their new pan-ethnic personal and collective identities while still being deeply rooted in their particular island cultures. Micronesian islanders are experts in sharing and using material resources. What they learned from fishing and gardening in their island communities, they now apply to their houses, apartments, and cars in the communities to which they migrate. The reciprocal networks of familial and kin relationships include those who earn money and those who don't, and those who live on their home islands and those who have migrated to Guam, Hawaii, or California. The ongoing exchange of money, household work such as child and elderly care, and other services within families and kin ensures that those who do not succeed in their search for income-generating employment still have shelter, food, and transport in their home islands and in the communities to which they have migrated. Not only does this system of "trans-Pacific householding" minimize relative poverty within communities, it also generates a high degree of community participation and sense of belonging for everyone.

In conclusion, we question the effects of the politically strategic use of imported social welfare programs on indigenous ways of organizing social welfare. We contend that indigenous peoples in Micronesia hold valuable bodies of knowledge pertaining to organizing sustainable communities in general and advancing social work theory and practice in particular.

The Emergence of Social Work as a Profession

The emergence of social work as a profession in the Micronesian islands, specifically Guam, is a direct consequence of the introduction of U.S.

formal social welfare institutions, substantial investments in higher education by local and U.S. federal governments, and the provision of social work
education by the University of Guam.

The formation of the Guam Association of Social Workers and the development of baccalaureate social work education at the University of Guam
occurred simultaneously and in a synchronistic fashion during the late
1970s. By this time social-services training and education had been identified as a critical need throughout the Micronesian islands. Since then, the
Guam Association of Social Workers, which transformed itself into the
Guam Chapter of the U.S. National Association of Social Workers (NASW)
in 1998, has provided an organizational nexus for social work activity and
professional identity development. It sponsors the annual regional social
work conference in March, recognizes outstanding social workers, raises
funds for social work scholarships, and engages in professional advocacy
related to specific community issues. The annual regional social work
conferences provide a historical account of how social workers in the Micronesian islands are forging professional identities and articulating their
mission.

In 1983 Dames presented a paper at the annual regional conference not-
ing that the major challenges for social workers in Micronesia are similar
to those of social workers everywhere else, but with the additional challenge of recognizing and strengthening the social welfare functions of traditional healers, religious leaders, indigenous chiefs, and culturally diverse
families and kinship systems.

In 1989 the conference on Uncle Sam in Micronesia: Social Benefits,
Social Costs, provided "a forum for analysis and discussion of the American
legacy in Micronesia . . . and the duality of the velvet glove of paternalistic
beneficence and the iron fist of military imperialism" (Dames 1991:viii).

The conference in 2011, with the theme of "Human Rights and Social
Justice in Micronesia," again looked at the social implications of the current U.S. military buildup in light of core social work values. Social workers in Guam clearly and publicly continue to oppose the military buildup
as proposed by the U.S. military and have launched community education
activities such as a weekly radio program —Beyond the Fence—analyzing
and discussing issues pertaining to the military buildup.

In addition to organizing the annual social work conferences, social
workers gradually have involved themselves more in professional and pub-

lic policy development processes. For example, through a national advocacy campaign by Guam social workers in 1998, the U.S. NASW amended its constitution to include Guam as its own chapter. Shortly thereafter, Guam was represented for the first time at the National Delegate Assembly and played an active role in drafting and advocating for adoption the NASW policy statement on Sovereignty and the Health of Indigenous Peoples. This represents the first formal recognition by NASW of the common experience of colonization by the United States and the effects of colonization on the sovereignty and health of indigenous peoples.

Currently the NASW Guam Chapter also more frequently articulates and publishes statements on public policy issues in Guam and actively lobbies for and against specific bills in the Guam Legislature regarding issues such as drinking age, sex offenders, mental health services, gambling, same-sex domestic partnership, and the U.S. military buildup. Additionally, one of Guam's most experienced social workers, Sarah T. Nedodog, is the first social worker in Guam to campaign for a seat in the Guam Legislature.

Social Work Education

The University of Guam has provided the institutional context for social work education in the Micronesian islands for more than thirty years. It is the only U.S.-accredited four-year institution of higher learning in the Micronesian islands. Its mission statement describes the university as being in the "Pacific crosscurrents of East and West" and as offering "a unique opportunity to discover and acquire indigenous and global knowledge." This mission statement provides a philosophical framework supportive of a generalist social work education.

The Bachelor of Social Work (BSW) Program was established in 1980, was granted initial accreditation by the U.S. Council on Social Work Education (CSWE) in 2003, and had its accreditation status reaffirmed in 2007 for eight more years. The BSW Program seeks "to prepare individuals to develop a global perspective of social welfare and social development, to actualize the concept of social caring, to demonstrate belief in the intrinsic value, dignity, and worth of all humankind, to serve those in need, and to act with conviction in advancing the principle of social justice and human rights within the communities of Guam, Micronesia, and the neighboring regions of the Pacific and Asia" (University of Guam 2010:79).

This program statement is rooted in the program's unique context of the Micronesian islands and the novel and contested relationships of the various Micronesian political entities with the U.S. government. Since 1980 the program has graduated more than 250 students, most of whom are working in health and human services in the region. An estimated 10 percent have earned graduate degrees in social work, including three individuals who have earned doctorates. From 2008 to 2010 the University of Guam launched a pilot project to examine the feasibility of a master's program in social work. The University of Guam also communicates with the University of Hawaii to advance graduate-level social work education for Micronesian students.

Toward an Indigenous Paradigm for Island Sustainability

We view the University of Guam as a promising intellectual and institutional site for further development of a multidimensional and sustainable model and practice of social work in Micronesia. We envision this developmental process to consist of social-cultural, economic-cultural, and political dimensions within Micronesian cultures.

The social-cultural dimensions of a developmental process toward island sustainability must use indigenous concepts and be based on indigenous bodies of knowledge and practice wisdom. It needs to recognize and value the many forms of reciprocal relationships within and among familial and kinship systems. At the same time, we believe that indigenous theorizing needs to be linked with the bodies of knowledge of current social and natural sciences. We contend that the acquisition of indigenous and global knowledge does not suffice to meet our challenges ahead. Rather, we need to facilitate and nurture broad interactions among these bodies of knowledge, primarily through respectful dialogue among the people who have access to one or both of these bodies of knowledge.

The economic-cultural dimensions of such a developmental process toward island sustainability need to redefine economic activity primarily within the indigenous concepts of connectedness of land and people, the common good, and reciprocal obligations. Thus economic activities must orient themselves toward meeting the needs of others and of their lands, meeting social obligations, and advancing the common good. The goal of these economic activities ought not to be individual profit. This way, local economies are reenergized and are able to link indigenous noncash economies with national and global economic systems. For example, the Guam local chenchule' system can be further developed to complement both noncash economic activities and obligations within Guam's cash economy. People may provide community service cleaning a restroom at a public park and in return get their water bill reduced by a certain amount, or somebody may provide a few hours of care for an elderly person or a child in return for a specific number of rides with people who are part of a carpooling cooperative.

The political dimensions of such a developmental process toward island sustainability need to focus on examining and developing more permanent modes of relationships with the United States than the current time-limited compacts. Most urgently, political development in Guam needs to afford the indigenous people of Guam, the Chamorros, the opportunity to exercise their inalienable right for political self-determination.

As this chapter illustrates, social welfare institutions and policies in the Micronesian islands are driven and determined primarily by political relations and status as well as cultures, which again are intrinsically linked with both the social and economic fabric of island communities.

Social Workers as Cultural and Political Workers

Social work has an important role to play in the development of social welfare in the Micronesian islands. The developmental paths and current welfare situations in this region highlight the importance of cultural and political contexts of social work practice and education. We are called to actively participate in the critical analysis of the systemic interactions of these diverse contexts and to engage collectively in the advancement of Micronesian island communities. We need to contribute to and at times lead the analysis and exploration of why life and living conditions in the Micronesian islands are the way they are, and how they relate to regional and global contexts. For example: Why is it that some 16-year-old girls in Guam get brand-new luxury cars as birthday gifts and attend expensive private schools, while others depend on food stamps and attend underfunded public schools? Why do many 16-year-old girls throughout Micronesia work hard in gardens and homes with no further educational opportunities, and why are other 16-year-old girls in Asian cities selling their bodies for sexual favors to support their families?

This chapter reminds us of the importance of continuous learning, not only from books and professional journals, but especially from the people with whom we work. Clearly "social" work is human work, and therefore we need to engage in cultural and political work to live up to our professional ethical standards. For social work educators and practitioners in Micronesia, this means celebrating human life by engaging constructively in the daily reconstructions of our many cultures and in the daily decolonizing of our political structures and human minds.

In this chapter we described social welfare in the Micronesian region within the context of complex U.S. federal-territorial relations and the ongoing decolonization of young and emerging island nations. We provided an overview of the history of social welfare originating in indigenous social networks along centuries of colonization by Spanish, German, Japanese and American governments. We described and discussed major cultural concerns related to land-kin bonds and identity, subsistence and sustainable living, and reciprocity. We then focused on three main social issues and problems: the fragmentation and transformation of indigenous kinship and familial structures, public and environmental health problems, and social problems associated with and caused by dramatic demographic changes.

The public policy and programmatic responses of island governments and nongovernmental organizations were illuminated as anchored in particular sets of various colonial administrations, as young and evolving bureaucratic structures, and within complex and dynamic political and institutional environments. Of particular importance are the strategic military interests of the United States in this region, expressed in the various forms of Compacts of Free Associations between emerging island nations and the United States as well as the current and massive U.S. military buildup in Guam. The evolution and development of social work and social work education are deeply imprinted with the Americanization of Micronesian island societies.

The chapter concluded by outlining the dimensions for the development of a sustainable model and practice of social work in Micronesia as well as a call to actualize social work as cultural and political work.

References

Centers for Disease Control and Prevention (2009). *Sexually Transmitted Disease Surveillance, 2008.* Atlanta: U.S. Department of Health and Human Services.

———— (2010). *HIV Surveillance Report, 2008.* Atlanta: U.S. Department of Health and Human Services.

Dames, V. (1991). "Uncle Sam in Micronesia: Social Benefits, Social Costs." In Uncle Sam in Micronesia: Social Benefits, Social Costs, ed. Rubinstein & V. Dames, 7–9. Guam: University of Guam Micronesian Area Research Center.

———— (1992). "Political Status, Citizenship and Dependency: The Children of the United States Insular Areas." Children and Youth Services Review 14:323–45.

———— (1998). "Key Events in the Chronology of Social Welfare Development in Guam, 1916–1998." In *Guam Association of Social Workers 1998 Conference Program Booklet.*

———— (2000). "Rethinking the Circle of Belonging: American Citizenship and the Chamorros of Guam." PhD. dissertation, University of Michigan.

Davies, G. (2008). An Overview of the Compact of Free Association Between the United States and the Federated States of Micronesia. Statement Before the House Committee on Natural Resources, Subcommittee on Insular Affairs. Washington, D.C.: U.S. Government Printing Office, June 10.

Dodge, C. (1991). "Views from Both Sides of a Fence: Attitudes That Promote Disharmony Between the Civilian and Military Communities in Guam." In Uncle Sam in Micronesia: Social benefits, Social Costs, ed. D. Rubinstein & V. Dames. Guam: University of Guam Micronesian Area Research Center.

Ewalt, P. L., & N. Mokuau (1995). "Self-determination from a Pacific Perspective." Social Work 40 (2): 168–73.

Federated States of Micronesia Government and World Health Organization (2008). Federated States of Micronesia (Pohnpei) Non Communicable Disease Risk Factors: STEPS REPORT. Suva, Fiji: WHO Regional Office, December.

Fox, M. (1978–79). "Social Development in Micronesia." Journal of Asian-Pacific & World Perspectives 2 (2): 11–22.

Government of Guam, Department of Commerce (2002). Profile of General Demographic Characteristics for Guam: Comparison 1990 and 2000. Bureau of Statistics and Plans. Hagåtña: Government of Guam.

Government of Guam, Department of Public Health and Social Services and the University of Guam (2009). Guam Cancer Facts and Figures 2003– 2007. Mangilao: Guam Comprehensive Cancer Control Program.

Guampedia (2008). "Chamorro and Other Micronesian Migration to the U.S." Retrieved on December 12, 2010, from http://guampedia.com/chamorro -migration-to-the-u-s/.

———— (2008). "Chenchule': Social Reciprocity." Retrieved on January 10, 2010, from http://guampedia.com/chenchule.

Hanlon, D. (1998). Remaking Micronesia: Discourses over Development in a Pacific Territory 1944–1982. Honolulu: University of Hawaii Press.

Hayes, G. (2010). "International Migration Patterns and Trends in the Pacific Islands." Paper presented at the United Nations ESCAP Conference on Strengthening National Capacities to Deal with International Migration, Bangkok, April.

Hezel, F. X. (1989) "Suicide and the Micronesian Family." Contemporary Pacific (1) 1: 43–74.

———— (2001). The New Shape of Old Island Cultures. Honolulu: University of Hawaii Press.

———— (2004). "Health in Micronesia over the Years." Micronesian Counselor 53. Pohnpei, Federated States of Micronesia: Micronesian Seminar.

———— (2009). "Playing the Numbers Game." Micronesian Counselor 79. Pohnpei, Federated States of Micronesia: Micronesian Seminar.

Iyechad, L. P. (1998). An Ethnography of Reciprocity Among the Chamorros in Guam: An Historical Perspective of Helping Practices Associated with Birth, Marriage, and Death. New York: Edwin Mellen Press.

Kihleng, K. (1996). "Women in Exchange: Negotiated Relations, Practice, and the Constitution of Female Power in Processes of Cultural Reproduction and Change in Pohnpei, Micronesia." Ph.D. dissertation, University of Hawaii.

Mabuchi, K. (2005). "Testimony of Dr. Kiyohiko Mabuchi." Hearing Before the Committee on Energy and Natural Resources United States Senate, First Session on Effects of U.S. Nuclear Testing Program in the Marshall Islands. Washington, D.C.: U.S. Government Printing Office, July 19.

Manis, F. (1981). "Views Out of Micronesia on Social Welfare Services and Social Work Education: A Report Based on Eighty Interviews in Six Micronesian States." Mangilao: University of Guam, Bachelor of Social Work Program, Western Pacific Studies Program.

Midgley, J. (1995). Social Development: The Development Perspective in Social Welfare. Thousand Oaks, Calif.: Sage.

Miles, G. (1991). "The Micronesian Catastrophe: The Role of Land in the Subversion of Indigenous Peoples." In Uncle Sam in Micronesia: Social benefits, social costs, ed.. Rubinstein & V. Dames. Guam: University of Guam Micronesian Area Research Center.

Naik, R. (2008). "An Assessment of Local Food Production in Pohnpei, Federated States of Micronesia." M.A. thesis, Emory University, Atlanta.

Nufer, H. (1978). Micronesia Under American Rule. Hicksville, New York: Exposition Press.

Petersen, G. (2009). Traditional Micronesian Societies. Honolulu: University of Hawaii Press.

Ridgell, R. (2006). Pacific Nations and Territories: The Islands of Micronesia, Mela-nesia, and Polynesia. Honolulu: Bess Press.

Rogers, R. (1995). Destiny's Landfall: A History of Guam. Honolulu: University of Hawaii Press.

Rubinstein, D. (1983). "Epidemic Suicide Among Micronesian Adolescents." Social Science and Medicine 17 (10): 657–65.

Rubinstein, D., & V. Dames, eds. (1991). Uncle Sam in Micronesia: Social benefits, Social Costs. Guam: University of Guam Micronesian Area Research Center.

Samuel, E. (2003). "The Silent Cry for Help: Spouse Abuse in Micronesia." Micro-nesian Counselor 46. Pohnpei, Federated States of Micronesia: Micronesian Seminar.

Sanchez, P. C. (1990). Guahan Guam: The History of Our Island. Agana, Guam: Sanchez Publishing House.

United Nations, Department of Public Information (2001). United Nations and Decolonization. New York: UN.

United States Census Bureau (2004a). Population and Housing Profile: 2000 Guam. Washington, D.C.: U.S. Census Bureau.

——— (2004b). 1990 and 2000 Guam Census. Retrieved on September 10, 2010, from http://factfinder.census.gov/home/saff/main.html?_lang=en.

United States Department of the Navy (2010). Final Environmental Impact State-ment Guam and CNMI Military Relocation. Retrieved on July 15, 2010, from http://www.guambuildupeis.us.

United States Government Printing Office (1941). GUAM Population Agriculture. Prepared under the supervision of LeVerne Beales, chief statistician for terri-torial, insular, and foreign statistics. Washington, D.C.: United States Govern-ment Printing Office

University of Guam (2010). Undergraduate Catalog. Mangilao: University of Guam.

Untalan, F. (2009). Chamorro Migration to the U.S. Retrieved January 11, 2011, from http://guampedia.com/chamorro-migration-to-the-us.

Wright, R. (1947). "Let's Not Civilize These Happy People." Saturday Evening Post, May 3, p. 23.

10

Social Welfare in the Samoan Islands

A Comparison of Two Models

KENNETH E. GALEA'I

There are two distinct political entities of Samoa: the unincorporated U.S. territory American Samoa and the Independent State of Samoa. Just as the political states of Haiti and the Dominican Republic represent independent countries, and Thailand and Malaysia are on a connected peninsula but are separate states, so too are the Samoas independent locations. For ease of reference throughout the chapter, we will use American Samoa for one and Samoa for the other. Samoa refers to the constitutional monarchy on the western parts of the islands of Samoa in the South Pacific. American Samoa lies to the southeast of Samoa. While these two regions share the same ocean, culture, and language, they differ in governance and approach. For example, Samoa uses the metric system for measurement and its own currency, the tala, for price calibrations. American Samoa uses the U.S. standard of a yard, pound, and gallon, and the dollar to purchase consumables. Other differences are described as they arise throughout the chapter.

History

Early History

The Manu'a Islands in American Samoa were once the ruling and spiritual capital of Polynesia and are an important part of Samoa's creation myths. Samoans have legends of having descended from the god Tagaloa. Many Polynesian peoples have inherited a similar story of a deity arising from the sea and pulling the islands up from the ocean. As the Samoan story goes, Tagaloa first touched Earth on the island of Ta'u in Manu'a, where the first Tagaloa Chiefly House was built, called Fale Ula (Abode of the Gods). The Fale Ula became the palace of the king and deity Tui Manu'a, the first leader of the South Pacific. Legends also indicate that Manu'a Samoa warriors and kings conquered other islands such as Tonga, the Niuas/Niue, the Marquesas, Rotuma, the Cook Islands, Uvea, Futuna, Tokelau, and Rurutu. All Polynesian islands then paid tribute to Manu'a kings. However, the rise and fall of these regional empires took place well before Samoa's contact with Europe (Galea'i 2010).

Samoa

New Zealand occupied the German protectorate of Western Samoa at the outbreak of World War I in 1914. New Zealand continued to administer the islands as a mandate and then as a trust territory until 1962, when the islands became the first Polynesian nation to reestablish independence in the twentieth century. The country dropped the "Western" and has continued as the Independent State of Samoa since becoming autonomous.

Slightly smaller than the U.S. state of Rhode Island, which is 2,800 square kilometers (1,736 square miles), Samoa has two main islands, Upolu and Savaii. Several smaller islands include rocky coastal terrain with rugged volcanic mountains sweeping back into the islands' centers.

American Samoa

American Samoa is a set of small islands located 3,012 kilometers (about 4,850 miles) from Hawaii. The year 1772 marked the first recorded European contact with American Samoa by a Dutch explorer. Two additional explorers from France and a Christian missionary from England followed between 1768 and 1830 (American Samoa Historic Preservation Office, n.d.).

In 1900 the islands of Tutuila and Aunu'u were ceded to the United States. By 1924 the Manu'a Islands and Swains Island were annexed by the United States. The U.S. Navy oversaw the territory of American Samoa until 1951. Since 1956 the U.S. Department of the Interior (DOI) has had authority over the islands (U.S. Department of the Interior 2009). This U.S. territory, which is 76 square kilometers (123 square miles), is about the size as the District of Columbia.

While American Samoa as a U.S. territory under the DOI adopted its own constitution on July 1, 1967 (DOI 2009), becoming in essence self-governing, this status is not recognized officially by any contract (One Laptop per Child American Samoa 2010).

Population Demographics

The UN Population and Vital Statistics Report (2010) indicates many unique findings when comparing the two Samoas. Some of these census data, vital statistics, and demographic data follow.

Population

The midyear census estimate for the American Samoan population from 2007 to 2008 was 68,200, while the number of people living in Samoa was 188,359. Reports since 2000 have consistently indicated the population of American Samoa to be about one-third of that found in Samoa.

The population growth rate for American Samoa during this period was reported at 1.6 percent, and for Samoa it was 0.5 percent. American Samoa reported 92 percent of the population living in urban areas; Samoa, 22.7 percent. The population density gives some insight into this distribution. The population density in American Samoa is 330.5 persons per square kilometer (127.6 per square mile), and in Samoa it is 64.07 per square kilometer (24.7 per square mile). This fact is critical for professionals planning social service delivery and for program administrators attempting to reach consumers in outer villages. Access and delivery of services are especially important in a remote island setting.

Birthrate

The live birthrate for American Samoa is 21.6 percent per 1,000 women. The comparable live birthrate for women in Samoa is 9.2 percent (Rural Assistance Center 2010). The infant mortality in American Samoa was reported at 11.9 percent, and for children ages 1 through 5, it was reported at 4.9 percent. The infant mortality rate in Samoa is 20.4 percent, significantly higher at nearly twice the rate as that of American Samoa. Samoa reported a mortality rate of 13 percent for children ages 1 to 5 (Rural Assistance Center 2010). These figures provide grave indications of the differences of life and death at birth for the two countries. Babies born in Samoa statistically have twice the chance of dying as an infant compared to those born in American Samoa.

Literacy

American Samoa and Samoa report similar literacy rates of the population at 90 percent and 92 percent, respectively (Ministry of Education Sports and Culture 2008; NationMaster 2010). However, the per capita gross domestic product in American Samoa is U.S. $8,052 (18,772 Western Samoa tala). On the other hand, the per capita gross domestic product in Samoa is barely one-third that of American Samoa, reported at U.S. $2,892 (6,742 Western Samoa tala) (UN Development Programme 2009).

Life Expectancy

According to the UN Population and Vital Statistics Report (2010), the life expectancy in American Samoa is 72.4 years while in Samoa it is 73.2 years. Further review of local data indicates more variance. The Samoa Bureau of Statistics (2008) reported the life expectancy for males in Samoa to be 72 years, and 74 years for females. The life expectancy for males in American Samoa is 68.5 and for females, 76.2, according to the *American Samoa Statistical Yearbook* (2007).

Thirty percent of women in American Samoa and Samoa use contraceptives. In American Samoa, 20 percent of the women report breast-feeding at six months while Samoa reports nearly 60 percent. This difference may contribute to diphtheria, pertussis, and tetanus (DPT) immunizations, where differences in health care may affect choices to access professional care or more traditional options. In American Samoa, 99 percent of children receive DPT shots, compared to 50 percent of the children of Samoa. The differences in maternal child care practice and immunizations could be explained by the difference in the number of nurses. In American Samoa there are 127 nurses serving a population of roughly 60,000 residents, but there are only 136 nurses in Samoa serving nearly 180,000 people. In American Samoa, 59 physicians reported for work but only 50 physicians went to work in Samoa. Given the population, population density, and distribution, the number of medical professionals is a major difference in how health and human service programs are staffed in the two Samoas. The average annual expenditure on health per family in American Samoa is U.S. $500 (1,165 Western Samoa tala), which is almost three times what families spend in Samoa (U.S. $144.90 or 335 Western Samoa tala). The American Samoa government dedicates 14 percent of its budget for health care compared to 10 percent in Samoa (United Nations 2010).

Social Welfare Challenges: Two Systems, One Culture

The Samoas' systems of social welfare services reflect an example of dual societies or societies with different systems that are transposed on each other. According to Valdez (2009), in dual-economy societies, wealthier societies intersect and coexist with relatively poorer, more traditional, labor-oriented societies. This dual-economy theory came about in studies reflecting colonization. This chapter expands the concept to framing dual cultures as well, as the Samoas have different economic, political, and cultural systems as a result of colonialism and geographic isolation.

Colonialism brought about these dual societies through socialization and institutionalization of the colonial powers' cultures, educational systems, and forms of government. Duality became formalized after World War I when the Samoan Islands were redistributed between the British and the Americans. The currently emerging distinct island nations still share a unique culture, language, and fiercely protected traditions; however, they now have different political structures and governing networks as a result of their colonial experiences.

Economic Development

Samoa

Mapp (2008) says that underdevelopment and poverty in a country are internal social problems; and the source of the problem is located within the country itself and may include the lack of democratic institutions, capital, technology, or initiative on the part of its citizens. She is quite correct in describing the approach to human services in Samoa, where underdevelopment is a state or condition that is synonymous with tradition. The traditionalists in Samoa attempt to maintain control to continue the status quo, inadvertently maintaining its stagnant development. This is relevant at the micro level for life choices people make in the villages and how they live the Samoan way of life, or the *fa'a Samoa*.

At the macro systems level, Samoa has spent years attempting to change its UN status from a least developed country to an emerging nation. Changing the world's perceptions about Samoa required major organizational and bureaucratic steps monitored by the United Nations. These steps were critical for a country anxious to conduct business in the global community with many different countries as partners. Samoa reported to the UN High Level Meeting on the Brussels Program that its global inequality was due to technological and cultural differences. By completing the status change process prescribed by the United Nations, Samoa now can take formidable steps in economic development to reverse long-standing poverty by new types of cooperation with wealthier nations such as China, New Zealand, Australia, and even Germany. In theory this modern amalgam of new economic partners will operate in a free-market economy to achieve maximum good for all citizens.

This very optimistic approach to the goal of economic growth in Samoa is well intentioned but must take into account lessons of the past. Today, fewer people control wealth in Samoa than ever before. Mary Aufutaga (2000), a Samoan author and respected social work practitioner, makes this point when she says, "Exclusion is felt when one sector of society cannot fully participate in employment, education, civil and political society because they do not understand the nuances and metaphors of the English language and therefore European culture. Exclusion can be seen and recorded everywhere. Exclusion reaches into your soul because isolation and marginalization can drive a person to despair."

It appears from reports and data presented by the government that economic development is meant to build capacity (Ministry of Health 2009; Ministry of Women, Community, and Social Development 2006; UNESCAP 2010; UN Conference on the Least Developed Countries 2001; WHO 2009). There is a sense that the correct formula for internal corrections combined with efficiency savings and foreign investment can achieve the desired social developments. However, the low level of males completing school, in spite of a reported 92 percent literacy level nationwide, projects a very limited workforce (UN Population and Vital Statistics Report 2010).

American Samoa

American Samoa's social development strategists believe that underdevelopment is a process, not a state of being. They consider their predicament an outcome of the current situation and relationship with their major partner, the United States. Power nations like the United States have developed their current level of prosperity because they have depended on the resources of the less-developed nations for cheap raw materials. Pago Bay in American Samoa is the world's largest natural deep harbor and once served as a strategic naval possession. Under the U.S. Navy, an expanded form of colonization was put in place. The navy used the harbor for its own purposes and then provided navy personnel with prime positions in the transition from military to civilian administration.

The U.S. Navy occupied but may never have intended to build up Pago Bay. Development for a burgeoning community would have provided the local human resources to realize the potential of the harbor. When the navy left American Samoa, all the railways, roads, and trails were left unattended and unstaffed. Infrastructure by the military, with all the roads and railroads leading to the harbor, was designed to benefit an import-oriented economy as opposed to providing inland access for villagers. Today the trains are gone, but there remain train tracks that lead to no specific direction or village. Villagers had no cars when the navy left, let alone the knowledge of how to maintain the highways in the mountains next to the railroad tracks. Engineers, specialists, and technicians left when the navy base in American Samoa closed in the 1950s. American Samoa has been a dependent state of the U.S. Department of the Interior since the early to mid-1900s.

Though colonialism is gone, orientations such as the above remain, and poor countries like American Samoa continue to be dependent on the United States. Tuna is the only major product that American Samoa exports. The tuna canneries build companies to can the tuna and pay workers less than the minimum wage they would pay other workers doing the same work in the United States. American Samoa gives canneries and food conglomerates tax incentives and federal government regulations. The workers in American Samoa lead the international fishing industry in every standard for safety, production, and performance. After twenty years, it seems that the tuna industry, like the economy, is going to be fickle by relocating the cannery and taking its business elsewhere (Faleomavaega 2010).

More than half the personnel at the American Samoa canneries are employees from the Independent State of Samoa. They have come for jobs and remit much of their income to family members living back home. These people work hard for a living, contribute to the American Samoa tax base, and import the health and human service challenges of a growing population minority in a dual society.

Social Welfare Services Structure

The health care and human service systems of the Samoas have evolved predominantly along independent paths. These structures are described below.

Samoa

The Independent State of Samoa has an executive, legislative, and judicial branch. There is a chief of state. The head of government is the prime minister, who serves with a deputy prime minister. The cabinet consists of twelve members appointed by the chief of state on the prime minister's advice. The chief of state is elected by the Legislative Assembly to serve a five-year term (with no term limits). Following legislative elections, the leader of the majority party is usually appointed prime minister by the chief of state with the approval of the Legislative Assembly. Samoa operates a unicameral Legislative Assembly or Fono, with forty-seven of the forty-nine seats elected by voters affiliated with traditional village-based electoral districts and two seats elected by independent (mostly non-Samoan or part-Samoan) voters who cannot (or choose not to) establish a village affiliation.

Samoa health and human services are addressed under the Ministry of Health and the Ministry of Women, Villages, and Youth. Samoa's health and human services were originally largely segregated by geography, ethnicity, and occupation, including disparate care for upper-class and

Upolu-based families. With so few trained personnel in health and human services for the diverse and dispersed population, the leadership decided on a community-based model. Much of the focus and funding for these ministries goes directly to nongovernmental organizations to provide the direct services of planning, evaluating, and training in the villages. Several NGOs provide guidance on community building and training about solving challenges. The system then provides support for these village-based initiatives.

American Samoa

American Samoa's government is a presidential representative democratic dependency. This generally means that the territory has a head of government and state elected to represent the people, but it is not completely independent politically. American Samoa's government is similar to that of the United States. The executive branch consists of the chief of state, head of government, and a cabinet of twelve department directors. Its chief of state is the president of the United States, and its head of government is the governor. The governor serves for a four-year term.

The legislative branch, referred to as the Fono, has two branches, the House of Representatives and the Senate. Representatives are elected by popular district vote to two-year terms. Senators are nominated and confirmed through the traditional village chief's council. There is also a judicial branch, called the High Court.

The U.S. secretary of the interior appoints a chief justice and associate justices to the High Court (Central Intelligence Agency 2010). A citizen of American Samoa is not a U.S. citizen but is instead a U.S. national or "an individual who owes his sole allegiance to the United States." Because of this, American Samoans have travel access into the United States by showing their American Samoa passports, do not pay federal taxes, and do not have the right to vote in federal elections (U.S. Department of Interior 2009).

The navy used to be the sole health and human services provider for all residents. Today American Samoa presents a new emerging pattern of services. The U.S. colonial regime neglected the development of comprehensive health and human services and kept the territory effectively isolated from patterns of service delivery and financing prevalent on the

U.S. mainland. Many Samoan elders thus were born into a society where traditional healing arts continued to be practiced. Since the government determines and provides all services, access to health care was enshrined as a right rather than a commodity. The concept of health insurance was described as being a dubious scheme by even the highest elected official. In effect, the absence of a coherent policy for developing health and human services for the territory allowed a focus on individual needs. Organized health care emerged very slowly in American Samoa, facilitating retention of traditional healing practices. Religious missions and public health facilities provided virtually all health care until an investor-owned hospital opened in 1999. Territorial law now guarantees government-financed access to health care as provided at the government-owned Lyndon B. Johnson Hospital and human services to all Samoans without charge (Legislature of the American Samoa Government 1998, Public Law 25–22). Not surprisingly, private insurance is not widely accepted, as evidenced by the 2001 State of the Islands address of Governor Tauese Sunia:

> Our health care services have improved facilities and certainly some of the services. We still need more specialized doctors and definitely more nurses. The basic solution is to provide adequate compensation. That adequate compensation for professional medical personnel would be a strong first step to assuring that competent and relevant health and human services could be provided on the island. With the compensation not approaching the levels of pay in other parts of the world, or even the Pacific jurisdictions, quality health and human services are at constant risk.

The Social Work Profession: Data Differences

Samoa

An examination of technical papers of each Samoa manifests the organizational differences between the two approaches. The technical papers of the Samoa ministry include updates actually produced by NGOs. These technical reports indicate developments in the villages, updates on functions delivered that are related to program initiatives, and the number of partners contracted locally, regionally, and internationally for a particular goal or priority. This indicates data generated by the service providers to meet larger systemic goals.

American Samoa

The American Samoa programs typically report as government agencies. These reports on direct services provided are compiled by agency personnel on individual outcomes, number of eligible persons served, number of services provided, average cost per successful case, number of referrals, and number of grievances, for example. A large number of personnel providing services do not have advanced degrees in social work. Graduate- trained social workers are frequently in supervisory positions overseeing direct services and compiling mandated reports and quality assurance data, an indication of a system utilizing micro data to meet official reporting requirements for funding from external sources.

Social Work Education

Samoa

Samoa coordinates with the University of the South Pacific to offer a bachelor's degree and professional certificate in social work. Students in social work at the University of the South Pacific gain specialized skills and knowledge in social and community work methods, professional practices, and social policy. They can choose a flexible program of study that can result in a bachelor's degree with a social work major, a certificate in community development after completing six additional courses, and/or a diploma in social and community work after completing ten courses, all by distance methods, including both asynchronous and synchronous programs.

The local university, the National University of Samoa, not only offers a bachelor's degree in nursing but also provides an opportunity for further study on island for a postgraduate certificate in leadership and management, acute care, and mental-health high dependency.

American Samoa

The American Samoa Community College Department of Human Services provides a unique opportunity for students considering this field. The mission of the department is to support and prepare students who are interested in pursuing careers in the fields of health or human services. The department offers an associate of science degree in health science, an associate of arts degree in human services, and a certificate of proficiency in guidance and counseling. The health science degree enables students to continue into a specialized area in allied health, obtain local employment as a medical support staff member, or serve as a public health educator.

The human services degree can be used as a career ladder into a bachelor's degree program or for employment on island in the areas of counseling, rehabilitation, and disabilities. The certificate of proficiency in guidance and counseling can be used to enrich an occupational skill for professional development or job training. American Samoa Community College coordinates other professional education programs with institutions of higher education on the island, including San Diego State University for the master's degree in rehabilitation counseling and education, the master's degree in administration, and the bachelor's degree in vocational education.

Understanding Samoan Social Structures and Culture

The common notion of *O Samoa o le atunuu ua uma ona toti* is important to understanding Samoan social structures and culture. Translated, this means "Samoa is an already defined society; that is, everyone understands his or her role(s)." *Fa'a Samoa*, the "Samoan way" or the Samoan culture, determines these roles. Fa'a Samoa has been called the wheel upon which Samoan society turns (Galea'i 2010).

Samoan culture teaches the importance of family. Adolescents see themselves as an integral part of that collective. The role of the social worker as a helper from outside the family is difficult because of the emphasis on family and less on outsiders. Most clinicians who treat adolescents and their families are used to the difficulty many families experience in permitting a clinician into their "private family business." The Samoan culture, where individuals stay connected to the collective, argues for a rethinking of common Western individual and family therapy techniques. The social welfare planner or administrator developing services for the Samoan community would do well to identify these potential areas of conflict between the more collectivist values of the Samoan culture and the more individualist orientation of the U.S. health care system.

It would not be unusual for service providers in the Samoas to prioritize attention to and direct services for the elderly population. If there is an order of selection, it will be modified according to the needs of older people. Young people, although valued and prized in most families, will wait to be helped in programs and offices to allow older people to receive services first. Although children are highly valued, rank is more important in the Samoan culture. The concept of triage according to severity of illness is less important to the staff than the cultural imperative to treat the chief first.

A Key to Samoan Social Work Success: Fa'a Samoa

Samoan culture is based on respect (*fa'aaloalo*), and formal language plays an essential part in expressing this respect. Fa'a Samoa refers to visible symbols such as the '*ava* (kava) ceremony, speeches, feasts, the exchange of gifts in the form of food, large amounts of '*ie toga* (fine mats), and money. It also involves such things as births, marriages, deaths, visiting parties called *malaga* (or a group making a journey), and the dedication of church buildings (Galea'i 2010).

Fa'a Samoa highlights Samoan ways instead of non-Samoan ideas. The fa'a Samoa includes not only the unwritten traditions that are the core of the oral culture but also the social ethics and protocol of day-to-day activities. The responsibilities and values that make Samoans unique are all part of the fa'a Samoa (Lesa 2009).

Understanding Samoan communal values and familiar institutional structures within the community is essential to understanding Samoan views of mental health and the *Samoan self,* a term described by Tamasese, Peteru, and Waldegrave (2005:3) as "relational self and mental wellness as a state of relational harmony, where personal elements of spiritual, mental, and physical are in balance." This is critical in social work, as mental health has sometimes been linked to breaches of forbidden and sacred relationships, which could be addressed effectively only within protocols laid down by the culture. The Samoan concept of self as defined by Tamasese et al. provides a theoretical foundation for understanding the mental health needs of the Samoan people and a basis for developing appropriate services.

Aufutaga (2000) cautions us that English-language usage can perpetuate colonizing behavior and defeat efforts to assist families and individuals in need owing to efficiency and language. The English language has been a monumental force and institution of oppression. Too often Samoans strive to master the language and push families to speak English, but they must be careful not to replace their own language. Lesa (2008), a linguist and professor, provides the insight of current Samoan language users when he observes that there is a lack of confidence and a sense of uncertainty among Samoans of all ages in using their own language. He found great resistance and avoidance of Samoan cultural functions by many young adult Samoans because of their perceived incompetence in the Samoan Language of Respect or Gagana Faaaloalo. Many young adult Samoans with a limited ability to speak the Samoan language may find it a burden to speak in formal settings and participate in cultural functions, church meetings, and public events such as in government, media, and education.

Consequently, incompetence in the Samoan language in general has a great impact on the cultural identity of young Samoans today. Professional Samoans, scholars, practitioners, and linguists are calling for a return to the basic use of the native language as a means for personal, social, and cultural healing. Social work professionals must consider this discussion in approaching individual clients. What is their level of acculturation? What is the balance of familial pulls and cultural responsibilities that are embedded in native language use?

Effective human service strategies should include components of fa'a Samoa, which provides communities with the capacity to act collectively and pragmatically in relation to their own social issues (Lesa 2008). Any social development needs to consider the traditional collectiveness of the Samoan people when addressing the harmony and equilibrium of being a Samoan person.

Current Social Welfare Problems

Two major events occurred several years ago that affected the welfare of both Samoas. In 2010, when a tsunami hit the islands, the devastation and residents telling their stories through picture, text, and audio over the Internet were chronicled for the world. A tsunami hitting the islands was not a new phenomenon, but the fact that people from Samoa had the technology and know-how to tell the world was a revelation. Unfortunately, entire villages were run-off victims into the ocean because of the failure of technology warning systems and natural barriers. Not long before, in the same year, the wake of the global economy crisis hit American Samoa as one of the tuna canneries, the major private employer on the island for twenty years, closed. The carnage of these events has yet to be finally determined. However, signs of long-lasting impact and delayed recovery are evident and could affect the territory for generations. The loss of commerce and jobs may not be replaceable.

Former child protective service worker Celeste Annandale (2010) wrote about the struggle of young people as they also try to cope with the meeting of Western values and traditional society: "The conflicts created by these influences are stronger for young adults (post–high school) than for adolescents. For younger adolescents, lack of transportation, distance between villages, and existing village ties all combine to reinforce bonds within their families and villages. But, when introducing an external intervention to interrupt dangerous and abusive behavior, the village collectivism can be a powerful inhibitor even to the safety of those reaching out for help."

Although outside the scope of this discussion, it is interesting to note the effects of personal mobility on the development of individuation on a rural island. According to Annandale, community-based domestic violence services are new to the islands, and the number of incidents and requests for assistance has climbed astronomically since onset in the early 2000s. Sadly, the number of individuals served has not achieved the same levels because of low funding, poor training of very dedicated personnel, and lack of service options. Where does one put a safety transition house when everybody knows everyone in the village?

A special adviser to the American Samoan delegate to the U.S. Congress and former human-service counselor and program supervisor said, "Sometimes we send our kids from the states home to be part of the *aumaga* [village young men], to immerse them in the daily life activities of making the *umu* [Samoan traditional cooking] and fishing for the family, to get away from problems and city life. But, these gangbangers just react as if they were dealing with a new set of gangsters and reject the notion of village for urban life" (Faamuli 2010).

The emphasis on affiliation and family loyalty also affects young people's ability and willingness to discuss (or perhaps even to consider) conflicts with their elders. In the same communication, Annandale described a young woman she knows well: "Despite the fact that she is torn apart over the issue, she will not say anything 'bad' or 'disrespectful' about her family or the village" (Annandale 2010).

Lata (2003) seems to confirm Annandale's lament. Sex is not openly discussed in Samoan society. Lata gathered baseline data on reproductive health information and service needs of adolescent girls between 16 and 19 years of age in Samoa. The opinions and attitudes of these girls toward the provision of reproductive health services and availability of health services were investigated. Access to age-specific education, information, and health services was identified as a reproductive health need for Samoan adolescent girls. Promotion of condom use by sexually active adolescents was also identified as a need. Including biological and psychosocial aspects of reproductive health in the school curriculum may improve knowledge. Lata argues that reproductive health education involves all strata of society, such as governments, churches, communities, and families, with each playing a vital role. Annandale (2010) emphasizes the impact of culture on this practice area:

In the states how casually we may bad-mouth our elders (anyone from our parents to the president). She needs help, her child may be at risk for abuse and it amazes me that this person requesting assistance can exercise so much restraint with her emotions. Sometimes, working with people in the village I can help them to let their guards down by using the language of *faaloalo* and respect so we can clearly plan and move on for help; but I could just as easily be surprised by the number of young women and mothers who will not speak adversely or file charges against their abusers.

Government and NGO Responses to Social Issues

The Pacific Islands Association of Non-Governmental Organizations (PIANGO) indicates that NGO functions are active in Samoa. PIANGO is a regional network of NGO focal points or coordinating bodies known as National Liaison Units based in twenty-two Pacific Island countries and territories. Both American Samoa and Samoa are members of this association (PIANGO 2010). Both governments contract with human-service organizations, and nonprofits in both countries work with multiple government agencies to deliver services. While it is difficult to ascertain the volume of grants and contracts given to NGOs for human services, there are clusters of NGOs on record that focused on crime- and legal-related functions, housing and shelter, human-service multipurpose activities, employment, public safety and disaster relief, youth development, community development and food, and agriculture and nutrition.

Opportunities for People with Disabilities

Recent history includes examples of cultural conflicts and human-service-system collisions that are residues of colonialism. In the late 1970s and early 1980s, grants from the U.S. government funded programs in American Samoa. These grants were formula awards that were provided to reverse discrimination (as in Section 504 of the Rehabilitation Act), increase education (as in the No Child Left Behind legislation), and improve the employment of persons with a disability (Rehabilitation Act of 1973 as amended).

In 1980 the UN Decade of the Disabled was enacted to reverse the discrimination and stigma faced by people with disabilities throughout the world. In the 1990s the Americans with Disabilities Act in the United States changed employment for people with disabilities and increased access to public settings and services. However, when initial steps were taken to decrease the barriers to employment for individuals with disabilities in American Samoa, the vestiges of colonial thinking were hard to break. The efforts by certain government agencies, including the Department of Human Resources in equal employment opportunities and the Division of Vocational Rehabilitation in transitioning persons with a disability from the plantation to the community, were initially met with organizational barriers. Such a change in service protocol ignited the typical organizational barriers presented in the form of rigid implementation of established bureaucratic procedures and practice.

As a result of the programs and funding initiatives to address the needs of people with disabilities, sensibilities about how to care for people with disabilities and how to include them in daily life were challenged directly and traditionally with sentiments like, "How dare those people bring the handicapped out into public! Why are you making those poor kids work so hard? That's not right. We don't want that. No, you can't do that!" Programs with federal funding to provide recreation, counseling, employment, and education to people with disabilities were established by those who learned the system of grant application. Legislation tied to grant-formula awards for funding was now mandating the implementation of the guiding principles of inclusion, independence, and integration.

Initial steps at collaboration between the special education part of the Department of Education and the newly established, grant-funded vocational rehabilitation program within the Department of Human Resources failed. Vocational rehabilitation attempts to expand the opportunities for persons with a disability to get, find, and keep a job faltered. An eligible individual with a disability now had a choice to go to school or to work. But the special education faculty and administration who had worked with these individuals for most of their lives did not trust their well-being to nonfaculty workers. As a result, special education personnel did not want students to participate in a separate vocation-focused program. The educators were oblivious to the reality for so many of their students with a disability—that the next stage was not to be found in the classroom. The efforts of vocational rehabilitation personnel to collaborate and coordinate initially with special education were tainted by the lens of old colonial thinking and the traditional slow pace of change. The eventual outcome of successfully employed people with disabilities overcame the new barriers to employment and the old colonial thinking in Samoa. When students actually heard from their peers that wages were being earned at the vocational rehabilitation program, they came and brought their parents with them to see if it was true. Old thinking does not always stifle new dreams.

Social Service Response to an Aging Society

As the basic demographic data indicate, people are living longer in both Samoas, and this is presenting a new set of issues for elderly care in a manner consistent with the culture. There are no nursing homes on the islands. American Samoa has the Territorial Agency on Aging (TAOA), which receives U.S. federal funding, but there are few if any trained gerontologists and no trained geriatrics doctors. Like other U.S. state government "aging departments," the TAOA provides senior citizen services, elder care services and resources, and family caregiver support. It is also the planning entity that coordinates issues regarding long-term care, health, legal protection, abuse, and so forth. Some specific services the TAOA provides include caregiver counseling, caregiver training, meals, respite care, care companions, homemaker, medical help, transportation, shopping, support groups, home modification, and legal services through the territorial attorney general's office.

The Catholic Church, through its charities program, provides respite-care with a few beds for older people, and nuns provide immediate care for frail elderly persons. The respite-care program provides an opportunity for collaboration via the Community Service Block Grant Program, where competitors for separate funds coordinate and collaborate on joint proposals to help the Church continue to provide these needed services. Government vocational rehabilitation, independent living centers, public health programs, and the TAOA collaborate to provide basic assistive equipment and materials and durable medical supplies.

Mulatilo et al. (2000), in a study of hospital care options and the impact of a shortage of nurses to care for older people, found that Samoa is focusing on helping families to better care for their elderly loved ones. This qualitative study used informational workshops to educate community members regarding care for their elderly family members and then evaluated the effects of the workshops on participants. The authors explored the different avenues for changes in polices related to elderly people in Samoa.

Program reports indicate discussions regarding feelings of both parties, their concerns, and techniques to help them to bathe, eat, and move from place to place. Nurses addressed what to possibly expect in terms of physical and mental changes in older people and the importance of caregiver self-care. The workshops were offered for a low cost and proved to be a success and relief for participants. Suggestions about (a) a change in policies regarding the continuation of such workshops annually, (b) nurse and professional involvement in continuing elderly care, and (c) support for family caregivers were submitted to the government at the completion of the study. There was also a response in the community, not only from members of families who were caregivers but also from organizations wanting to support those families (Mulatilo et al. 2000).

The above is an example of culturally appropriate approaches that seem to have worked out well. Others have argued for more culturally relevant approaches that may diminish the colonial effects of Western-based models (McLaughlin & Braun 2009). These authors suggest that a seemingly realistic idea of cultural attentiveness in language, behavior, and perspective could be implemented in other countries with a design pertinent to Samoan cultural values.

The Public and Private Social Service Model in American Samoa

In American Samoa elderly people can qualify to receive the same social welfare services provided in the United States, such as Medicare, food stamps, and social security. The Department of Human and Social Services (DHSS) oversees government-funded social welfare programs offered in American Samoa. The DHSS describes itself as a "dynamic, innovative, compassionate, and professional organization of social work and human services such as counseling, client protection and advocacy, family preservation, child care, nutrition counseling and education, assistance in vocational rehabilitation, substance abuse awareness and education, and nutrition assistance for at-risk community members" (U.S. Department of Human and Social Services 2006). Within this department, consumers are treated with dignity, honesty, courtesy, and respect. Government partner agencies include the attorney general's office, the Department of Public Safety, the Department of Health, the LBJ Hospital social services (related to medical services), the Department of Education, and the Psychiatric Clinic (U.S. DHSS 2006).

In 2002 the Center for Medicare and Medicaid Services (CMS) of the DHSS studied "health beliefs and health related information preferences among Pacific Islander Medicare beneficiaries" (Stoil, Murthy, & Kuramoto 2006). In terms of health-seeking behaviors, Samoans said they were unlikely to go to a doctor when first noticing symptoms of sickness. Women showed a preference to initially seek religion rather than a physician, while men preferred self-medication rather than hassle with costs and the inconvenience of seeking medical care. When asked about their views of Medicare, many respondents seemed to positively recognize how it can be used to cut health costs; however, there still seemed to be some wariness about clinicians' treatments and suspicion about profit motives. Respondents also appeared to be confused about how the Medicare system works.

Several organizations that partner with government agencies to meet the needs of elderly and poor people in the villages include charitable organizations such as the Faleasao Village Council, which helps with food services and food distribution; Flaming Sword of Samoa Association, which helps fund cultural and ethnic awareness programs; and Goodwill Industries of American Samoa, which provides charitable donations and programs that employ people with disabilities, train people who are severely disabled or homebound, and implement respite-care services upon request. The Governor Tauese Sunia Leadership Foundation, an educationally focused organization, helps with historical societies and related activities where elderly people are key in reciting customs and traditional family histories and other authentic cultural practices.

There are a growing number of community-based organizations and civic groups that provide assistance. According to the most recent report by the U.S. Internal Revenue Service, there are sixty-five private and nonprofit tax-exempt organizations in American Samoa. The total income for these organizations in the territory is U.S. $3.2 million. The total assets of the organizations with tax-exempt status as nonprofits amount to U.S. $5.8 million. However, a large portion of services are conducted under the auspices of and provided for by the American Samoa government. Failure to meet the requirements for qualified professionals working for the government program could jeopardize continued funding for human and social services in the territory. In response, American Samoa's efforts to develop its own professionals are beginning to show results. The dependency on contract employees in human, health, and education services to meet competency criteria for federal funding is diminishing. Even with the risk that professionally trained Samoan social service employees may eventually chase the more lucrative opportunities in other, higher-paying environments, the number of returning educated Samoans is a dividend to the consistent budgeting for scholarships and professional training in the territory and now allows for the continued flow of U.S. federal funds for human and health services.

The Public and Private Social Service Model in Samoa

The Samoa model uses NGOs extensively. The national government contracts with NGOs to actualize government goals and objectives. This model allows for government resources to be utilized directly by the community. The majority of government program initiatives funded by various internal and external sources, the reports of these programs, and even the ministry boards and advisory groups are all focused on nongovernment talent and knowledge to guide and direct the affairs of the government in its service to residents. The startling piece to this is the low number of professionally trained service personnel. Despite this, however, Samoa continues to provide for its own, on its own terms. This model provides for limited resources to be dedicated directly to the community and includes community input in delivery of services.

An example of an NGO is the Help Samoa Disaster Relief Coalition for American Samoa and Samoa, which operates in Samoa. The coalition includes more than twenty nonprofit organization members. The Samoa Umbrella for Non-Governmental Organisation acts as a focal point for coordination of technical program reports. One such project listed twenty-four partners collaborating to submit the technical product. These partners included, among others, Women for Peace, Understanding, and Advancement; Inclusion International; National Council of Women, Avanoa Tutusa; Catholic Women's Association; Faasao Savaii Society; Faataua Le Ola; Loto Taumafai Society for the Disabled; Mapusaga O Aiga; Rotaract; Samoa Association of Manufacturing Enterprises; Society for the Intellectually Handicapped; and the South Pacific Business Development Foundation.

The U.S. territory American Samoa and the Independent State of Samoa are joined by the same culture, language, and traditions but differ in a number of other ways. The social welfare system of Samoa, for example, while based in the Ministry of Health and the Ministry of Women, Villages, and Youth, extensively contracts out social services to NGOs. American Samoans, meanwhile, qualify for almost all federal social welfare programs available in the United States. In addition, there are sixty-five private and nonprofit tax-exempt organizations providing services in American Samoa.

There are a limited number of social workers practicing in American Samoa, and there are virtually no professionally trained social workers functioning in Samoa under the social worker title for the government. Nevertheless, some human service workers may still be found helping Samoans recover from the global economic crisis and the tsunami of 2010.

More detailed and culturally relative research is needed to ascertain just what impact the natural and human-caused disasters have left as a legacy. Additional research on the impact of the different social service systems to needy, disabled, elderly, young, and otherwise marginalized people in

Samoa must be undertaken to provide insights for potential coordination, collaboration, and continued improvement.

Future Considerations: Purposeful Collaboration

Since the onset of programs funded through the U.S. Administration for Children and Families, the American Samoa programs for domestic violence, child welfare, adoption, foster care, and day care located in the DHSS have been documented for efficiency. The Child Care Program of the American Samoa DHSS spends an inordinate amount of time and resources on training personnel. The department brings in outside contractors with expertise in short-term contracts to assure that the agency meets its requirements and addresses the child-care needs of the community. The training program has successfully moved from a heavy presence of contract personnel from other countries to few non-Samoan contract specialists in professional ranks of the human and social services. Human and social services operations are now hiring locals and, in unique instances, developing local personnel through advanced training.

As a model of efficiency and a service well received in most political circles, the Child Care Program has positioned itself for local federal stimulus resources (Grohse 2010). The U.S. government was using funds to spike the economy by investing in special programs of note, including the Child Care Program. At the same time, the U.S. Administration for Children and Families was being replenished for budget encumbrances with its own federal stimulus awards. As such, the data-driven and efficiency-modeled Samoan Child Care Program was to receive another supplement. Aufutaga (2000) and others have warned against the colonial dependence that comes with learning the system. Too often Samoans have learned systems and models from other countries and neglected to build their own indigenous systems of services. The future for the Samoas cannot exclude the Samoan indigenous ways and thinking.

In response to indigenous models for service delivery, personnel are trained in Samoan family dynamics and community organization. These participants are recruited and selected because they know and love their culture. As culturally relevant personnel providing a needed community service, they have decided that the best way to target these short-term funds is to create three cohorts across the territory. These cohorts, with input from community resources and guidance from key stakeholders in the villages and districts, develop customized plans to use the stimulus resources for child care. Special training, education, care, and tools are part of the plans for child care, and the outcomes are locally developed targets for improved communities.

American Samoa seems to be skilled in recognizing and returning to the values and potential for village input for Samoan models of service. In this situation where native values determine a future, could this be the end of colonial imperialistic controls? This could be the reality of the vision of the U.S. Council on Social Work Education in "fostering mainstream development of international content in social work to increase the cross organizational collaboration in project development as well as research and data collection" (Council on Social Work Education 2010). As social work education in the Pacific produces more practitioners trained in evidence-based practice, further study and detailed analysis will be needed to see if we can bring forward a new model for social welfare in this part of the world. Perhaps it is time to include purposeful collaboration to solve continuing problems.

References

American Samoa Department of Commerce (2007). *American Samoa Statistical Yearbook 2006*. Government Printing Office.

American Samoa Department of Human and Social Services (2006). Retrieved from http://www.dhss.as/.

American Samoa Historic Preservation Office (n.d.) *Cultural History of American Samoa*. Retrieved from http://www.ashpo.org/history.htm.

American Samoa Legislature (2010). PL 25-20 History. Retrieved from http://www.asbar.org/Newcode/Title%2013.htm.

American Samoa Territorial Agency on Aging (2010). Retrieved from http://www.acronymfinder.com/Territorial Administration-on-Aging-%28American-Samoa%29-%28TAOA%29.html.

Annandale, C. Personal communication. July 2010.

Aufutaga, M. (2000). Conference Speeches from Tidal pools. New Zealand Electronic Text Centre, NZTEC. Retrieved from http://www.nzetc.org/tm/scholarly/tei.NZTEC.

Central Intelligence Agency (2010). *The CIA World Factbook*. Retrieved from https://www.cia.gov/library/publications/the-world-factbook/geos/aq.html.

Council on Social Work Education (2010). *Global Education Initiative.* Retrieved from www.cswe.org/centersinitiatives/kaki.aspx.

Faamuli, J. Personal communication. July 2010.

Faleomavaega, E. H. (2010). Press release: "Faleomavaega Calls for Walter Williams, Nationally Syndicated Columnist, to Apologize for His 'Breathtakingly Stupid' Comments About the Productivity of Samoa Cannery Workers," May 26. Retrieved from http://www.house.gov/list/press/aso0_faleomavaega/Enicallsforwalterwilliams.html.

Galea'i, L. Personal communication, July 2010.

Grohse, C. Personal communication. July 2010.

Lata, S. (2003). "Decisions and Dilemmas: Reproductive Health Needs Assessment for Adolescent Girls in Samoa." *Pacific Health Dialog* 10 (2): 53–61.

Lesa, F. (2008). "The Impact of Samoan Christian Churches on Samoan Language Competency and Cultural Identity." PhD. dissertation, University of Hawaii. Retrieved from http://micro189.lib3.hawaii.edu/ezproxy/details.php?dbId=320.

Mapp, S. (2008). *Human Rights and Social Justice in a Global Perspective. An Introduction to International Social Work.* New York: Oxford University Press.

McLaughlin, L.A., & K. L. Braun (2009). "Asian and Pacific Islander Cultural Values: Considerations for Health Care Decision Making. *Pacific Health Dialog* 15 (1): 138–46.

Mulatilo, M., T. Taupau, I. Enoka, & M. A. Petrini (2000). "Teaching Families to Be Caregivers for the Elderly. *Nursing and Health Sciences* 2:51–58.

NationMaster (2010). *Oceania: American Samoa Education Statistics.* Retrieved from http://www.nationmaster.com/red/country/aq-american-samoa/e.

One Laptop per Child American Samoa (2010). *One Laptop per ChildWiki.* Retrieved from http://en.wikipedia.org/wiki/American_Samoa.

Pacific Islands and Non-Government Organizations (2010). *PIANGO Members.* Retrieved from http://www.piango.org/members.html.

Rural Assistance Center (2010). *Rural Health and Rural Human Services Resources.* Retrieved from http://www.raconline.org/states/americansamoa.php.

Samoa Ministry of Education, Sports and Culture Samoa (2008). *Education Statistical Digest—2008.* Government of Samoa.

Samoa Ministry of Health (2009). *Samoa Demographic and Health Survey, 2009.* Samoa Bureau of Statistics and ICF Macro. Government of Samoa.

Samoa Ministry of Women, Community and Social Development (2006). *Annual Report to the Legislative Assembly of Samoa.* Government of Samoa.

Stoil, M. J., S. Murthy, & F. H. Kuramoto (2006). "Psychocultural Influences on Health Care Acceptability Among Elderly U.S. Pacific Islanders." *Journal of Health & Social Policy* 22.

Sunia, T. (2001). "2001 State of the Islands Address of Governor Tauese Sunia." Samoa: American Samoa Government Office.

Tamasese K., C. Peteru, & C. Waldegrave (2005). "Ole Taeao Afua, the New Morning: A Qualitative Investigation into Samoan Perspectives on Mental Health and Culturally Appropriate Services." *Australian and New Zealand Journal of Psychiatry* 39 (4): 300–309.

United Nations (2010). *Population and Vital Statistics Report.* Department of Economic Affairs Statistics Division. New York: United Nations.

United Nations Conference on the Least Developed Countries (2001). *Report of the Third UN Conference on the Least Developed Countries, Brussels, Belgium,* May 14. Retrieved from http://www.un.org/special-rep/ohrlls/ldc/Contributions/Report%20of%20the%20LDC%20III_E.pdf.

United Nations Development Programme (2009). *The Global Financial Crisis and the Asia-Pacific Region: A Synthesis Study Incorporating Evidence from Country Case Studies.* New York: United Nations.

UNESCAP (2010). *Social Services Policies in the Asian and Pacific Region,* 165. Economic and Social Division for Asia and Pacific. New York: United Nations.

United States Congress (2010). *Rehabilitation Act of 1973 as amended.* Retrieved from http://www.access-board.gov/enforcement/Rehab-Act-text/intro.htm.

United States Department of Education (2001). *No Child Left Behind Executive Summary.* Retrieved from http://www2.ed.gov/nclb/overview/intro/execsumm.html.

United States Department of Human and Social Services (2006). *Department of Human and Social Services.* Retrieved from http://www.dhss.as/index.html,

United States Department of the Interior (2009). *Insular Area Summary for American Samoa.* Retrieved from http://www.doi.gov/oia/Islandpages/asgpage.htm.

Valdez, M. (2009). "Resources, Motivation, and Work: Family Interface as Antecedents of Entrepreneurial Success." Ph.D. dissertation, University of Hawaii. Retrieved from http://micro189.lib3.hawaii.edu/ezproxy/details.php?dbId=320.

World Health Organization (2009). *Country Health Information Profiles: Statistical Tables.* New York: World Health Organization.

11

Cambodia

Social Welfare Renewed

THY NAROEUN, AMMON PADEKEN, AND SHARLENE B. C. L. FURUTO

From the tenth to the thirteenth century in what today is Cambodia, the Angkor Empire was the dominant political, economic, and cultural center throughout much of Southeast Asia. However, several centuries later the king asked for French protection in 1863 against the Cham and Thai people. Four years later the country became French Indochina. French Indochina gained independence from France in 1953 and became known as Cambodia. From 1975 to 1979 Pol Pot attempted to reform society by killing two million Cambodians or about one-third of the population through warfare, starvation, overwork, disease, and executions (Chandler 1991; Shawcross 1985; Vickery 1988). In 1979 Vietnamese forces invaded Cambodia for political reasons, captured Phnom Penh, forced the Khmer Rouge into the countryside, and remained in power for ten years (Office of Electronic Information 2011). A peace settlement was reached in 1991, and two years later the people voted for a constituent assembly to govern along with the presence of the royal family. In 2009 a tribunal began hearing the first of several court cases against senior leaders responsible for the atrocities committed by Pol Pot's Khmer Rouge.

Cambodia today is a country of diversity. The 2011 population was 14,805,000, and the life expectancy at birth was 57 years for males and 65 years age for females (World Health Organization 2011). The Khmer or Cambodian ethnic group constitutes 90 percent of the population, and the remaining population includes Vietnamese, Chinese, and other ethnicities. The majority of Cambodians are Theravada Buddhists; only 5 percent are Christian, Muslim, or members of other religions. Buddhism is the state religion, and its influence is felt throughout the country and culture.

Of residents 15 years of age or over, 74 percent are able to read and write. About 75 percent of the people live in rural areas (CIA 2011), and the gross national income per capita was US$1,870 according to the World Health Organization (2011).

While life in Cambodia for the majority of the people is a struggle, some conditions seem to be slowly improving for part of the population. The history of social welfare is an extensive one.

History of Social Welfare in Cambodia

Steinberg (1959) marks the beginning of the history of social welfare in Cambodia as the twelfth century, under the rule of King Jayavarman VII, who built public rest houses along the roads, distributed rice to the needy, and banned tax collectors from places where the sick resided. Traditionally family members and business associations have long provided a variety of assistance to needy family or association members.

Laws were passed in 1936 affecting the hours of work, wages, and workers' compensation for employees, and a few welfare organizations were established in Cambodia under the regime of King Sihanouk. In 1949 the National Mutual Help Association was founded to provide money, food, and clothing for the needy. Two years later, in 1951, the Cambodian Red Cross was organized and started helping disaster survivors, especially those suffering from floods during the monsoon season. The most prominent of the organizations established during this period was the Association of Vietnamese in Cambodia, which opened a dispensary in Phnom Penh in the 1950s. The Women's Mutual Health Association, formed in 1953, provided prenatal and child care at the Preah Ket Mealea Hospital in Phnom Penh. Finally, a system of family allotments was instituted in 1955 whereby employers were required to contribute monthly for the welfare of their workers' families.

During the genocide and civil war years, the government leadership decentralized social welfare and gave it minimal attention. Small amounts of resources were distributed to local government committees, and leaders of these groups were able to evaluate actual needs and distribute a variety of services, from in-kind assistance to employment opportunities.

Today the Ministry of Social Affairs, Veterans, and Youth Rehabilitation serves the social welfare needs of the people. Within this ministry are the Departments of Social Welfare, Child Welfare, Rehabilitation, Youth Rehabilitation, Pensions, Veterans, and Veteran Development (Ministry of Social Affairs, Veterans, and Youth Rehabilitation n.d.).

Nongovernmental organizations today provide the bulk of the social and medical services, particularly in Phnom Penh. The three thousand NGOs in Cambodia provide shelter, food, medical attention, education, and employment for a wide cross section of the population through orphanages, housing for rescued child prostitutes, employment for battered women, and treatment for acid burn survivors (Monireth 2011).

A unique feature of the social welfare system in Cambodia is the system of Buddhist monks and wats, or temples, which have been found throughout all of Cambodia from ancient times to today. It is the monks in the wats who have consistently been the source of assistance for average as well as poor Cambodians, except in the mid-1900s, when the government followed socialist policies, and later under Pol Pot and the Khmer Rouge, when the wats were summarily destroyed and monks went into forced hard labor.

Today the wats again feed the hungry, educate the poor, and house those with dementia. For example, the monk Chheang Phalla from Wat Preah Dak founded the Cambodian Child and Hope Association, which now sponsors eight schools and underwrites partial expenses to teach, shelter, and feed 721 impoverished children and orphans (Cambodian Child and Hope Association 2011). Other wats have built schools, planted trees, installed water pumps for villages, cared for sick and elderly, and taught people how to be happy.

Culture

The Cambodian people continue to manifest great respect for extended family members, elders, the village chief (brahtean poom), natural healers (krou Khmer), and monks. The extended family is the key social unit in the Cambodian society, and individual members work collaboratively for the benefit and success of the family as a unit. There are strong bonds and considerable interaction between and among both nuclear and extended family members.

Elders are perceived as being the source of wisdom, culture, and knowledge, and they are treated with distinct honor and respect in a caring and gentle manner. Grandparents and older parents reside at home where they provide counsel for troubled families or those making major decisions.

The village chief is an elected individual accorded authority to keep the village running smoothly. He is sought after by villagers in time of land disputes, natural disasters, family conflicts, and neighborly disagreements over animals. His signature or his stamp is needed when land is purchased or sold, divorces are processed, and marriages are announced. The village chief is also responsible for collecting the census and publicizing information given him from the local wat. Battered women may seek the assistance of the village chief if family members are unable to help.

Because many people believe in the natural healers and certified medical doctors are usually unaffordable and unavailable outside of Phnom Penh, the sick readily seek the services of natural healers for conditions such as mumps, cancer, diarrhea, broken bones, backaches, asthma, ringworm, malaria, poisoning, fever, and stomachaches (Yorn 2011). Villagers trust that natural healers will help them to recover by restoring the yin-yang balance or the wind-water-earth-fire body balance. Natural healers use a number of herbs, potions, amulets, ointments made from animals and minerals, offerings, and rituals to heal a sick person.

Monks, actively engaged in following Buddha by doing good, feeding the poor, and teaching the people how to be happy, are highly revered in Cambodia. Some monks may be natural healers (by sprinkling water, for example), while others may foretell the future. All monks who participate in marriage ceremonies bring good luck to the couple while driving away bad spirits. Above all, monks resolutely promote peace and goodness for all while encouraging the people to do likewise.

Many clients prefer to seek help from extended family members, the village chief, natural healers, and monks rather than from an unfamiliar social worker practicing in the unknown social work profession that is part of an unfamiliar, international NGO. This traditional assistance network has helped Cambodians to rebound from natural and unnatural disasters.

Social Welfare Issues and Services

Cambodia, with only two decades of peace in its immediate past and with low Human Development Index (HDI) and Gini index rankings, continues to struggle with a number of social issues, including poverty, human trafficking, health, child welfare, aging, a poor economy, insufficient jobs, and corruption in and outside of government.

With limited income from taxation at this time, the government is able to fund few social welfare services through the Ministry of Social Affairs. On the other hand, NGOs have a dominant presence in Phnom Penh and some rural areas. Moreover, traditional sources of aid such as wats, village chiefs, natural healers, and family members play a significant role in providing social welfare services throughout all of Cambodia.

Poverty

Cambodia is considered to be among the poorest countries in Asia. In fact, Cambodia and Myanmar ranked the lowest of the Asian countries on the HDI in 2010. The gross domestic product based on purchasing power parity per capita in 2008 was $2,033 (8,193,396 KHR), with a projected increase to $3,248.17 (13,090,255 KHR) in 2016 (International Monetary Fund 2011b). UNICEF (2010) estimates that poor people in Cambodia earn a maximum of about U.S.$1.25 (5,112 KHR) per day.

The Ministry of Social Affairs (n.d.) estimates the poverty rate in Cambodia to be 32 percent, while the United Nations (n.d.) estimates the rate to be 30 percent. Most of the poor live in the countryside as subsistence farmers who face natural disasters, insect infestations, poor infrastructure, low yield, and other challenges, and a bad crop results in further hardship. Poor families live in underprivileged villages with minimal educational and employment facilities, usually no formally trained medical personnel, and few opportunities. Crises that befall one family usually affect other families, making most survivors unable to help relatives and friends in an ongoing, meaningful way.

Since 1996, there has been progress in a number of major areas: internal peace and security, democracy taking roots, and spectacular and steady macroeconomic growth, all of which have reduced poverty. Between 1993 and 2004 the poverty rate dropped from 39 percent to 28 percent in the 56 percent of the country surveyed. In 2004, 90 percent of the poor were in rural areas, and, among the poor, a larger share was closer to the poverty line (International Monetary Fund 2006).

The Royal Government of Cambodia has subscribed to the Socio-Economic Development Plans (1996–2005), Public Investment Programs

(1996–2002), National Poverty Reduction Strategies (2002), Cambodia Millennium Development Goals (2003), and National Strategic Development Plan of 2006–10 (International Monetary Fund 2006). The current antipoverty program, the comprehensive Rectangular Strategy IV (2008–13), addresses governance and socioeconomic development issues and government efforts (Ministry of Social Affairs, Veterans, and Youth Rehabilitation n.d.). This plan includes the government advocating for passage of two laws that would underwrite not only the national social security fund but also the national pension fund for veterans.

The Royal Government of Cambodia is also working on programs that help the poor. The Homeless Social Concession Program provides homeless people temporary shelter in social centers, psychological education services, health services, vocational training services, and reintegration back into the community services (Ministry of Social Affairs, Veterans, and Youth Rehabilitation n.d.).

The government accepts funds and programs from NGOs. In 2011 the Asian Development Bank announced that it would invest U.S.$500 million (2,009,999,968,000,000 KHR) in an antipoverty plan to improve Cambodia's agricultural sector and rural infrastructure. Plans include improving irrigation systems, creating farm jobs, advancing food security, making secondary education more accessible throughout Cambodia, and strengthening transportation and therefore business links between Phnom Penh, Ho Chi Minh City, and Bangkok. This investment is in addition to the U.S.$100 million (401,999,999,744,000 KHR) the Asian Development Bank and Australian government are already providing to help rehabilitate Cambodia's national railroad and improve business opportunities from Sihanoukville in the south, through Phnom Penh, and up to the northern border with Thailand (Radio Free Asia 2011).

According to its website, the NGO Tabitha Cambodia (n.d.) fights poverty by working with groups of poor families to help them attain a better life by developing sustainable cottage industries and administering family development programs. Tabitha has helped more than 500,000 Cambodians out of poverty and become self-sufficient by starting cottage industries, which can vary from baking bread to sewing rag rugs.

The 2009–10 Tabitha Cambodia *Annual Report* describes the organization's achievements as follows: (a) working with 33,466 families with 267,728 dependents in community development and with 641 families with 5,128 dependents in cottage industries; (b) helping 28,754 families achieve food security (of these families, 19,153 now are able to eat three meals a day); (c) installing 1,561 wells, ponds, or reservoirs that enabled another 3,610 families to have clean, potable water and to earn incomes that averaged U.S.$2,000 (8,180,000 KHR) per year (an increase from U.S.$300, or 1,227,000 KHR, per year); (d) helping 2,224 families to buy bicycles; (e) building five schools; (f) enabling 189,333 children to attend school; and (g) coordinating 2,280 global volunteers to build 1,053 houses.

Orphanages play a unique role as an antipoverty strategy in Cambodia. Poor families who cannot feed and educate their children sometimes place one or more children in an orphanage (Friends International n.d.). A number of children living in orphanages have parents who feel the orphanage offer their children an opportunity for a better life.

Human Trafficking

Cambodia is a source, transit, and destination country for human trafficking of men, women, and children who are survivors of forced labor and forced prostitution, according to the U.S. Department of State *Trafficking in Persons Report 2010*. Many Cambodian men, women, and children migrate to Thailand, Malaysia, and other countries for work, and a number of them are subsequently forced into commercial sexual exploitation or forced to labor in the Thai fishing and seafood processing industry, agricultural plantations, factories, or domestic industries. Some must turn to begging and street selling.

For more than ten years the U.S. Department of State (2010) has placed Cambodia in the unenviable Tier 2 or Tier 3 category in its annual *Trafficking in Persons Report*. In addition, the *Trafficking in Persons Report 2010* noted that some law enforcement and government officials, police officers, military officers, and military police are believed to be complicit in or to have accepted bribes in facilitating the trafficking and sex trade.

The number of children involved in the sex trade varies from thirty thousand, according to the Cambodian minister of women's affairs, Mu Soc Hua, in 2005 (*Dateline NBC*), to the unofficial count of fifteen thousand prostituted children, some as young as four years of age, in Phnom Penh. Up to 35 percent of them have been smuggled into Cambodia from China or Vietnam (Coalition Against Trafficking in Women 2011).

Some Cambodian children are trafficked to Thailand and Vietnam to beg, sell candy and flowers, and shine shoes. Within the country Cambodian and ethnic Vietnamese women and virgin children are trafficked from rural areas to Phnom Penh, Siem Reap, and Sihanoukville for commercial sexual exploitation (King 2004). The sale of virgin girls continues to be a serious problem in Cambodia, with foreign and Cambodian men paying as much as U.S.$4,000 (16,360,000 KHR) to have sex with virgins.

Some Cambodians who migrate to Taiwan and South Korea through brokered international marriages may also be subsequently subjected to prostitution or forced labor.

While the Law on Suppression of the Kidnapping, Trafficking, and Exploitation of Human Persons was passed in 1996 and criminalizes debt bondage, slavery, and forced child labor in Cambodia, the law has limitations in terms of (a) the effective definitions of trafficking and its survivors, (b) controlling restrictions on prostitution, (c) an absence of a protection clause for trafficking survivors, and (d) gaps between the law and the practice of the law. Since passage of the law, Cambodia has not been vigilant in fighting human trafficking (Yasunobu 2004).

Based on the seriousness of the human trafficking problem in Cambodia, the government needs to take a strong leadership posture and do much more to fight it. It would helpful for the international arena to collaborate with Cambodia on this issue. While the Cambodian government met with five member states of the Coordinated Mekong Ministerial Initiative Against Trafficking in Phnom Penh and agreed to approve the plan of action developed in March 2005 in Hanoi, more attention needs to be paid to implementation and enforcement of the plan itself.

The U.S. Department of State (2011) recommends that the Cambodian government investigate and prosecute offenders of both labor and sex trafficking; conduct robust investigations and prosecute government officials involved in trafficking activities; institute and enforce a law to better regulate the recruitment, placement, and protection of migrant workers going abroad; hold labor recruitment companies criminally responsible for illegal acts committed during the recruitment process, such as debt bondage through exorbitant fees, detention of workers during predeparture training, and recruitment of workers under age 18; increase efforts to make court processes sensitive to the needs and best interests of both child and adult trafficking survivors; expand efforts to proactively identify survivors of trafficking among vulnerable groups; increase engagement with governments of destination countries on the protection of migrant workers, as well as the safe repatriation of Cambodian trafficking survivors and the prosecution of their traffickers; increase efforts to train and sensitize law enforcement, prosecutors, and court officials about trafficking, proactive identification of survivors, referral procedures, and sensitive handling of cases; improve interagency cooperation and coordination between police and court officials on trafficking cases; and conduct a public awareness campaign aimed at reducing demand by the local population and Asian visitors for commercial sex acts.

The Cambodian government operates two temporary shelters, and survivors of human trafficking have been provided with education, health services, and other services without discrimination (Ministry of Social Affairs, Veterans, and Youth Rehabilitation n.d.). Law enforcement and immigration officials implement formal procedures to identify survivors among vulnerable groups, such as girls in prostitution, and refer them to provincial and municipal departments of social affairs, where they are interviewed and then referred to short- or long-term shelters.

The Cambodian government has made efforts to raise awareness of human trafficking through posters, television, radio, and local movie theaters. In 2006 the police conducted an awareness campaign among twenty thousand students in Siem Reap and three thousand students in Phnom Penh, according to the 2007 U.S. Department of State *Trafficking in Persons Report*.

The government also collaborates with NGOs such as the Cambodian League for the Promotion and Defense of Human Rights (LICHADO) and End Child Prostitution, Abuse, and Trafficking in Cambodia (ECPATC) to assist trafficked survivors in reintegrating into society. According to ECPATC's website, the group sponsors a number of activities to address human trafficking, including an annual meeting to target common issues faced by local partners; training seminars for NGO and government officials to increase awareness and understanding in the tourism sector; a petition drive that recently resulted in five thousand signatures; workshops for staff and volunteer capacity building; and special programs such as the Child Protection Tuk-Tuk projects in both Phnom Penh and Sihanouk Province. These concerted efforts are aimed at increasing campaign awareness and training stakeholders to better address human trafficking on the macro level.

NGOs in Cambodia

The Cambodian social welfare system has been depending more on NGOs than on the government Ministry of Social Affairs for social services largely because of the challenging economy and some corrupt government officials (Office of Electronic Information 2011; Global Organization of Parliamentarians against Corruption n.d.). Since the Vietnamese occupation ended in 1989, NGOs have become increasingly visible in Cambodia. A description of several key NGOs in Cambodia follows.

Cooperation Committee for Cambodia

The Cooperation Committee for Cambodia (CCC), according to its website, is the preeminent membership organization for NGOs in Cambodia. Since 1990 the CCC has taken a lead role in representing the combined voices of NGOs to the government and donors. It is known to provide high-quality information management, information sharing, and capacity development. The approximately 126 NGO members of the CCC provide a breadth of services, from labor-law training to medical and psychosocial services.

NGO Forum on Cambodia

The NGO Forum on Cambodia is composed of approximately 93 local and international NGOs working in Cambodia (NGO Forum 2011a). Its purposes are to share information, debate issues, and advocate for those priority issues that affect Cambodia's development. The forum's three programs—the Development Issues Program, Environment Program, and Land and Livelihood Program—focus on issues ranging from the national budget to sustainable agriculture to housing and minority rights, respectively. Member organizations of the NGO Forum provide services ranging from farmer education to child prostitution rescue. It should be noted that a considerable number of NGOs are neither members of the CCC nor the NGO Forum.

LICADHO

Since 1992, LICADHO has been at the forefront, advocating not only for human rights but also for civil and political rights in Cambodia. LICADHO advocates for the people and monitors the government through a broad range of human-rights programs in Phnom Penh and twelve provincial offices. LICADHO pursues its mandate through its seven offices: the Advocacy, Documentation, and Resource Office, the Human Rights Education Office, the Monitoring Office, the Medical Office, Project Against Torture, the Children's Rights Office, and the Women's Rights Office. LICADHO regularly addresses issues regarding women and children, land, prison, rape, acid attack, and torture. In addition, LICADHO was involved in conducting voter-education campaigns and monitoring political violence in the 1993, 1998, and 2003 elections.

LICADHO is also concerned about corruption in the government and, like many other local and international observers, was dissatisfied with the swift passage of the country's first Law on Anti-Corruption in March 2010 because it lacked input from the general public and international standards (Cambodian League for the Promotion and Defense of Human Rights 2010). The law is considered to be "seriously flawed" by Global Witness (2010).

Transparency International agrees with LICADHO that corruption remains a significant issue in Cambodia. Last year Transparency International ranked Cambodia 154th out of 178 countries, or a 2.1 (where 0 is highly corrupt and 10 is highly clean), in its Corruption Perceptions Index 2010 results (Transparency International 2010). Corrupt government officials at all levels must continue to be challenged by organizations like LICADHO so that dishonesty in the government can be curbed and eventually Cambodians can benefit.

Social Services of Cambodia

The SSC has a prominent social work presence in Cambodia. The SSC (Administrator 2011a, b, c) provides a number of services including mental health and psychosocial services. The Community-Based Livelihood Enhancement Program employs innovative learning technologies such as community psychosocial assessment, oral histories, and participatory drama to facilitate community dialogues whereby villagers are able to build on their own resilience.

The SSC also sponsors a Sexual Assault Center, a residential facility for survivors of domestic violence and human trafficking that provides counseling, information, legal referrals, and medical care. A unique feature of the SSC is that since 2003 it has been rigorously offering social work training to staff members of other NGOs (Padeken 2011). In 2004 a basic social work skills training course for survivors of gender-based violence was initiated, and a building in Phnom Penh was renovated for educational purposes. The following year the SSC offered an intermediate social work curriculum. Students enroll in this popular thirty-day, six-week social work skills course for a fee.

Social Work Education and the Social Work Profession

While social work education and the social work profession are present in Phnom Penh, the general public is not very familiar with them. The few social work positions are found in NGOs rather than in the Ministry of Social Affairs. Most human service professionals have no training in social work and do not have social work job titles. Nevertheless, these human service workers are making a valiant and commendable effort in delivering social services to a population with multiple needs within a fledging social welfare structure.

The three thousand NGOs found primarily in Phnom Penh provide general social welfare services, including child welfare, education, employment, health care, and community development. More NGOs are needed, particularly in the provinces, to provide basic social welfare and health services.

Social work education on the university level is also very new in Cambodia. In 2004 the Royal University of Phnom Penh (RUPP) and the University of Washington in Seattle began a relationship that resulted in Cambodian students studying in the United States at the graduate level in social work. Upon returning home these students established and began teaching in the RUPP social work department in the fall of 2008 (University of Washington School of Social Work n.d.a).

As RUPP graduates its own baccalaureate students, more NGOs and the government will be able to employ trained social workers to work with their clients on many levels and with a keen sense of cultural sensitivity relevant to the indigenous population. Indeed, RUPP has recently drawn attention to social development by establishing the first social work training program in the country. The RUPP social work department has twelve social work faculty members and a field learning program manager, according to the University of Washington's School of Social Work's website (n.d.b).

The social work profession is beginning to be recognized in Phnom Penh with the establishment of the social work department at RUPP. It is likely that as students graduate in social work from RUPP, these alumni and social workers who were trained abroad will collaborate to form a professional social work association. In time it is anticipated that this professional association will become the recognized voice for the profession and will interface with the Cambodian government, NGOs, international organizations, and traditional social service institutions such as wats. There is much good the social work profession will be able perform in Cambodia.

This chapter examined social welfare in Cambodia from the Angkor Wat period to the present. We have seen the constant presence of assistance from family members and wats throughout the centuries. Poverty and human trafficking were discussed in the context of current strategies and programs. While statistics indicate that poverty is decreasing, it remains a serious problem, particularly in the provinces.

Today several thousand NGOs are the primary forces for social, educational, medical, health, employment, and training programs in Phnom Penh, and these services need to expand into the provinces. With recent political stability and steady economic growth, the future for government social welfare services looks promising but cautious in the shadows of corruption. The major social welfare stakeholders, government, NGOs, international aid, the social work profession, and social work academia, need to collaborate to enhance social development for the benefit of the people.

Future Perspectives

Currently the Cambodian government seems to be transitioning between prioritizing its efforts to build a strong economy and stabilize politics to improving infrastructure such as roads, water, and electricity. While corruption continues to exist in the government, and money can buy position, status, and services, there is hope that this can be curbed in the future through a concerted effort by the people through anticorruption laws. The U.S.$4 billion (16,079,999,999,918,082 KHR) national debt (Index Mundi 2011) is high and is about 30 percent of the gross domestic product while per capita income is low.

On the other hand, a successful confluence of three favorable aspects of the economy could result in a stronger fiscal position for the government and subsequent improved education, health, and living conditions for the people: first, the 6 percent economic growth from 1993 to 2003 and the 11 percent economic growth from 2004 to 2007 (Business-in-Asia 2008; United Nations in Cambodia n.d.); second, the government's intent to begin pumping oil and natural gas deposits from its territorial waters in December 2012 (*Straits Times* 2010); and third, the possibility of more bilateral and multilateral donors to fund pressing needs. A more honest government also may promote the country economically, socially, physically, and educationally (U.S. Department of State 2010).

NGOs need to remain in Cambodia, and the expansion of current NGOs and establishment of new NGOs in the provinces could empower the people to work toward social justice. Providing social work education at RUPP is an important step toward adding trained social workers to the field of social services in NGOs and the government. At some point a national organization of social workers is anticipated. As the economy becomes stronger, it is anticipated that health, education, and social development will also grow, and funds will be granted to the Ministry of Social Affairs for income and social service programs.

The economic status of the majority of Cambodians has been dismal; however, a look at the recent past suggests optimism for the future growth of the overall economy, particularly in the areas of textiles, tourism (CIA 2011; United Nations in Cambodia n.d.), oil, and natural gas. Additionally, GDP averaged almost 10 percent over the past decade. For Cambodia's urban population, this is heartening; however, the majority of the poor and extremely poor rural farmers are constrained by insufficient access to the market and to arable land.

While the Cambodian government has not prioritized the development of a social welfare system at this time, there is a plan to reduce poverty in the National Poverty Reduction Strategy (International Monetary Fund n.d.), and it is hoped that this will be a start for further services as the economy becomes more robust. The National Poverty Reduction Strategy outlines the government's plans to collaborate with NGOs by first establishing a viable economy that will then be able to support the much-needed public social welfare services.

The Cambodian government may want to consider enacting comprehensive legislation that more effectively combats human trafficking. Robust investigations should be conducted in departments and among government officials who allow or personally gain from criminal activities such as human trafficking. In addition, the government may choose to support the more traditional and indigenous social service efforts provided by extended family members, village elders, village chiefs, natural healers, and monks in the wats.

Indeed, it is essential that there be collaboration among good and honest governance at all levels, including the Ministry of Social Affairs, Veterans, and Youth Rehabilitation, trained social service providers in partnerships with NGOs and indigenous entities, and RUPP's social work program to address the social welfare needs of each Cambodian citizen. Cambodia has a brighter future as the economy expands, government is refined, social welfare progresses, and the social work profession develops. As one RUPP social work faculty member noted: "I hope social work education and the social work profession will grow as more young people learn and help restore our country and help build trust again in each other and in the country. They need to accept what happened in the past and work towards the future" (Ngoum 2010:1).

References

Administrator (2011a). "Psychosocial Services." Social Services of Cambodia, January 28. Retrieved November 11, 2010, from http://www.ssc.org.kh/index .php?option=com_content&view=article&id=108&Itemid=224&lang=en.

——— (2011b). "Sexual Assault Services." Social Services of Cambodia, January 26. Retrieved November 1, 2010, from http://www.ssc.org.kh/index.php? option=com_content&view=article&id=107&Itemid=223&lang=en/

——— (2011c). "The SSC Story Thus Far." Social Services of Cambodia, January 21. Retrieved November 14, 2010, from http://www.ssc.org.kh/index.php?option=com_content&view=article&id=101&Itemid=212&lang=en.

Business-in-Asia (2008). "Cambodia's Economic Growth." Retrieved November 21, 2011 from http://www.business-in-asia.com/cambodia/cambodia_constructions.html.

Cambodia Ministry of Social Affairs, Veterans, and Youth Rehabilitation (n.d.). *The Ministry of Social Affairs, Veterans, and Youth Rehabilitation Flow Chart.* Retrieved November 20, 2010, from http://mosvy.gov.kh/English/minister_english.php.

Cambodian Child and Hope Association (2011). *Cambodian Child and Hope Association—CCAHA—Poor Children & Orphans School Cambodia.* Retrieved October 20, 2010, from http://www.causes.com/causes/333190-cambodian-child-and-hope-association-ccaha-poor-children-orphans-school-cambodia/about

Cambodian League for the Promotion and Defense of Human Rights (LICADHO) (n.d.). *About Us.* Retrieved November 18, 2010, from http://www.licadho-cambodia.org/aboutus.php.

———. (2010a). "Cambodia Still Ranking Low on Corruption Index." *Cambodia Monthly News Summary—October 2010.* LICADHO, November 1. Retrieved December 4, 2010, from http://www.licadho-cambodia.org/articles/20101101/127/index.html.

——— (2010b). "UN Secretary General Ban Ki-moon Visits Cambodia." *Cambodia Monthly News Summary—October 2010.* LICADHO, November 1. Retrieved November 18, 2010, from http://www.licadho-cambodia.org/articles/20101101/127/index.html.

Central Intelligence Agency (n.d.). "East & Southeast Asia: Cambodia." In *The World Factbook.* Retrieved March 8, 2011, from http://cia.org/.

Chandler, D. P. (1991). *The Tragedy of Cambodian History.* New Haven: Yale University Press.

Coalition Against Trafficking in Women (2011). *Factbook on Global Sexual Exploitation: Cambodia.* Retrieved November 21, 2011 from http://www.uri.edu/artsci/wms/hughes/cambodia.htm.

Cooperation Committee for Cambodia (n.d.). "Who We Are." Retrieved February 9, 2011 from http://www.ccc-cambodia.org/.

Dateline NBC (2005). "Children for Sale: Undercover in Cambodia." Retrieved November 21, 2011, from http://www.msnbc.msn.com/id/4038249/#.TssDSVYVTTp).

End Child Prostitution, Abuse and Trafficking in Cambodia (2009–10a). "Petition Signature Collection During the Water Festival." Retrieved March 14, 2011, from http://www.ecpatcambodia.org/index.php.

——— (2009–10b). "Child Protection Tuk-tuk in Phnom Penh." Retrieved December 1, 2010, from http://www.ecpatcambodia.org/index.php.

——— (2009–10c). "Child Protection TukTuk in Sihanouk Province." Retrieved December 4, 2010, from http://www.ecpatcambodia.org/index.php.

Friends International (n.d.). "Myth and Realities About Orphanages in Cambodia." Retrieved November 21, 2011, from http://www.friends-international.org/resources/alternative-care/mythrealities_FINAL.pdf.

Global Organization of Parliamentarians Against Corruption (n.d.). "Corruption: Case in Cambodia." *South East Asian Parliamentarians Against Corruption— SEAPAC.* Retrieved February 16, 2011, from http://www.gopacnetwork.org/chapters/SEAPAC_chapter.htm.

Global Witness (2010). "New Cambodian Anti-corruption Plan Will Not Stop High-Level Offenders." Retrieved October 12, 2010, from http://www.globalwitness.org/library/new-cambodian-anti-corruption-plan-will-not-stop-high-level-offenders.

Index Mundi (2011). "Historical Data Graphs per Year: Cambodia, Economy Debt-External." Retrieved on November 21, 2011, from http://www.indexmundi.com/g/g.aspx?c=cb&v=94.

International Monetary Fund (n.d.). "Cambodia: National Poverty Reduction Strategy." Retrieved February 7, 2011, from http://www.imf.org/external/np/prsp/2002/khm/01/.

——— (2006). "Cambodia: Poverty Reduction Strategy Paper." *International Monetary Fund Country Report,* no. 06/266. Retrieved from http://www.imf.org.

——— (2011a). "Cambodia: 2010 Article IV Consultation—Staff Report." *International Monetary Fund Country Report,* no. 11/45. Retrieved November 21, 2011, from http://www.imf.org/external/pubs/ft/scr/2011/cr1145.pdf.

——— (2011b). "World Economic Outlook: GDP Based on PPP per Capita GDP." Retrieved November 21, 2011, from http://www.google.com/publicdata/explore?ds=k3s92bru78li6_&ctype=l&strail=false&bcs=d&nselm=h&met_y=ppppc#ctype=l&strail=false&bcs=d&nselm=h&met_y=ppppc&scale_y=lin&ind_y=false&rdim=country_group&idim=country_group:001&idim=country:KH:CN:HK:ID:MY:WS:TW:TH:KR&ifdim=country_group:parent:&hl=en&dl=en.

King, G. (2004). *Woman, Child, for Sale: The New Slave Trade in the 21st Century.* New York: Chamberlain Brothers Pub.

Monireth, T. (2011). Personal interview, November 21.

NGO Forum (2011a). "List of the NGO Forum on Cambodia's Memberships." NGO Forum on Cambodia. Retrieved October 12, 2010, from http://www.ngoforum.org.kh/eng/core/sublistmembership.php.

——— (2011b). "Introduction." NGO Forum on Cambodia. Retrieved October 15, 2010, from http://www.ngoforum.org.kh/eng/core/introduction.php.

Ngoum, S. (2010). Personal interview, Phnom Penh, March 12.

Office of Electronic Information (2011). *Background Note: Cambodia.* Retrieved November 4, 2010, from http://www.gopacnetwork.org/chapters/SEAPAC_chapter.html.

Radio Free Asia (2011). *"Cambodia: ADB Unveils Poverty-Reducing Strategy."* July 7. Retrieved November 18, 2011, from http://www.unhcr.org/refworld/docid/4e23 f48529.html.

Padeken, A. (2011). Personal interview, September 29.

Shawcross, W. (1985). *The Quality of Mercy: Cambodia, Holocaust and Modern Conscience.* New York: Simon and Schuster.

Steinberg, D. J. (1959). *Cambodia: Its People, Its Society, Its Culture.* New Haven: Human Relations Area Files Press.

Straits Times (2010). "Cambodia to Pump Oil in 2012." *Straits Times:* A Singapore press holding website, July 1. Retrieved November 13, 2010, from http://www .straitstimes.com/BreakingNews/SEAsia/Story/STIStory_548327.html.

Tabitha Cambodia (n.d.). "About the Tabitha Foundation." Tabitha Foundation Canada. Retrieved October 25, 2010, from http://www.tabitha.ca/about.html

Transparency International (2010). "Corruption Perceptions Index 2010." Transparency International: The Global Coalition Against Corruption. Retrieved December 20, 2010, from http://www.transparency.org/policy_research/surveys_ indices/cpi/2010/results.

UNICEF (2010). "Cambodia: Statistics." Retrieved July 17, 2010, from http://www .unicef.org/infobycountry/cambodia_statistics.html.

United Nations in Cambodia (n.d.). "Cambodia: Country Information." Retrieved November 11, 2010, from http://www.un.org.kh/index.php?option=com_conten t&view=article&id=47&Itemid=66.

United Nations in Cambodia Economic Growth and Poverty Reduction (n.d.). Retrieved August 17, 2010, from http://www.un.org.kh/index.php?option=com_co ntent&view=article&id=47&Itemid=66.

United States Department of State (2010). *Trafficking in Persons Report 2010.* U.S. Department of State: Diplomacy in Action. Retrieved October 14, 2010, from http://www.state.gov/g/tip/rls/tiprpt/2010/.

——— (2011). *Trafficking in Persons Report 2011.* U.S. Department of State: Diplomacy in Action. Retrieved November 21, 2011, from http://www.state.gov/g/tip/ rls/tiprpt/2011/.

University of Washington School of Social Work (n.d.a). "First Class of Social Work Students in Cambodia Finish Their Freshman Year." Retrieved March 14,2011, from http://depts.washington.edu/sswweb/rupp/updates.html.

——— (n.d.b). "Royal University of Phnom Penh and University of Washington Social Work Partnership." Retrieved March 14, 2011, from http://depts .washington.edu/sswweb/rupp/facstaff.html.

Vickery, M. (1988). "Correspondence." *Bulletin of Concerned Asian Scholars* 20 (1): 73.

World Health Organization (2011). *Cambodia: Statistics.* Retrieved November 21, 2011, from http://www.who.int/countries/khm/en/.

Yasunobu, T. (2004). "Combating Human Trafficking in Cambodia: Establishing a Legal Environment for the Effective Counter Trafficking Measure." Ms, May 1. Heller School of Social Policy and Management, Brandeis University, Boston.

Yorn, S. (2011). Personal interview, January 20.

12

Social Welfare Contrasted in East Asia and the Pacific

SHARLENE B. C. L. FURUTO

This final chapter analyzes and compares social welfare in Cambodia, China, Hong Kong SAR, Indonesia, Malaysia, the Micronesian region, South Korea, Samoa and American Samoa, Taiwan, and Thailand. The many similarities and differences among them, beginning with the histories of social welfare in these political entities, have resulted in a number of intriguing components in their social welfare systems today. The chapter also discusses some thriving indigenous social service models that the local populations have accepted and that could be considered for implementation in the United States and Europe. The chapter ends with a discussion of future social welfare challenges.

Comparison of Social Welfare

Historical events laid the foundation for and influenced the direction of social development in East Asia and the Pacific. The lands and islands discussed in this book, except for China and Thailand, were colonized (usually by European countries), exploited, and subjected to similar experiences that resulted in barriers to their social welfare development.

Colonization and Social Welfare History

All the islands in the Pacific were colonized by European countries except for the Kingdom of Tonga. From the 1700s and well into the 1800s,

England, Germany, France, Japan, and the United States laid claim to or occupied the Pacific Islands. After exploiting the islanders and nearly decimating their populations with the introduction of new diseases and superior weapons, the new motherland failed to provide for the health and educational needs of the local people. Today ethnic Samoans and Micronesians, along with other Pacific Islanders, are disadvantaged, oppressed groups. Social services for these beleaguered groups are uneven at best and lacking at worst.

The Asian political states reviewed in this book, except for China and Thailand, were former colonies of France, the United Kingdom, the Netherlands, or were occupied by Japan. Like their counterparts in the Pacific, the exploited Asians also suffered and were subjugated economically, politically, socially, and emotionally. Asians and Pacific Islanders have been attempting to catch up from this disadvantaged position with varying levels of success. Cambodia, Indonesia, the Micronesian region, and Samoa are not faring well economically, while Hong Kong SAR, Taiwan, and South Korea continue to improve their standards of living.

These many colonies eventually moved toward independence, and today Indonesia, South Korea, and Samoa are republics; American Samoa, Cambodia, Hong Kong SAR, and Taiwan are democracies; Malaysia and Thailand also are democracies but with constitutional monarchies; some islands in the Micronesian region have a constitutional government in free association with the United States; and China is Communist. When the United Kingdom turned Hong Kong over to China in 1997, Hong Kong was made a Special Administrative Region with continued self-governance and a capitalist economic system. Today, Hong Kong SAR continues to enjoy autonomy and many freedoms and overtly seems to have changed little. Most people in East Asia and the Pacific Islands appear free to express their opinions and opposition against government policies, except perhaps for the Cambodians and the Chinese, where memories of past incidents may restrain their present voices. Concern about government retaliation, among many other reasons, may have resulted in the people of Cambodia and China enjoying fewer social welfare programs and benefits today. The overall development of a country and the development of social welfare seem to be better established in the countries whose government is more honest, economically stable, fiscally sound, and social-policy-oriented, among other attributes.

While all the countries studied have progressed in the last hundred years, perhaps today there is a new form of repression that might be called "colonization of the social work profession." The profession of social work started in Europe before moving to North America in the early 1900s. Since then, many international social work students have learned about social work in European and U.S. classrooms, and this perspective accompanies international students who return home. In Europe and the United States, little, if any, tribute is given to social work knowledge, models, paradigms, or indigenous practices from Asia and the Pacific. Until these countries further develop their own indigenous models and publish their findings, European and U.S. domination will continue in the field of social work, even with the best of intentions. This book has not only allowed more Asian and Pacific Island colleagues to be heard but also provided the opportunity to contrast social welfare in these regions.

Cultures and Values

The Asian and Pacific Island cultures seem to be more similar to each other than to cultures in Europe and the United States. There is archaeological, genetic, and linguistic evidence that points toward the majority of Polynesians originating from Southeast Asia about six thousand years ago. Arguably many cultural aspects of Asia and the Pacific have become Westernized; nevertheless, Asians and Pacific Islanders in general continue to demonstrate strong adherence to their core values of filial piety and male preference. In ancient times Confucius taught that filial piety, a respect for one's parents and ancestors, is the virtue to be held above all others. Filial piety means to be good to one's parents by taking care of them and to perform sacrifices for one's ancestors to ensure an honorable name for the family. Pacific Islanders also feel a strong desire and responsibility to respect and care for their parents, as is evidenced by the scarcity of care homes in the Pacific.

A second significant value in Asia, and to a noticeably lesser degree in the Pacific, is to prefer and reward males over females. In poorer Asian families, boy babies and young boys are more likely to be given preferential treatment in terms of food, education, and health care. The oldest son usually inherits his family's farm or business, works hard to support his parents, produces an heir to carry on the family name, and later cares for his aging parents through the efforts of his wife. A young woman, conversely, loses her value to her biological family when she marries and moves into her in-laws' home. The 1979 one-child or family-planning policy in China, which restricts urban married couples to one child while allowing rural couples to apply for approval to have a second child, often further solidifies this value.

Male preference is also evident in the Pacific, where the many societies are patriarchal and men are valued for their roles and responsibilities as chiefs, title holders, physical laborers, protectors or warriors, inheritors of land use, and, through their wives, caregivers for aging extended family members. On the other hand, certain customs in the Pacific, such as the importance of the *fahu*, or oldest sister, in the Tongan family and recent bestowals of chief titles to women in American Samoa and Samoa, do give formal recognition and respect to some women.

Social Welfare Issues and Professional and Traditional Responses

The East Asian and Pacific regions face a number of social welfare issues, some of which all political entities share to some extent, and others that seem to be more localized. Three social issues that bind the East Asian nations more than those of the Pacific Islands are poverty, child welfare, and aging. In addition to these three issues, there are other serious local problems, such as human trafficking, discrimination, health, conflict with neighboring nations, and undocumented laborers.

Poverty

Poverty is a serious problem in East Asia and the Pacific. The contributors to this book indicate that poverty is an issue in Cambodia, China, Hong Kong SAR, Indonesia, and South Korea (where the poverty rate has increased dramatically since 2000), while data from the CIA *World Factbook* (2011) and the International Monetary Fund may lead some to add Thailand, the Micronesian region, and Samoa. The *World Factbook* ranks Cambodia at 187 (when compared with other countries in terms of their gross domestic product per person), the Federated States of Micronesia at 159,

Indonesia at 154, Samoa at 143, China at 125, and Thailand at 118. Of the nations discussed in this book, only Hong Kong SAR, Taiwan, and South Korea, which are ranked at 12, 33, and 44, respectively, seem to have much higher incomes per capita. Malaysia ranks in about the middle, and American Samoa is not ranked at all. Most observers would consider poverty to be a problem in American Samoa.

Poverty is perceived differently across East Asia and the Pacific. In East Asian states many observers in the cities and urban areas do not readily witness extensive poverty until they travel to the countryside. In the rural parts of Cambodia, Indonesia, China, and Thailand, sometimes entire villages fall below the poverty level. Many homes are small, sparsely furnished, and without electricity or potable running water. Poor people living in countries without strong government social programs depend instead on their clan and neighbors, who may also be poor, and on local traditional means for assistance.

Cambodia. Since the 1970s Cambodia has been devastated by the U.S. war, by genocide and Pol Pot, and by the war with the Viet Cong of Vietnam until 1991. Since then, the Cambodian government has been focusing primarily on the economy rather than on education, health, and social welfare. While the economy is improving owing to the garment and tourism industries, the government does not yet sponsor any major antipoverty program on a large-scale basis. Family, NGOs in Phnom Penh, indigenous health healers, and the local temples or wats seem to provide the minimal public social services available. Two potential natural resources for government revenue are extracting oil deposits from Cambodia's territorial waters and mining bauxite, gold, iron, and gems from the north. As corruption is curbed, the government will be able to begin to address poverty.

Hong Kong SAR. While Hong Kong SAR has long been incredibly successful economically and the wealthy are very prosperous, more recently the disparity between well-to-do people and low-income people has been worsening at an alarming rate, as discussed in chapter 4. In 2005 there were 1.22 million low-income families in Hong Kong SAR out of a population of nearly 7 million. Ten years earlier there were 890,000 low-income people. The unemployment rate has also been increasing as more factories move to China and deindustrialization continues. The Comprehensive Social Security Assistance Scheme is available for low-income people who have lived in Hong Kong SAR for at least seven years and, if able-bodied adults, are seeking employment. Those with severe disabilities or those over age 65 may qualify for the Social Security Allowance Scheme by show-ing documentation of disability and seven-year residency.

Indonesia. Indonesia, like Cambodia, suffered for decades with eco-nomic crises, political instability, natural disasters, and corruption after gaining independence in 1945 from Japan. Regional separation has also made it difficult for the leadership to unite. Today about 48 percent of the population falls below the poverty level, according to chapter 5. Those with low income may apply for the government Cash Transfer Assistance Pro-gram for financial help or the Hope Family Program for a conditional cash transfer through the bank or post office.

Indonesia is reported to have had a growing economy since at least 2007, leading one to surmise that government services should begin to be more readily available; however, the contrary seems to exist, due in part to corruption continuing in the government. Today Transparency Interna-tional ranks Indonesia relatively high on its corruption scale (at 110 out of 178 countries), a position well above the majority of other nations. Mauro (1995) implied that corruption had a negative correlation with government spending for social programs. Indonesians, like the people of Cambodia, China, and Thailand, seem to be victims of corrupt leaders.

China. Politics in China has had a great impact on the poor sector. Losses incurred from the Chinese Civil War, which ended in 1949, and the Cultural Revolution of 1966–76 caused serious setbacks in social develop-ment and thrust millions into poverty. Corruption in China's past perhaps has kept the government from making social services available to poor people. It is interesting that China is ranked 78 by Transparency Interna-tional (2011).

The social issue of poverty in China is similar to its counterparts in Cambodia, Indonesia, and Thailand in that most poor people live in the countryside. In addition, a disproportionately large number of poor people reside in western China, near the deserts and away from rivers and the coastline. Most poor people today are farmers who lost their land because of industrialization or urbanization, are migrant workers living in cities, or are former workers now laid off from their jobs. There are very few social welfare programs for poor people in the vast rural areas, and these people are left to depend on themselves, their clan, and the other villagers for help.

Thailand. Thailand has had fewer human travesties when compared to Cambodia, Indonesia, and China, since it neither was colonized nor ever engaged in a civil war and has had only a few wars with its neighbors; however, Thailand's twelve coups d'état in the last seventy years, internal political conflicts, and corruption have disrupted social development. In the recent past the political situation in Thailand has been undergoing rapid changes, and much more change is expected to occur.

Fortunately Thailand has had generous, benevolent kings who have been involved in caring for their subjects. Furthermore Thailand is strengthened by its abundant agricultural and natural resources and the benefits of having had democracy for a number of years. While only an estimated 9.6 percent of the population in 2006 was considered poor, the gap between the wealthy and the poor in Thailand is large and growing, similar to the situation in Hong Kong SAR.

Since 2009 the living allowance for aging people has expanded, and a living allowance for persons with disabilities has been initiated. While the Thai economy is favorable and its poverty rate is bearable, an expansion and addition of social programs could better address the huge wage gap between the rich and the poor. The social welfare outlook for Thailand is encouraging, but much of the future depends on the outcome of the current political situation.

The Pacific Islands. While the International Monetary Fund and the *World Factbook* (2011) may rank Samoa, the Federated States of Micronesia, Palau, and the Marshall Islands between 122 and 183 in terms of poverty when compared with other countries, very few Pacific Islanders consider themselves to be poor. Traditionally much of the land in the Pacific was not purchased but rather used by the subjects of the ruler. Today most families continue to be land stewards rather than owners, use the land for crop farming, sell their produce in the local open markets, and use that income for small purchases. Costly expenses are often funded by remittances from family members living abroad. More European-style homes are found throughout the Pacific, although some homes are made from plant fronds. Pacific Islanders believe there are no poor in the islands. Rather, they believe that having food from their farms and the ocean, thatched or European-style homes, and clothing exonerate them from the Western concept of poverty. Not having a paid job is not necessarily a predicament since that person may be needed to care for grandparents and the farm, and remittances from family members working abroad come regularly. Everyone in the family, whether living abroad or locally, has a responsibility to the family members living in the islands despite distance and time.

The Micronesian nations that have political agreements with the United States (Palau, the Federated States of Micronesia, the Marshall Islands, Guam, and the Northern Mariana Islands) and the U.S. territories of American Samoa and Guam have access to most U.S. social welfare programs. The two income programs—Temporary Assistance for Needy Families and Supplemental Security Income—are designated for low-income families and seniors and people with disabilities, respectively.

While the Pacific Islanders from Samoa and people of the Micronesian region may not consider themselves to be poor, from the European and Western perspective they have low incomes, receive poor medical and dental care, consume a less nutritious diet, live in shelters that lack some basic amenities, attend marginal schools, have few opportunities for jobs with advancement potential, and so on. In the final analysis, Pacific Islanders continue to seek help first from their kin abroad and then from their villagers and church members.

Other political entities also provide social programs for low-income populations. Malaysia has social assistance and financial schemes for low-income families, needy children, older persons, and people with disabilities. South Korea is able to fund financial assistance and subsidies in education, medical services, emergency funding, and public housing for families, women and children, and people with disabilities. In Taiwan there is assistance for low-income families, orphans, elderly people, people with disabilities, and those who are unable to work.

Common causes of poverty. Poverty is a complex social issue present in all nations in some form and to some degree. Poverty is perhaps the most dominant, fundamental base condition contributing to the many derivative social ills and bears further scrutiny. In analyzing East Asian and Pacific states that are seriously affected by poverty, several common factors seem to stunt the social welfare development of a country and magnify the poverty level and needs of the people:

- Human travesties such as colonization, war, cultural revolution, genocide, and coups d'état
- Political leadership characterized as being corrupt, autocratic, authoritarian, or ineffective
- Economic stagnation due to untapped natural resources, a minimal private sector, insufficient jobs, and inadequate international trade agreements

- Barriers such as rural, isolated locations with few opportunities for education and health care, and negligible services

Conditions for alleviating poverty. In contrast, political entities that have the following characteristics and conditions seem to eventually offer a number of social welfare programs and services:

- Fewer travesties that happened in the distant past, or people who are better able to make a significant comeback from hardships such as civil war
- Strong, honest political leaders functioning in a stable government who give primacy to the interests of the nation and its people
- Government collaboration with NGOs and the private sector for the benefit of the people
- A vibrant economy with a growing private sector that results in more exports than imports
- More opportunities and services available to those living in rural, isolated areas

Child Welfare

Cambodia. A large percentage of Cambodian children are vulnerable to an array of problems: poverty, hunger, malnutrition, poor health, glue sniffing, sex trafficking, prostitution, forced labor, abandonment, lack of education, homelessness, abuse, begging, separation from parents and family, and so forth. Hundreds of waifs readily live in city dumps or on the streets until they die from exposure or worse. The lucky ones who live in any of the dozens of overcrowded orphanages receive food, clothes, and an education. A number of children with one or two parents are in orphanages because their parents are unable to feed them.

The year 2000 was encouraging as the government took the initiative to no longer grant visas to suspected child-sex tourists and to place a moratorium on adoptions owing to a one-third increase in adoptions between 1999 and 2000. This suspension allows the adoption process and almost nonexistent adoption laws to be reviewed; however, many believe that bribe money is being collected from hopeful adoptive parents. So far it seems that the government has been bypassing its children, particularly when it spends 40 percent of its budget on the armed forces and less than 10 percent on welfare programs (*Economist* 2000). Local and international NGOs are responsible for the care of most disadvantaged Cambodian children.

China. China has a unique child welfare situation. While the one-child policy has prevented four hundred million births, it has also introduced a network of problems that may worsen with time: illegal abortions, abandonment of female babies, orphanages populated essentially only with girls, an imbalance in the sex ratio, a low fertility rate, and now an inadequate number of brides and therefore wives and subsequent children. Incidents of bride or wife kidnapping have been reported.

Hong Kong SAR. In 2003 Hong Kong SAR responded to increases in child abuse and domestic violence by initiating a service delivery model that provides a continuum of preventive, supportive, and remedial services for families. Specialized services address child custody and guardianship disputes through outreach, investigation, early intervention, statutory protection, casework, and group work. Hong Kong SAR also provides robust comprehensive and integrated services at residential centers and schools.

Indonesia. Indonesia has more than seventy-six million children and approximately 20 percent are neglected or neglect-prone. Other major problems for children as reported by in chapter 5 include child prostitution and child sex trafficking in foreign countries, drug abuse, street children, and juvenile delinquency.

The national health care network does make available district medical centers, community and village health centers, and local community medical facilities, but there needs to be an expansion from offering medical programs to offering social welfare programs as well. In order for children to be safe, healthy, and educated, there is a need for changes in policies, initiation of programs focused on direct services to children and their families and communities, and a decrease in corruption.

Malaysia. Child abandonment and the tripartite problem of premarital sex–teen pregnancy–HIV/AIDS infection are notable problems in Malaysia. Baby dumping is a new issue in Malaysia, and chapter 6 indicates that this number is increasing. Baby abandonment, while illegal, may be done to avoid the social stigma of having a baby prior to marriage rather than to avoid paying costly government penalties as in China. As many as 60 percent of Malaysian teenagers, who are often without accurate sex education, engage in sexual activity on the average of 135 times a year. Most of these teenagers engage in unprotected sex and risk pregnancy and sexually transmitted diseases such as HIV/AIDS.

The government is concerned about abandoned babies, and perhaps with the recently established NGO Baby Hatch program, the lives of more babies will be preserved. Poster exhibits, mass media, and road shows are used to disseminate information about programs for moms and babies throughout the cities. NGOs actively sponsor seminars, workshops, and talks about sex information; the government and NGOs underwrite centers for unwed pregnant mothers; and Café-at-Teen centers highlight teens educating their peers about reproduction. Offering sex education in schools and establishing special schools for unwed pregnant teenagers are issues being debated now.

The Micronesian region. Micronesian children are affected by the fragmented and transformed indigenous kinship and family structures. Children learn to depend on U.S. government social welfare programs, experience stress moving from a matrilineal history to having the father as the nuclear household head, and migrate for economic opportunities or become part of the working poor. Health problems adults encounter, such as cancer, diabetes, heart disease, stroke, sexually transmitted diseases, and obesity, are awaiting the children. As the young people migrate abroad for educational and economic opportunities and as many elderly people move into the islands, the aging population is increasing. Children were expected to see social problems emerge from the U.S. military moving into Guam and thus increasing the island population by 30–40 percent by 2014.

Most Micronesian governments, with little tax monies and few philanthropists, do not have the fiduciary ability to provide costly social and health programs that can help children and families transition to independence and better health. Those political entities in the Micronesian region that have ties to the United States do have access to many social welfare benefits and services. By far the most stable, most competent, and strongest providers of social welfare in the Micronesian area are the familial and kinship networks. They work the farm in the islands and they work abroad and send remittances across the Pacific, according to chapter 7.

Samoa and American Samoa. The people of Samoa and American Samoa are like their Pacific neighbors in the Micronesian region in that they do not believe they are poor. Their cell phones may not have the largest capacities, but they may debate their poverty label. Samoa has chosen to help its poor children by partially funding selected NGOs, a practice implemented in Hong Kong SAR, Hawaii, and many other lands. These NGOs then provide direct services to the Samoan people in their villages.

American Samoa, in contrast, has access to programs funded by the U.S. federal government, such as Temporary Assistance to Needy Children, Medicaid, and the Federal Emergency Management Agency following natural disasters. Traditional healers are used in both Samoa and American Samoa, and the United States does offer partial compensation for sick people who need to be treated abroad. Some have asked the same question facing Micronesians: "Are the federal programs a fair trade for American Samoans?"

South Korea. Delinquent acts such as assault, peer victimization, fighting, sexual violence, gang involvement, homicide, and suicide have been increasing recently in South Korea. The government has responded by establishing counseling centers nationwide to help combat juvenile delinquency. Many school districts have implemented school-based intervention and prevention programs. Bullying-prevention and suicide-prevention programs have been developed and implemented, and a limited number of school districts have also hired school social workers.

Taiwan, Hong Kong SAR, and South Korea. Taiwan, Hong Kong SAR, and South Korea share the serious problem of having a low birthrate. The Taiwanese birthrate, which has been declining since 1950, was estimated to be 8.99 births per 1,000 in 2011 (CIA 2011). This low birthrate ranks Taiwan at 211 in comparison to the world, while South Korea is 216 and Hong Kong SAR is 220. Birthrates in these regions are low for many reasons, including a declining marriage rate and inadequate economic conditions. It appears that if the birthrate does not increase for Taiwan, there may be problems in the military service, marriage, and taxes to fund services for the rapidly growing aging population. Government enticements such as waiving hospital birth fees, childbirth allowances, tax breaks, and subsidized day care do not seem sufficient to entice an increase in the birthrate in these locations.

Thailand. To boost the national economy and encourage consumerism, the government and private enterprises continue to target the younger generation in Thailand. Teenagers are encouraged to purchase cell phones, motorcycles, clothing fads, fast food, and so on, and while some youth can afford it, a large number cannot. Peer pressure is strong, and there is growing concern that adolescents may be turning to prostitution, an open door to becoming pregnant, dropping out of school, being a single parent, or marrying at a very young age. Juvenile delinquency has been increasing in recent years in Thailand.

While some political entities address their child welfare issues in a somewhat comprehensive manner, others are not able to do so. The senior population also faces a number of challenges.

Aging

Almost all political entities discussed in this volume are addressing changing demographics and preparing for the millions of baby boomers who are beginning to retire and require more services, except perhaps for Cambodia. The Cambodian government is not keenly focused on the universal aging issue. Instead, Cambodian families will continue to care for their seniors, and some older people without families will find refuge in the wats, while others will resort to begging. China has been rebuilding homes, expanding the old-age pension, and improving the pension system in rural areas. Hong Kong SAR's aging-in-place policy is supported by neighborhood elderly centers, day-care centers, nursing homes, and residential services. The Indonesian government passed a law in 1998 that promotes age-friendly communities and bans age discrimination, and a 2009 law provides care for bedridden, poor, and neglected seniors.

South Korea has financial and medical services, public housing, and shelters available for the older population. Seniors in Taiwan can apply for home care, nursing homes, group homes, day care, respite for caregivers, community care stations, meals on wheels, assistive devices, support groups, and barrier-free home improvements as part of the 2007 ten-year plan for long-term care. Additional services in Taiwan include helping elderly people file lawsuits, installing emergency buttons or communication devices in homes, simulating for the general population daily inconveniences older people encounter, and telephone greeting services. Local government organizations in Thailand provide care for elderly people, and monthly subsidies are available to them. Family caring for older people at home is less possible in Thailand because many adult children work away from home.

Other Social Problems

The chapters also mention a number of other social challenges in East Asia and the Pacific. Cambodia and Thailand both suffer from sex trafficking and loss of life and property during the monsoon season. In Hong Kong SAR, Indonesia, South Korea, and Thailand, there is discrimination against immigrant workers from China, Indonesia, Vietnam, the Philippines, and Bangladesh. Meanwhile, in the Pacific, Micronesian and Samoan youths and young adults migrate from the outlying islands to the main islands for education and employment opportunities. The job seekers, crowding the cities and unable to find employment, often migrate abroad to New Zealand, Australia, or the United States to secure employment and be able to send remittances to family members remaining back home in the islands. Micronesians in the Bikini and Enewetok atolls, after having had sixty-seven nuclear bombs detonated on their islands by the United States, still cannot return to their islands and surrounding seas and instead die from unusually high rates of cancer and thyroid problems. Climate change or global warming may be causing the ocean water to rise, submerging the perimeters of islands and forcing Pacific Islanders to vacate their atolls when brackish water floods their farmland.

Incredibly, in 2009, 42 percent of Taiwan's population had an undergraduate or higher degree. A social challenge for Taiwan is unemployment and poverty of the educated. Currently there is corruption and extreme political unrest in Thailand, where ninety-one people died and more than two thousand were injured in the 2010 riots against huge wealth disparities and the gross misuse of political power.

There are calls for political advocacy in a number of nations. In Indonesia there is a growing demand for social and political participation, Micronesian colleagues are demonstrating against the military buildup entering Guam during the next four years, and Thai social workers are advised to fight for their professional positions or lose them. In addition, all political entities are threatened by terrorism and global warming or climate change. Social workers in East Asia and the Pacific must continue to work to identify successful paradigms and models for practice to address these issues.

Successful Practice Models

While "it is difficult to formulate a model for the progressive development of Asian-Pacific entities" (Mohan 2008:7), there are some practice models that have been used successfully in the nations discussed here, including the following:

- The strong familial and kinship systems in the Micronesian region, Samoa, American Samoa, Cambodia, Indonesia, and Thailand in particular, where family members actively help one another in the form of labor, goods, or money
- The indigenous *chenchule'* practice in the Micronesian region, a support system of exchange in which families express their care, concern, and obligation to help each other with food, labor, money, and so on
- The indigenous healers and helpers such as astrologers, priests, and clever men in Indonesia; acupressure, feng shui, fortune-telling, acupuncture, cupping, herbalism, and ancestor worship in China; amulets, village chiefs and healers, elders, and monks in Cambodia; and chiefs in the Pacific
- The temples in Cambodia and Thailand with food and shelter for seniors and others and occupational and medical care, drug programs, or care for HIV/AIDS last-stage patients and their orphaned children
- The communal self-help practices in Indonesia and Malaysia, *gotong royong* (which leads to cooperation in work, politics, and personal relations) and *tolong-menolong* (reciprocal assistance to complete community tasks such as maintaining rural roads, irrigation facilities, natural disasters, mutual help for home construction, and labor or funding to support important ceremonies)
- The self-help community organizations and self-reliant welfare services that collaborate with the Thai government Community Organizations Development Institute to establish cooperative stores, dams, clinics, radio stations, schools, income-generating groups, agricultural-processing facilities, and so on
- Community-based welfare banking schemes where the community saves for a welfare expenditure (such as medical care, education scholarship, funeral donation) that the Thai government matches

- The private enterprises in South Korea, Taiwan, and Thailand that partner with their respective governments to establish welfare programs and provide employment opportunities for people with low income
- The Hong Kong SAR government's comprehensive and integrated school-based and center-based model, which enhances the social, educational, cultural, and physical development of young people
- The aging-in-place approach to serving seniors with an array of services in Hong Kong SAR
- China's social welfare system, one of the basic aspects of the socialist market economic system
- Tax-reduction incentives in Thailand that target businesses and communities for delivering social services and for making social welfare expenditures (such as donations for educational purposes or for managing the firm's child-care center), hiring people with disabilities, and supporting income-generating and other social welfare projects.

Analysis of Social Welfare Systems

The social welfare development of a political entity varies according to a number of factors, including historical travesties, questionable and dishonest government officials, quantity and quality of natural resources, the financial ability to access and export these resources, the economy, presence of NGOs, and rural or urban settings.

States that have suffered a number of major travesties over an extended period of time in the last half-century or longer seem to still be recovering from those barriers to development. For example, Cambodia, China, Indonesia, and Malaysia, stymied because of years of civil war, world wars, neighbor wars, genocide, a cultural revolution, economic crises, and so forth, still wrestle today with inadequate social welfare services. Negative political influences and corruption have kept international donations and local monies from funding social welfare programs in Cambodia, Thailand, and Indonesia.

Social welfare seems to be more prominent in the regions that are more economically developed and thus better able to sponsor social programs.

The Thai, Hong Kong SAR, South Korean, and Taiwanese governments, followed by Malaysia and Thailand, have been able to access and export their natural resources and have taxes paid to the government, thus making it possible to initiate and finance numerous social welfare programs for all ages. Parts of the Micronesian region and American Samoa have access to most of the social welfare programs available in the United States. China is in an encouraging position economically but seems to be taking the policy approach rather than the direct-services approach to meeting the needs of its 1.3 billion people. The Cambodian and Indonesian governments perhaps offer the fewest social welfare programs and services in East Asia and the Pacific. The Samoan government contracts out its social service programs to NGOs.

While early NGOs were often church-based when they entered the colonized land to "help the natives," today many are not. Thousands of NGOs are present in Cambodia and Indonesia. The many NGOs that are centralized in Phnom Penh and Jakarta are perhaps the result of need and substitute for the government's low profile in providing social services. Cambodian and Indonesian farmers living in the countryside, where few NGOs are present, rely on their families, clans, villages, and indigenous models for help. Samoa also has a large number of NGOs because the government has chosen to contract out these services rather than provide them. On the other hand, Hong Kong SAR, as an NGO-based region, has the social welfare structures in place to accommodate well-established and stable social service agencies that are committed to human welfare. These NGOs render more than 90 percent of the social welfare services and provide three thousand service units throughout the geographically small Hong Kong SAR.

Social welfare seems to be well developed in the tiger political entities of Hong Kong SAR, South Korea, and Taiwan. These regions have a large number and wide variety of programs for all ages and many needs. These three locations have been at relative peace for the last fifty years, have stable governments and for the most part honest leaders, and have various natural resources and industries that generate income for their governments through taxation. The generally well-educated labor force is engaged in professional, service, and industrial employment and pays taxes that underwrite social welfare, education, and health programs. Conversely, Cambodians and Indonesians, in particular, and Samoans to a lesser degree, tend to rely on family, clan, village, and indigenous healers for assistance with social and medical difficulties because their nations as yet do not have similar services.

Macro Comparison of the East Asian and Pacific Region with the Developed West

Governments and politics in the region, with the monarchies and assorted types of democracies, seem to be just as varied as those in the economically developed West. One major difference, however, is the corruption level and sometimes open disregard for human rights of some Asian nations. Corruption, including government officials who keep international aid for personal use rather than public distribution, in all probability retards the overall progress of a nation, including its social development.

The economy in nations discussed in this volume is based more on agriculture than on industry, services, and information as in the West. The majority of the people in East Asia and the Pacific Islands are farmers living in somewhat homogeneous villages, many of which can be considered to be isolated. The farmers are stable, and when their land is devastated by natural disasters, the options for assistance are limited to kin, tribe, and village.

Formal social welfare programs are generally not available to the farmers or majority of the population. On the other hand, perhaps for many farmers their greatest asset is their relationships with other people. Each person belongs to a clan, tribe, village, and church, and these ties are often strong and loyal. Mutual assistance and relationships with many others empower the survivors of hardship and disasters. The majority of the people in these countries are highly developed socially, and villagers are actively engaged in communal projects, civil dynamics, and civic involvement as they care for one another and their community.

Social work in the West, on the other hand, can be described as a highly democratized, institutionalized machine with policies, programs, and organizations that make up a bureaucracy. Social welfare systems often are well developed, and programs frequently are available to both the urban and rural poor. While the developed Western families may live in cities or rural areas, they are not grounded to the earth owing to mobile employment in industry, services, or information. This mobility can be part of the social demise of many families in the developed West.

Indeed, many would believe that families in most of the nations studied have fewer opportunities for "a good education, adequate health, and medical and social services" than their counterparts in the developed West. On the other hand, others would prize the depth of an education steeped in the culture, ethnicity, and traditions of one's forefathers; value the curing powers of herbs, massage, and ceremonies practiced by traditional healers; and trust the unwavering collective sources of help from kin, clan, villagers, and chiefs.

For most of these states and their people, values, and behaviors, it seems that the macro social work practice approach may be more effective than the micro or mezzo levels of practice. Some governments are in the process of passing laws that better protect the vulnerable children, aging, and poor. Government and NGOs also seem to be making a difference in people's lives as they provide education for improving health; community mutual assistance projects for building homes and installing wells; microfinance for allowing mothers-turned-entrepreneurs to feed and educate their children; and joint projects with traditional healers that help to treat the physically and mentally sick. Many macro projects in these areas are atypical of those in the developed West.

Development of Social Work Education

The first social work education programs in the political entities discussed in this book were established in 1922 at Yanjing University in Beijing and Hujiang University in Shanghai. In 1952 they were closed until they began reopening in 1984. The other early social work education programs began in South Korea (in 1947 at Ewha Womans University), followed by Hong Kong SAR (in 1950 at the University of Hong Kong) and Taiwan (also in 1950 at Taiwan Provincial Junior College of Administration), Thailand (in 1954 at Thammasat University), and Indonesia (in 1957). Not quite twenty years later, social work education became available in Malaysia (in 1975 at the Universiti Sains Malaysia, Penang), the Micronesian region (in 1980 at the University of Guam), Samoa (in the 1990s), and Cambodia (in 2008 at the Royal University of Phnom Penh). Table 12.1 indicates when the social

Table 12.1 Social Work Education in East Asia and the Pacific Islands

	China	South Korea	Hong Kong SAR	Taiwan	Thailand	Indonesia	Malaysia	Micronesian Region	Cambodia	American Samoa
Year social work education initiated	1922	1947	1950	1950	1954	1957	1975	1980	1990	2008
Social work education currently not available										
Number of BSW programs	250	101	6	26	3	32	7	1	1	1
Number of MSW programs	35	77	4	23	3	4	1	1	0	1
Number of doctoral programs	2	NR*	NR*	4	1	2	1	0	0	0
Accreditation available	Yes	Yes	Yes	Yes	Yes	No	No	Yes	No	No
Hours required for BSW internship	400–800	120–130	400	400	270	400–800	900–1,000	540	NR	150

*Data were not reported.

work education programs were established and the number of bachelor's, master's, and doctoral programs in social work. Most programs participate in an accreditation process.

Geographically, social work education has traveled in a somewhat orderly route. Social work courses formally began in China with the missionaries, going on to the East Asian countries of South Korea, Hong Kong, and Taiwan, before moving westward to Thailand and then south to Indonesia and Malaysia. Finally social work education made its way toward the Pacific to Guam in the Micronesian region, south to Samoa, and then all the way back to Cambodia in Southeast Asia.

Universities intent on establishing social work academic programs have partnered with other well-established programs. Since the 1980s, for example, China formed relationships with social work education programs in Hong Kong SAR, Guam collaborated with the University of Hawaii at Manoa, Samoa aligned with the University of the South Pacific, and the Royal University of Phnom Penh joined with the U.S. University of Washington.

Today some social work education programs offer subbaccalaureate degree training (associate's degree and diploma), all the political entities except American Samoa have baccalaureate programs, all the states except Samoa and Cambodia have master's programs, and all the locations except for the Micronesian region, Samoa, and Cambodia have doctoral programs. In 2006 a professional certification program was established in China. In addition to the baccalaureate and graduate programs, there are sixty-four vocational schools in South Korea that offer a specialized social work program. Samoa also offers a professional certificate in social work. In time it is anticipated that the younger social work education programs in Guam, Samoa, and Cambodia will develop graduate programs, as have their predecessors.

The East Asia and Pacific Island entities are moving in the direction of accreditation. All three Thai social work education programs are accredited by the Ministry of Education Commission on Higher Education, the South Korean social work programs are accredited, and the Taiwan Council on Social Work Education was established in 1992 with the intent to accredit programs. Although Malaysia has established the National Joint Consultative Committee on Social Work Education, which consists of members from the seven public universities, to ensure that higher education has minimal social work education standards, the authors of chapter 6 believe there remains a recognized need for the Malaysian Social Work

Council to set and maintain standards for social work education programs at the university level. Currently the Universiti Sains Malaysia follows the international standards of social work education. The situation with accreditation in the Micronesian region is different. While the University of Guam started its undergraduate program much later (in 1980) than the East Asian schools, since Guam is a U.S. territory, the program was able to achieve accreditation in 2003 through the U.S. Council on Social Work Education.

Core components of social work education in most East Asian and Pacific island schools look similar to those found in the United States and Europe in terms of curriculum, textbooks, and sometimes faculty training. Several contributors reported that the curriculum is strong in the area of theory-policy but weaker in social work practice. In addition, it seems that many schools in economically struggling nations are more focused on community development and community work rather than on the micro and mezzo content and practice. Also, required hours for baccalaureate practicum programs vary from 120–130 hours in South Korea to 900–1,000 hours in Malaysia.

Indigenous social work content does not seem to be a priority concern in the region's social work education programs at this point. Some contributors claim to still have "one blood or one people" in their nations, while others note the influx of immigrants. It seems that Guam, Malaysia, and Hong Kong SAR may be the furthest along in working, for example, with various Pacific ethnic groups, local wisdom, and needs of the local Chinese community, respectively.

There are several other ways in which social work education differs in East Asia and the Pacific from the United States and Europe. A number of agency field instructors in the region are not trained in social work, necessitating more university input in educating the interns. Some agencies or agency field instructors require a practicum fee in Cambodia, Hong Kong SAR, and South Korea that the student or university underwrites, and universities in Indonesia have a policy to give agency supervisors an honorarium.

The U.S. Council on Social Work Education requires that baccalaureate- and master's-level social work faculty members be not only trained in social work but also be required to have had some work experience with clients if they instruct practice courses. However, because of the severe shortage of academicians trained in social work in East Asia, many faculty members do not have degrees in social work or social welfare or a comparable field. Malaysia and Taiwan have noted this academic limitation, and Cambodia, Indonesia, and Samoa, struggle with this constraint also. Nations that offer doctoral programs in social work or social welfare, or places where a number of residents study social work abroad and then return home, such as South Korea, Hong Kong SAR, Taiwan, and to a lesser extent Malaysia and Thailand, have a larger supply of social-work trained faculty members.

Development of the Social Work Profession

Status and Perceptions of the Profession

By and large in East Asia and the Pacific, the general public views the social work profession as usually in the middle of the professional range. Many people are unaware of this relatively new profession, especially in Samoa and Cambodia, where there are few "social worker" job titles. In China social work is not yet an official post, in Malaysia the social work position is not yet listed in the Public Service Department's category of jobs, and in Indonesia the government has not yet established social work as an independent profession; hence the social work salary is low in these locations. In Samoa the government contracts out the equivalent of social work positions to NGOs. In countries such as Indonesia and Malaysia, where volunteers, community, and religious leaders are often called social workers (owing to misconceptions and a poor understanding of the social work profession), many citizens give little credit to paid social workers. Thailand's problem is that *social worker* in Thai translates to "charity worker," and hence the assumption of a less qualified practitioner. Thailand, Malaysia, China, Indonesia, the Samoas, and Cambodia are moving toward professionalization.

Conversely, most of the countries that have long had the social work profession, such as Hong Kong SAR, South Korea, and Taiwan, are much more familiar with the social work community and seem to give it more respect and status. Chapter 9 states that social work was recognized as a legitimate profession in South Korea in the 1980s, and Bibus (2011) indicates that social workers already have established a solid professional identity there. Legislation has helped legitimize the social work profession in both Hong Kong SAR and South Korea, and social work graduates are elevated in Hong Kong SAR since only trained social workers can apply for professional social work positions. The Taiwan Social Worker Act of 1997 not only established the professional service system of social work but also promoted the professional status of social workers and ensured that clients are being helped by trained professional workers. While the Taiwanese people in general see the profession as growing and admire social workers, they ultimately do not view the social work profession with a high degree of respect. Currently Malaysia is working on a bill that would recognize the social work profession, and at this book's publication the outcome is pending. The draft social work professional licensure bill in Thailand may take years to pass.

The social work profession is visible and known in the U.S. territories of Guam and American Samoa since most U.S. social welfare programs are available there. A growing number of social workers are trained and employed in social work positions in Guam and to a lesser extent in American Samoa. Countries that have social work education programs seem to benefit from the steady supply of trained practitioners and from the access to another entity with which to collaborate on common social issues.

In East Asia and the Pacific it appears that the length of time the social work profession has been in a country is often related to the developmental extent of the profession. For example, Cambodia is not focusing on social welfare, and Samoa uses its traditional family-based system of helping, and yet Hong Kong SAR, South Korea, Taiwan, some of the Micronesian region, and American Samoa seem to have a variety of services. Nations that offer a number of social welfare services and policies seem to be viewed positively and are well regarded.

Professional Associations and Credentials

All the nations except Cambodia, Samoa, and American Samoa have established national associations for social workers. These associations of social workers strengthen the profession's identity, enhance the quality of service delivery, and allow for collaboration with other organizations. Some nations, such as Indonesia, have established additional organizations that also focus on social welfare. In addition to the Indonesian Association of Professional Social Workers (which is open only to professional social workers), Indonesia has the Indonesian Association of Social Workers (for social workers and volunteer workers), the Indonesian Association for Social Work Education, and the Indonesian National Council on Social Welfare. Unfortunately, political and fiduciary problems have made it difficult for these organizations to sponsor significant joint activities that promote social development, practice, and education. Hong Kong SAR has several recognized associations that collectively form a sturdy social welfare community. In addition to the Hong Kong Social Workers Association (which promotes professional development and is based on individual membership), Hong Kong also has the Hong Kong Council of Social Services (which serves as a platform for coordinating the NGOs) and the Hong Kong Social Workers General Union (which works for practitioners' rights as employees in NGOs and the government).

Social work credentials, which are intended "to protect consumers and increase credibility of social work practice" (Bibus 2011:60), are available in varying formats in Taiwan, China, Hong Kong SAR, Indonesia, South Korea, and Thailand. Taiwan in 1997 was the first of the states discussed in this volume to implement licensure. Licensure is granted to those applicants who hold a required social work or related degree and pass the social work license examinations in six areas: casework, group work, community organization, public policy and legislation, human behavior, and social environment. Social work credentials were advanced further when the Ministry of the Interior developed the Regulations on Specialty Certifications for Licensed Social Workers and Continuing Education in 2009. This regulation categorized five specialty social workers: medical social workers; social workers in mental health; certified children, youth, women, and family social workers; social workers in gerontology; and certified social workers for people with disabilities.

China began offering registration with a certificate in 2006 to those who are trained in social work, have one year of experience in personal care–related occupations, and have passed the National Examination for Social Workers. The Ministry of Civil Affairs oversees the examination. The first qualifying examination was given in June 2008 to 133,000 applicants, and 20,000 individuals passed (Bibus 2011). Registration has brought social and public recognition to the profession.

Registration has been available in Hong Kong SAR since 1997 to social workers who hold a degree or diploma in social work. This policy, based on the 1972 government stipulation that only persons with social work degrees could apply for social welfare officer positions, is one of the most important milestones in the professional development of social workers in

Hong Kong. The Hong Kong Social Workers Registration Board is autho-rized to oversee the registration of social work practitioners. In 2010 there were approximately fourteen thousand registered social workers in Hong Kong SAR.

Both licensure and certification have been available in South Korea since 2003. To be licensed, social work applicants must have majored in an ac-credited social work program or be employed in a social service agency for at least five years (for high school graduates) (Cheung 2010). The three levels of licensure are level 1 certification, the highest level, in which appli-cants are required to pass an examination provided by the government in cooperation with the Korea Council of Social Work Education; level 2; and level 3, in which certification is granted to applicants depending on their educational degree and number of years of social work experience. As of 2006 there were 157,228 licensed social workers in South Korea.

The Indonesian Ministry of Manpower and Transmigration oversees the Professional Certification National Board for professional workers, includ-ing professional social workers. Although this semigovernmental licensing system exists, there is a felt need for a licensing system specifically for social work practitioners in Indonesia. Certification and registration for social workers have been available in Thailand since about 2011, and social workers are now looking in the direction of getting a licensing bill passed.

Acquiring social work credentials based on education and examination is for the most part possible in places where the social work profession has had the extended time to grow, develop, and advance to the stage of credentials. Political entities that have had the social work profession and education available only in the last several decades, such as Cambodia, Malaysia, the Micronesian region, and the Samoas, are in the earlier stages of professional credentials. Legislation has played a key role in affecting credentials in Hong Kong SAR and Taiwan. While credentials protect the consumers, it may also be useful to consider areas where costly examina-tion fees may preclude an inordinately large number of trained social work applicants from applying.

Social Welfare Challenges for the Future

The challenge for governments, NGOs, and the social work profession in the twenty-first century in East Asia and the Pacific is to provide the various needed services to one-third of the world's population living in an area that constitutes one-fourth of the world's landmass, in nations with varying abilities to do so.

Government and NGO Tasks

In order for the social work profession and NGOs to be most effective and efficient, governments need to be positioned to do good for their people by passing appropriate laws. Corrupt government officials who misuse their power should not be in office. Legitimate, honest, and capable leaders need to be in key positions to help nations, NGOs, and the social work profession best address poverty and health issues.

Poorer nations' governments seem to focus on the economy, perhaps with the intent to expand to social development as the economy improves. The challenge for governments is to instead address economic issues simultaneously with social and health developments. All institutions—economic, social, health, education, and political—are important for the growth of nations and the well-being of their people.

NGOs perform commendable services in East Asia and the Pacific, but often these services are limited to the major cities. Usually the countryside has far fewer social welfare programs than the more urban areas. The challenge for NGOs is to expand their services and programs to the rural regions.

Social Worker Priorities

Social workers can play a key role in the development of a nation. There are a number of challenges facing social workers in East Asia and the Pacific, and we each must take our share of the responsibility for the common good of the general public. We social workers must do our best, whatever our position, title, and responsibilities:

- Social work students in their home countries should take their education seriously, be familiar with the overarching issues (such as poverty, child welfare, aging, immigrants, etc.), and experiment with the best practices and solutions while still in the classroom.

- Social work students abroad, especially those studying for graduate degrees, should return to their homelands, contribute to their nations, and work toward appropriate social welfare reform.
- Social work faculty members should be trained in social work and have macro practice experience.
- Social work faculty members need to make social work education more relevant given the particular social issues, government policies and laws, indigenous population, and practice methodologies that best strengthen individuals, families, communities, and organizations.
- Students need to be taught how to (a) organize (to gather people to rally for or against a social issue); (b) engage in campaign awareness (to combat HIV/AIDS, child trafficking, low birthrate, etc.); (c) advocate (against military buildup, corruption, poverty, and gender inequity and for social welfare programs, social work positions, and social work legislation); (d) change negative policies (such as those that allow for corruption and misuse of power); and (e) work with different government types (which may range from effective democracy to autocracy).
- Social work faculty members and students need to conduct meaningful comparative, cultural, and historical analyses that help politicians and policy makers to make decisions that best combat social issues and lay the basis for future social needs and directions.
- Social work faculty members and practitioners may want to conjointly identify the best social welfare practices, present these at conferences, and publish the findings. Indigenous models should be a priority topic.
- Students, faculty, and social work practitioners need to collaboratively venture into the field of politics and be a voice for social reform.
- Academicians and practitioners may want to continue the development of the social work profession in terms of social work core curriculum and accreditation of social work programs and professional associations for students, practitioners, and academicians.
- Other priority professional initiatives should include social work credentials (registration, certification, and licensure); national, regional, and international social work conferences; and social work journals.

Some view the challenges facing social workers in East Asia and the Pacific as daunting, while others are motivated by these deeply embedded situations. Whatever our individual attitudes toward these challenges, the issues of poverty, child welfare, aging, human trafficking, discrimination, immigration, and so forth will continue in East Asia and the Pacific and need to be addressed skillfully and collaboratively.

The renaissance of social welfare in Asia and the Pacific is in the future as we meet the upcoming challenges. India and China, half of the BRIC countries (Brazil, Russia, India, and China), stand ready with their power and potential in Asia. We social workers have the knowledge, technology, and people to make a difference where we are. Let us unite and work for the benefit of humankind in our own regions, nations, and ultimately the world. Fifty years ago, with a number of East Asian countries just beginning to establish the social work profession, this social welfare book was yet to be. Today, with social work a more established profession, may we in Asia and the Pacific continue to conduct research, publish, and share with our colleagues in the United States and Europe our best social work policies and practices for a more comprehensive understanding of global social welfare.

References

Apodaca, C. (2002). "The Globalization of Capital in East and Southeast Asia: Measuring the Impact on Human Rights Standards. *Asian Survey* 42 (6): 883–905.

Bibus, A. A., III, & N. Boutte-Queen (2011). *Regulating Social Work: A Primer on Licensing Practice*. Chicago: Lyceum Books.

Central Intelligence Agency (CIA) (2011). *World Factbook. Publications: East and Southeast Asia*. Retrieved on May 14, 2011, from https://www.cia.gov/library/publications/the-world-factbook/geos/th.html.

Cheung, M. (2010). Social Work Regulations in Selected Nations in Asia. In *Regulating Social Work: A Primer on Licensing Practice*, ed. N. Boutte-Queen & A. A. Bibus, 60–71. Chicago: Lyceum Books.

Economist (2000). "Cambodia: Saving the Children." *Economist*, October 5. Retrieved May 19, 2011, from http://www.economist.com/node/387392.

Hokenstad, M. C., & J. Midgley (2004). *Lessons from Abroad: Adapting International Social Welfare Innovations*. Washington, D.C.: NASW Press.

Holliday, I., & P. Wilding (2003). *Welfare Capitalism in East Asia: Social Policy in the Tiger Economies*. Hampshire, U.K.: Palgrave Macmillan.

Information Office of the State Council of the People's Republic of China (2002). "Labor and Social Security in China. *People's Daily*, April 30, p. 7.

International Monetary Fund (2011). *World Economic Outlook Database—April 2011*. Retrieved May 15, 2011, from http://www.ask.com/web?l=dis&o=16048&qsrc=2 870&gct=dns&gc=1&q=internationalmnoetaryfund.com.

Mauro, P. (1995). "Corruption and Growth." *Quarterly Journal of Economics* 110 (3): 681–712.

Mohan, B. (2008). "The End of the Third World: The Challenge of an Asian-Pacific Renaissance." Paper presented at the First National Asian and Pacific Islanders Social Work Education Conference, 54th Annual Program Meeting of the Council on Social Work Education, Philadelphia, November 2.

Ramesh, M., & G. A. Mukul (2000). *Welfare Capitalism in Southeast Asia: Social Security, Health, and Education Policies*. New York: Palgrave.

Samsung (2008). *Welcome to Noble County*. Retrieved May 10, 2011, from http://www.samsungnc.com/english/welcomeNc.asp.

World Bank (2011). "Poverty Headcount Ratio at $1.25 a Day (PPP)(% of population)." Retrieved May 14, 2011, from http://data.worldbank.org/indicator/SI.POV.DDAY/countries.

Human Development Index Rankings, 2010

Very High Human Development

1	Norway
2	Australia
3	New Zealand
4	United States
5	Ireland
6	Liechtenstein
7	Netherlands
8	Canada
9	Sweden
10	Germany
11	Japan
12	Republic of Korea
13	Switzerland
14	France
15	Israel
16	Finland
17	Iceland
18	Belgium
19	Denmark
20	Spain
21	Hong Kong SAR, China
22	Greece
23	Italy
24	Luxembourg
25	Austria
26	United Kingdom
27	Singapore
28	Czech Republic
29	Slovenia
30	Andorra
31	Slovakia
32	United Arab Emirates
33	Malta
34	Estonia
35	Cyprus
36	Hungary
37	Brunei Darussalam
38	Qatar
39	Bahrain
40	Portugal
41	Poland
42	Barbados

High Human Development

43	Bahamas
44	Lithuania
45	Chile
46	Argentina

47	Kuwait		Medium Human Development
48	Latvia		
49	Montenegro	86	Fiji
50	Romania	87	Turkmenistan
51	Croatia	88	Dominican Republic
52	Uruguay	89	China
53	Libyan Arab Jamahiriya	90	El Salvador
54	Panama	91	Sri Lanka
55	Saudi Arabia	92	Thailand
56	Mexico	93	Gabon
57	Malaysia	94	Suriname
58	Bulgaria	95	Bolivia
59	Trinidad and Tobago	96	Paraguay
60	Serbia	97	Philippines
61	Belarus	98	Botswana
62	Costa Rica	99	Moldova
63	Peru	100	Mongolia
64	Albania	101	Egypt
65	Russian Federation	102	Uzbekistan
66	Kazakhstan	103	Federated States of Micronesia
67	Azerbaijan	104	Guyana
68	Bosnia and Herzegovina	105	Namibia
69	Ukraine	106	Honduras
70	Iran	107	Maldives
71	Former Yugoslav Republic of Macedonia	108	Indonesia
		109	Kyrgyzstan
72	Mauritius	110	South Africa
73	Brazil	111	Syrian Arab Republic
74	Georgia	112	Tajikistan
75	Venezuela	113	Viet Nam
76	Armenia	114	Morocco
77	Ecuador	115	Nicaragua
78	Belize	116	Guatemala
79	Colombia	117	Equatorial Guinea
80	Jamaica	118	Cape Verde
81	Tunisia	119	India
82	Jordan	120	Timor-Leste
83	Turkey	121	Swaziland
84	Algeria	122	Lao People's Democratic Republic
85	Tonga		

123	Solomon Islands	145	Haiti
124	Cambodia	146	Angola
125	Pakistan	147	Djibouti
126	Congo	148	Tanzania
127	Sao Tome and Principe	149	Cote d'Ivoire
		150	Zambia
		151	Gambia
	Low Human Development	152	Rwanda
		153	Malawi
128	Kenya	154	Sudan
129	Bangladesh	155	Afghanistan
130	Ghana	156	Guinea
131	Cameroon	157	Ethiopia
132	Myanmar	158	Sierra Leone
133	Yemen	159	Central African Republic
134	Benin	160	Mali
135	Madagascar	161	Burkina Faso
136	Mauritania	162	Liberia
137	Papua New Guinea	163	Chad
138	Nepal	164	Guinea-Bissau
139	Togo	165	Mozambique
140	Comoros	166	Burundi
141	Lesotho	167	Niger
142	Nigeria	168	Democratic Republic of the Congo
143	Uganda		
144	Senegal	169	Zimbabwe

Sources: United Nations Development Programme, *Human Development Report 2010: The Real Wealth of Nations: Pathways to Human Development* (New York: Palgrave Macmillan, 2010); and United Nations Development Programme, "Human Development Index (HDI)—2010 Rankings," *Human Development Reports* (2010). http://hdr.undp.org/en/statistics/.

Index